Discarded by
Santa Maria Library

D0394169

973.9:
Kennedy, Randall, 1954-
The persistence of the color line :
racial politics and the Obama
presidency
c2011

SANTA MARIA PUBLIC LIBRARY

ALSO BY RANDALL KENNEDY

Interracial Intimacies:
Sex, Marriage, Identity, and Adoption

Nigger:
The Strange Career of a Troublesome Word

Race, Crime, and the Law

Sellout:
The Politics of Racial Betrayal

The Persistence
of the Color Line

The
Persistence
of the
Color Line

Racial Politics and the Obama Presidency

Randall Kennedy

PANTHEON BOOKS, NEW YORK

Copyright © 2011 by Randall Kennedy

All rights reserved. Published in the United States by Pantheon Books,
a division of Random House, Inc., New York, and in Canada by
Random House of Canada Limited, Toronto.

Pantheon Books and colophon are registered trademarks of Random House, Inc.

Library of Congress Cataloging-in-Publication Data
Kennedy, Randall, [date]
The persistence of the color line : racial politics and the Obama presidency /
Randall Kennedy.
p.   cm.
Includes bibliographical references and index.
ISBN 978-0-307-37789-0 (hardback)
1. African Americans—Politics and government. 2. Obama, Barack.
3. Presidents—United States—Election—2008. 4. United States President
(2009– : Obama) 5. Racism—Political aspects—United States—History.
6. Race awareness—United States—History. 7. United States—Race relations—
Political aspects—History. 8. United States—Politics and government.
9. United States—Social conditions. I. Title.
E185.615.K376 2011   973.932092—dc22   2010052056

www.pantheonbooks.com

Jacket design by Emily Mahon

Printed in the United States of America
First Edition
2   4   6   8   9   7   5   3   1

This book is dedicated to my wonderful children:
Henry William Kennedy
Rachel Elizabeth Love Kennedy
Thaddeus James Kennedy

Contents

The Persistence
of the Color Line

Introduction

The terms under which Barack Obama won the presidency, the conditions under which he governs, and the circumstances under which he seeks reelection all display the haunting persistence of the color line. Many prophesied or prayed that his election heralded a postracial America. But everything about Obama is widely, insistently, almost unavoidably interpreted through the prism of race— his appearance (light-skinned), his demeanor (*not* an angry black man), his diction ("articulate," "no Negro dialect"), his spouse (dark-skinned), the support he enjoys (anchored by blacks), the opposition he encounters (constituted overwhelmingly by whites).

For Obama himself, the consciousness of race is ever-present. It was evident on Election Night when he remarked on the miraculousness of an African American winning the White House. It was evident at the inauguration when he alluded to the fact that, during his father's lifetime, bigotry denied blacks service in Washington, D.C., restaurants. It was evident at the press conference of December 7, 2010, when, defending hotly disputed tax legislation, he maintained that compromise was central to America, including the Founding Fathers' compromise with slavery—a bargain that some thoughtful observers have condemned as immoral.*

* According to Obama, "This country was founded on compromise. I couldn't go through the front door at this country's founding. And if we were really thinking about ideal positions, we wouldn't have a union." Press conference by the president, Decem-

There was a time—now it seems long ago—when it appeared, momentarily, that America had taken a giant stride toward redemption. After all, the electorate selected Barack Hussein Obama, a black man, to be president of the United States. The hope, pride, relief, and astonishment generated by this unprecedented event provoked all sorts of optimistic declarations. People who had, in emotional self-defense, habitually eschewed patriotism, now waved American flags enthusiastically. People who had doubted that Americans would ever be able to overcome racial alienation now believed that they could. Expressions of exhilaration produced sounds and scenes reminiscent of reactions to such landmark events as the Emancipation Proclamation, Joe Louis's victory over Max Schmeling; the "I Have a Dream" speech of Martin Luther King, Jr.; and the landing on the moon.[1] Parties erupted featuring such anthems as "Ain't No Stoppin' Us Now," "A Change Is Gonna Come," and "We're a Winner." Strangers danced and cried with one another. People named newborns after the president-elect. On the day after the election, one of my students at Harvard Law School tearfully declared that in light of Obama's election she was reconsidering her career plans. His example, she said, made

---

ber 7, 2010. Others have condemned the compromise over slavery that Obama implicitly justifies.

> There is much declamation about the sacredness of the compact which was formed between the free and slave states, on the adoption of the Constitution. A sacred compact, forsooth! We pronounce it the most bloody and heaven-daring arrangement ever made by men for the continuance and protection of a system of the most atrocious villany [sic] ever exhibited on earth. . . . Such a compact was, in the nature of things and according to the law of God, null and void from the beginning.

William Lloyd Garrison, "On the Constitution and the Union," *The Liberator*, December 29, 1832. The compromise over slavery at the founding of the United States has long been debated among antiracist activists. See Randall Kennedy, "Afro-American Faith in the Civil Religion; Or, Yes, I Would Sign the Constitution," *William and Mary Law Review* 29 (1987): 163. For an excellent recent examination see Avishai Margalit, *On Compromise and Rotten Compromises* (2010), 54–61.

her want to be a better person. A few days later, I received a letter from an inmate of a maximum-security prison in Indiana that said the same thing.

On Election Night one heard repeatedly echoes of Maya Angelou's statement "I never thought I'd see a black president in the White House in my lifetime."* Oprah Winfrey exclaimed that Election Night was "the most electrifying" moment she had ever experienced. People commonly remarked that they felt as if they were dreaming. The day after the election, on a Listserv organized by racial-minority law professors, a distinguished black jurist remarked, "When I woke up this morning, I said to my husband, 'I had the weirdest dream last night. I dreamed that a black man named Barack Hussein Obama became president of the United States. Is that weird or what?'"[2]

Blacks were not the only ones feeling and expressing pent-up emotion. Responding to a column in which the black journalist Eugene Robinson explained why he wept on Election Night, numbers of white readers noted that they, too, had been moved to tears.† In an open "Letter to a New Neighbor," Washingtonian Betsy Karasik poured out feelings of gratitude:

---

* Seventy-one percent of black respondents to a poll conducted one week after the election (and 41 percent of white respondents) said that they had doubted that they would witness in their lifetime the election of an African American to the presidency. See Paul Steinhauser, "Poll: Racial Divides Persist After Obama's Historic Win," CNNPolitics .com, November 11, 2008.

See also Gary Fields, "Racial Significance of Vote Looms Large for Many at Polls," WallStreetJournal.com, November 5, 2008 (quoting a 101-year-old black voter who stated, "I never believed that I'd see a black man as president in my lifetime"). This reaction has now become a cliché. See Colson Whitehead, "Finally, a Thin President," *New York Times*, November 6, 2008.

† See Eugene Robinson, "Morning in America," WashingtonPost.com, November 6, 2008. Responses included the following: "I'm white and 56. All my friends cried and we are still emotional today"; "I'm 66 years old and white, but I, too, cried tears of joy when I heard that my next president would be . . . Barack Obama"; "Mr. Robinson, please know that this white woman wept with you."

You proved that Americans are not nearly as narrow-minded as most of us believed; that speaking to us adult-to-adult about race trumps playing the race card; that sticking to the issues and taking the high road do not make you a sucker; that being an intellectual is not a liability . . . and that appealing to the best in people brings out the young, the old, the dissatisfied, minorities and even the opposition in record numbers.[3]

In newspapers and Web sites people posted messages by the thousands displaying ways in which Obama's victory deeply moved them. A reader of *The Washington Post* wrote, "We still have a long way to go to erase the sin of slavery and end racism. But maybe, just maybe, this is the beginning of the end of race as a major issue. Today, I can truly say, God Bless America, and mean it."[4] A reader of *The New York Times* stated that Obama's election "does nothing less for me than heal my chronic young boyhood wound of November 22, 1963"—the assassination of President John F. Kennedy. "And also the wounds of Bobby and Martin"— the assassinations of Robert F. Kennedy and Martin Luther King, Jr., in the spring of 1968.[5] A reader of the Web site Jack & Jill Politics wrote, "This morning I woke up and realized that what I saw last night was not a dream. . . . I realized I woke up in a new time, in a new era. I woke up in A.B.—After Barack."[6]

Euphoric statements made in the grip of the postelection high are painful (and sometimes embarrassing) to recall. Even seasoned observers were swept up by a delusionary millenarianism. Many racial Panglossians, however, have been sobered by realities—the substantial number of Americans who simply refuse to acknowledge Obama's political legitimacy (for example, the allegation believed by tens of millions that he was born abroad),* the open contempt

---

* In May 2010, 14 percent of Americans polled said that they believed that President Obama was born abroad. See "Sizing Up the 'Birthers,'" *Washington Post*, May 7, 2010. This matters, of course, because the Constitution makes birth in the United States a

displayed by antagonists not only on the airwaves of right-wing talk radio but also in the inner sanctum of Congress (for example, Joe Wilson's infamous shout of "You lie!"), and the stark polarization that characterizes the racial demographics of support for and opposition to Obama. That the opposition is overwhelmingly white is a fact that no one can reasonably dispute.* What is disputed, however, is that racial sentiment is an important ingredient in the opposition. "America has turned the page on race," wrote a correspondent for *The Economist*. "The electorate may be divided by race, but no longer mainly because of race."[7]

It is, of course, true that there are many potential nonracial reasons for rejecting Obama, including disagreement with his domestic policies (his stance on abortion, financial regulation, immigration, taxation, etc.), foreign policy (his prosecution of the wars in Iraq and Afghanistan, for instance), and also objections to Obama himself. Even some who formerly supported him enthusiastically have subsequently voiced doubts about his mettle as a leader.[8] Racial sentiments, moreover, are devilishly difficult to isolate and quantify in specific instances. In gross, however, the evidence is overwhelming, that racial attitudes affect judgments pervasively—from the administration of justice to support or opposition to social welfare programs, to dating and the marriage market, to employment decisions.† African Americans, for in-

---

requirement for the presidency. "No person but a natural born Citizen . . . shall be eligible for the Office of the President." The Constitution of the United States of America, Article II.

"Much of the driving force behind the dogged unwillingness of so many to acknowledge that Obama was born in the United States is not just simple partisan opposition to a Democratic president but a general ethnocentric suspicion of an African American president who is also perceived as distinctly 'other.'" Michael Tesler and David O. Sears, *Obama's Race: The 2008 Election and the Dream of a Post-Racial America* (2010), 153.

* Around the time of the midterm elections of November 2010, Obama's approval ratings among whites hovered around 37 percent. Among blacks it stood at more than 90 percent. See gallup.com/poll/124922/presidential-approval-center.aspx.

† See, e.g., Ian Ayres, *Pervasive Prejudice? Unconventional Evidence of Race and Gender Discrimination* (2001); John A. List, "The Nature and Extent of Discrimination in the Marketplace: Evidence from the Field," *Quarterly Journal of Economics* (February

stance, are not only discriminated against in many settings; they are more discriminated against the blacker they are perceived to be.* Against that backdrop, it is wholly implausible to think that racial attitudes would not significantly affect assessments of politicians.

That Obama won the White House in 2008 does not mean that racial prejudice is no longer a potent force in American politics. The political scientists Michael Tesler and David O. Sears argue persuasively that the election of 2008 "was anything but post-racial. Instead, the racial hopes and fear evoked by [Obama's] potential to become the country's first black president sharply divided racial conservatives from racial liberals. Public opinion and voting behavior . . . were considerably more polarized by racial attitudes than at any other time on record."[9] Racial attitudes, they conclude, are "one of the most important determinants of how the American public responded."[10] Racial liberals supported Obama more than they would have backed an ideologically similar white candidate while racial conservatives opposed Obama more than they would have opposed an ideologically similar white candidate. Furthermore, there are some who voted for Obama in 2008 *despite* their disinclination to vote for a black candidate. It should be unsurprising that they would turn against him more quickly and sharply than they would have done under identical circumstances if he were white.

2004); Jennifer Doleac and Luke Stein, "Race Has a Hand in Determining Market Outcomes," Voxeu.org, June 29, 2010; Marianne Bertrand and Sendhil Mullainathan, "Are Emily and Greg More Employable Than Lakisha and Jamal? A Field Experiment on Labor Market Discrimination," *American Economic Review* 94 (2004); Martin Gilens, *Why Americans Hate Welfare: Race, Media, and the Politics of Antipoverty Policy* (1999); Elizabeth F. Emens, "Intimate Discrimination: The State's Role in the Accidents of Sex and Love," *Harvard Law Review* 122 (2008), 1307; Christian Rudder, "How Your Race Affects the Messages You Get," OKcupid.com, October 5, 2009.
* See Jennifer L. Hochschild and Vesla Weaver, "The Skin Color Paradox and the American Racial Order," *Social Forces* 86 (2007): 643.

The 2008 postelection racial euphoria stemmed from an array of sources, including denial of the breadth, depth, and subtlety of racial divisions in American life. Despite the epochal nature of the election, it should have been understood from the outset that something as thoroughly ingrained as American racial prejudice, particularly its antiblack variant, would not suddenly dissipate despite the goodwill effectively summoned by Obama's skillful campaign.* Much of what he had to surmount in order to win was rooted in America's racial traumas. He had to overcome doubts lodged deep in the psyches of blacks, some of whom were so afraid of the lengths to which they thought whites would go to prevent the election of a black president that early on they refrained from supporting him, convinced that he would be assassinated if he emerged as a serious contender.† He had to overcome Negrophobia that made it difficult, if not impossible, for some whites to vote in favor of entrusting a black man with the fate of the nation— regardless of the caliber of the white alternatives. A wide variety of biases confronted Obama—from paranoia about his origins and loyalties, to resentment that made a black man's ambition appear inappropriately "uppity," to a hypercritical attitude that magnified his perceived missteps, to lowered expectations that revealed the dismal image many observers have when they think of black politicians. When Senator Joseph Biden mused early in the campaign season that Obama was "the first mainstream African American [running for president] who is articulate and

---

* Obama himself recognized this: "I have never been so naïve as to believe that we can get beyond our racial divisions in a single election cycle, or with a single candidacy— particularly a candidacy as imperfect as my own." Barack Obama, "A More Perfect Union," speech given on March 18, 2008.
† "Time and again I encountered [black people during the early primaries] who believed they were doing Obama a favor by not supporting him. 'He has two small children,' they would point out. 'He needs to be around to see them grow up.'" William Jelani Cobb, *The Substance of Hope: Barack Obama and the Paradox of Progress* (2010), 6–7. See also David Remnick, *The Bridge: The Life and Rise of Barack Obama* (2010), 462, 499, 500.

bright and clean,"[11] he was simply giving voice to a widespread perception. Obama, moreover, had to overcome the taint of a long association with an Afrocentric spiritual adviser whom the country saw screaming from a pulpit "God damn America!" He had to overcome fear that the Democrats would once again "blow" a winnable presidential contest—this time by nominating a candidate who, partly because of his race, would be unable to persuade working-class whites to vote for him. He had to overcome detractors who complained that he is not black enough as well as those who complained that his wife is too black.

That Obama won despite these impediments shows undeniable racial progress. But the presence of these obstacles and the special circumstances under which he prevailed should have counseled caution in interpreting his election as the ultimate racial breakthrough that some saw it as representing. He was helped by the surprising ineptitude of Senator Hillary Clinton's campaign; a dramatic economic collapse; two unresolved military conflicts; the evident flaws of his elderly Republican opponent, Senator John McCain; the conspicuous unpreparedness of McCain's running mate, Governor Sarah Palin of Alaska; President George Bush's discreditation of Republican competency; and a strong electoral tide in favor of Democrats. "Do we honestly believe," one of my students wrote in the wake of the election, "that, under 'normal' circumstances, a black person [can] be elected to the highest office in the land, or do we think [that] this was simply an aberration?"[12]

Obama did prevail decisively in the Electoral College, winning 365 to 173. He was the first Democrat since Jimmy Carter to win a majority of the popular vote, and his 52 percent take was the largest slice for a Democrat since Lyndon Johnson's landslide in 1964. Obama also captured a larger share of the white vote than either Al Gore or John Kerry had and beat John McCain 54 percent to 44 percent among whites under thirty.[13] Obama lost to

McCain, however, in the competition for the white vote overall. While Obama won 95 percent of the black vote, 66 percent of the Latino vote, and 62 percent of the Asian-American vote, he won only 43 percent of the white vote (to McCain's 55 percent).[14] These polarities reflect more than voters' racial attitudes. They also show ideological preferences, partisan loyalties, perceptions of character, and religious proclivities. Whatever the race of the candidates, whites tend to vote Republican in presidential contests while blacks and other racial minorities tend to vote Democratic. Racial sentiments interact with and influence other dispositions—such as attitudes toward taxation, social-welfare programs, expressions of patriotism, governmental protection of traditionally oppressed groups—that have contributed to a situation in which, by and large, the Democratic Party is a refuge for blacks while the Republican Party is conspicuous in the degree to which blacks are absent from its ranks, especially in presidential elections.* While racial prejudice is not the only explanation for racially distinctive voting patterns, it is indisputably an important one. Surely it is no coincidence that the states in which racial polarization in voting was most stark—Alabama, Mississippi, Louisiana, Georgia, and South Carolina—are also the states with the most infamous histories of racial subjugation.†

---

* In 1980, nearly 98 percent of Ronald Reagan's voters were white. In 2000, 91 percent of George W. Bush's voters were white. In 2008, 89 percent of John McCain's voters were white. Nate Silver, "GOP Has Always Been Dominated by White Voters," FiveThirty/ Eight blog, June 1, 2009.

† In the presidential election of 2008, 10 percent of the white vote in Alabama went to Obama, while 98 percent of the black vote went to him. Eleven percent of the white vote in Mississippi went to Obama while 98 percent of the black vote went to him. Fourteen percent of the white vote in Louisiana went to Obama while 94 percent of the black vote went to him. In Georgia, 23 percent of the white vote went to Obama while 98 percent of the black vote went to him. In South Carolina, 26 percent of the white vote went to Obama while 96 percent of the black vote went to him. See Kristen Clarke, "The Obama Factor: The Impact of the 2008 Presidential Election on Future Voting Rights Act Litigation," *Harvard Law & Policy Review* 3 (2009): 59, 70.

This racial differentiation in partisan loyalties is largely rooted in self-conscious decisions made by party leaders. Since the 1960s, ascendant Republicans have chosen to make their party the white man's party, while ascendant Democrats have chosen to make their party the diversity party.

Obama's victory was a marvel because nowhere has resistance to the empowerment of racial minorities been more stubborn and intense than in the domain of electoral politics. In the pages that follow I address the way in which, for most of American history, blacks have been snubbed—or worse—when they have run for elective office. On only three occasions have voters selected blacks as United States senators (Edward Brooke in Massachusetts in 1966, Carol Moseley Braun in Illinois in 1992, and Barack Obama in Illinois in 2004), and on only three occasions have they elected blacks as governors (Douglas Wilder in Virginia in 1989 and Deval Patrick in Massachusetts in 2006 and 2010). That is why triumph for Obama seemed so improbable at the outset and, for many, tasted so sweet at the end.

An inflated sense of accomplishment is part of the racial predicament in which Americans find themselves. Electing a black American as president is treated as remarkable. In a sense it is—but only against the backdrop of a long-standing betrayal of democratic principles. When Shirley Chisholm ran for president in 1968, she declined to portray her pioneering candidacy as a reason for celebration. Why should it be such a big deal, she asked, for a black woman to run for the presidency? Forty years later the low expectations to which Chisholm objected were poignantly revealed at the moment of Obama's victory. When people exclaimed that they never thought that they would live to see the day a black man was elected president, they were indicating how little they expected of their fellow Americans. They were saying that they didn't anticipate that within their lifetimes a predominantly white electorate would be willing under *any* circumstances to entrust to a black, *any* black, the highest office in the land. For many, the joyful tears of November 4, 2008, reflected surprise that a sufficient number of whites would be willing to vote for an African American to enable him to become president. That surprise was founded upon a realistic appreciation of the extent to which the color line has cruelly thwarted talents and aspirations. The tears of Election Night were a reflection of that somber reality.

Nowadays, when Obama's most loyal and fervent followers are African Americans, it is easy to forget that there was a time, not so long ago, when he had to work hard to persuade blacks to support him. Congressman John Lewis, for example, the iconic representative of the black-freedom struggle of the 1960s, initially backed Hillary Clinton over Obama. The same is true of many other African Americans (including Andrew Young, Maya Angelou, Johnnetta Cole, Vernon Jordan, Calvin Butts III, and Charles Rangel). After the first few caucuses and primaries of the nomination contest, however, black officials, following their constituencies, broke toward Obama overwhelmingly. I will describe how he successfully courted black voters and retains their allegiance.* He does so by identifying himself as a black man, by carrying himself in a dignified manner as the loving spouse of a black woman, by associating himself with struggles for Afro-American empowerment, and by showing that his candidacy was "for real" in the sense that he could garner sufficient support from whites to prevail. I will also consider blacks whom Obama has failed to win over. Among his most vitriolic detractors are black conservatives and leftists whose views warrant a hearing and a response.†

---

* See pages 66–105.
† See pages 95–103.

What about the Obama way of dealing with those outside of black America? I will show how he assures them that he appreciates their concerns, that he is devoid of resentment, and that he is able to lead and represent the whole of the American nation. I will compare Obama's outreach to nonblacks with John F. Kennedy's outreach to non-Catholics.* Just as JFK had to convince Protestant America that it was safe to put a Catholic in the Oval Office, Obama had to convince white America that it was safe to put a black in the Oval Office. That Obama has had to work so hard to make himself and his family acceptable to white America and that he has had to continue to work so persistently to overcome the perceived burden of his blackness is a sobering lesson.

The presidential contest of 2008 witnessed numerous allegations of racial wrongdoing. Hillary and Bill Clinton were accused of "playing the race card." So, too, were John McCain and Obama himself. Did any of these figures engage in racial demagoguery? Did all of them? I conclude that there was considerably less racial misconduct in 2008 than much of the election commentary has contended. What is most notable about that election season is not how much racial demagoguery there was but how little. For reasons that are unclear, John McCain refused to pull out all of the racial stops at his disposal in his fight with Obama. He refrained, for example, from revisiting the Obama–Reverend Wright connection though Republican backers and his running mate beseeched him to do so. Moreover, McCain could have done more to create a problem for Obama by calling attention to their differences over the volatile issue of racial affirmative action. McCain could have at least raised the issue, making Obama openly distance himself from affirmative action (thereby disappointing enthusiastic supporters) or openly embrace the

* See pages 125–132.

policy (thereby alienating hesitant supporters). As it turned out, McCain never seriously broached the matter; remarkably, in three nationally televised presidential debates, the issue of affirmative action never surfaced.

This is not to say that Obama was free of the burden of his blackness, or that opponents did nothing to exploit that "weakness" in his political persona, or that McCain's forbearance will likely be emulated. Sometimes the racist motivation behind opposition or behind appeals for opposition has been explicit—referring to the president as a "nigger," portraying him as a monkey or an ape, calling for him to "go back to Africa." But often the prejudice has been sublimated and expressed via a code that provides a cover of plausible deniability: "He's not one of ours"; "He's not like us"; "He's alien"; "He's a Muslim"; "He's a socialist."

Ever since Obama emerged as a serious contender for the presidency, he has had to contend with racially inflected insinuations questioning his Americanism and patriotism. He has responded by stressing his "normalcy." Like his predecessors, Obama repeats time-worn versions of the American national narrative—celebratory stories that venerate the Founding Fathers (despite their slaveholding), laud the pioneers who "won" the West (despite their participation in the ethnic cleansing of the Native Americans), and applaud America's soldiers (despite their involvement, often as draftees, in imperialistic or otherwise misguided ventures). Like his predecessors, Obama sends flowers to commemorate the Confederate war dead.* Like his predecessors, Obama expresses

* Although Obama continued the tradition, begun by President Wilson in 1914, of sending a presidential wreath of flowers to the Confederate Memorial at Arlington National Cemetery, he also became the first president to send a wreath to the memorial in Washington, D.C., that honors the African-American veterans of the Civil War. See Kathy Kiely and Judy Keen, "Nation Salutes Its War Dead on Memorial Day," *USA Today*, May 25, 2009. See also Kirk Savage, "The President and the Confederacy," *Washington Post*, May 23, 2009.

belief in the divinely ordained superiority of the United States. Like his predecessors, Obama proclaims loudly, unreservedly, and often that he loves his country.

There is, however, an alternative opinion that African Americans ought *not* to love the United States. Holders of this view see African-American patriotism as a pathology akin to the "love" that exploited wives feel toward their battering husbands or that mistreated children feel toward their abusive parents. Often ignored, this tradition attracted a bit of attention during the frenzied controversy over Obama's association with Reverend Jeremiah Wright. I know this tradition well. My father espoused it. His view of the United States was more unforgiving than that voiced by Reverend Wright. Some will think that my father, too, was "crazy." They are wrong. He was an intelligent, thoughtful, loving man, who, tragically, had good reason to doubt his government's allegiance to blacks, and thus to himself. I ruminate on the Wright-Obama controversy through the prism of my father.*

A revealing episode during Obama's early years as president was his elevation of Sonia Sotomayor to the Supreme Court. This event shed light on several topics, including the rivalry between Democrats and Republicans for the favor of Latinos, the special challenges and advantages that affect people of color in competitions for society's most coveted positions, and the salient place that racial politics have played in Supreme Court confirmation hearings. I applaud Obama for making a selection that elevates the Latino community while recognizing and utilizing the talents of an able "Nuyorican" jurist. I criticize the president and his nominee, however, for the way in which they handled the confirmation process. Displaying tendencies that are all too likely to be repeated, they needlessly

---

* See pages 161–195.

ceded ideological ground to the right, ratifying a model of judging that is appallingly misleading.

Finally, I evaluate the state of the country's racial situation and Obama's influence upon it. Americans are deeply confused and conflicted regarding racial strategies and goals. Some Americans insist upon "color blindness" *now*, demanding an end immediately to all race-conscious selectivity, including programs designed to assist designated racial minorities. Others seek an eventual move to color blindness but believe that a wholesale disregarding of race in allocating opportunities can only be done justly after obstacles stemming from past and present racial wrongdoing have been removed. Still others reject color blindness as a strategy or goal, insisting that a decent respect for pluralism requires recognition of and deference to differences and boundaries that distinguish groups.

Obama provides little in the way of clarification, though some have expected that he would attempt to explicate the great American racial dilemma. This is an expectation that Obama periodically encourages. In his "A More Perfect Union" address, made in the midst of the controversy over his relationship with Reverend Wright, Obama declared that "race is an issue . . . this nation cannot afford to ignore."[15] Later, during the controversy over his criticism of the (white) police officer who arrested the (black) celebrity-academician Henry Louis Gates, Jr., Obama defended his remarks, saying, "I think that me commenting . . . and hopefully contributing to constructive . . . understandings about [racial issues] is part of my portfolio."[16] Actually, though, Obama is loath, at least in public, to expatiate seriously upon racial matters. When forced to do so, his comments are notably vague and unilluminating.

Though President Obama avoids directly confronting racial issues, he inescapably affects America's racial environment. Without drawing attention to the racial import of what he is doing, Obama consciously promotes racial minorities to high office—as in his appointment of the first Latina justice, the most Asian-American judicial nominees in the country's history, the first black attorney general, and the first black directors of the Environmental Protection Agency and the National Air and Space Administration. He does not expend political capital vocally defending affirmative action and rejects demands to create explicitly race-targeted programs to address the long-standing problem of disproportionate unemployment among certain racial minorities, particularly blacks. One of the few occasions on which Obama has been publicly challenged by black elected officials involves complaints stemming from frustration with distinctly high levels of unemployment among African Americans and the apparent absence of any concerted effort by the administration to grapple specifically with that problem.[17] Obama refuses, however, to conceptualize "minority unemployment" as a discrete issue warranting special treatment apart from the overall treatment of unemployment in general. He insists that by raising the economic fortunes of all, regardless of race, he is necessarily raising the economic fortunes of the black poor who suffer disproportionately in hard times. Sometimes this formulation accords with realities. Sometimes, however, rising fortunes *accentuate* inequalities, leaving behind those on the bottom or raising them much less than other groups higher on the socioeconomic-political pecking order. Depending on the circumstances, a rising tide might only lift the yachts, stranding the rowboats.*

* See James R. Hines, Hilary W. Hoynes, and Alan B. Krueger, "Another Look at Whether a Rising Tide Lifts All Boats," National Bureau of Economic Research: NBER Working Paper No. 8142, August 2, 2001.
    Gene Sperling, director of the National Economic Council, the top economic policy job of the White House, once remarked that "the rising tide will lift some boats, but

The president is in overall charge of the enforcement of federal law; the United States Attorneys, the Federal Bureau of Investigation, and the Bureau of Prisons report directly to the president's attorney general. Nothing more increases avoidable misery in black America than wrongheaded policies regarding the criminalization of conduct, the administration of prosecution, and the severity of punishment.

> Black men for a quarter century have been five to seven times more likely than white men to be in prison, are much more likely to receive decades-long sentences or life without the possibility of parole, and are much likelier to be on death row. . . . Blacks in 2005 constituted 12.8 percent of the general population but nearly half of prison inmates and 42 percent of death row residents. About a third of young black men ages twenty to twenty-nine were in prison or jail or on probation or parole on an average day in 2005. [According to some estimates] 32 percent of black baby boys born in 2001 would spend some part of their lives in a state or federal prison.*

The mass-incarceration disaster that so starkly and disproportionately burdens black communities dramatically decreases opportunities for employment, civic engagement, or family life. And nothing more reinforces the stigmatization of African Americans than their pervasive association with imprisonment and recidivism and all of their many dismal consequences. Yet little has been done or will likely be done by the Obama administration to address this massive problem. Challenging the destructive American romance with hyper-punitiveness would be risky for any politician. For

---

others will run aground." "How to Refloat These Boats," *Washington Post*, December 18, 2005.
* Michael Tonry, *Punishing Race: A Continuing American Dilemma* (2010), 1, 11.

Obama, though, the risk would be greater still, since taking a strong stand against mass incarceration would encounter intense opposition, invite association with the most despised sector of colored America, and prompt complaints of racial partiality.* This is a risk that Obama is unwilling to take.

I am not blaming Obama—at least not solely or even mainly. The problems are beyond the capacity of any single person to remedy, even a president. They include a deeply flawed Constitution, prevalent strains of bigotry, and defective institutions, most importantly public schools and the Fourth Estate, that miseducate an appallingly ignorant populace.† The social critic Eric Alterman is correct when he argues that, unless the obstacles that confront liberal reformism are removed, a presidency capable of delivering upon a truly progressive agenda may well be impossible.‡

Alas, despite the urgency of the situation, there appears to be no force on the horizon that is capable of implementing the reforms needed. Some rallied to Obama hoping that he would become a transformational figure. Disappointment has ensued. This was inevitable, as promise, with all its imagined potentialities, gave way to performance, with all its unavoidable deficiencies. As the columnist Frank Rich observes:

---

* "Every time the President does or says anything to press for the cause of racial justice, it risks being interpreted as nothing more than racial loyalty or special pleading. In his effort to avoid this characterization, there is a natural . . . tendency for Obama and those around him to try to distance the administration quickly and forcefully from anything that looks like racial spoils or reverse racism." David B. Wilkins, "The New Social Engineers in the Age of Obama: Black Corporate Lawyers and the Making of the First Black President," *Harvard Law Journal* 53 (2010): 557, 635.

† See, e.g., Rich Shenkman, *Just How Stupid Are We? Facing the Truth About the American Voter* (2008); Michael X. Delli Carpini and Scott Keeler, *What Americans Know About Politics and Why It Matters* (1996); Michael Schudson, "America's Ignorant Voters," *Wilson Quarterly* 24 (2000): 16.

‡ See Eric Alterman, "Kabuki Democracy: Why a Progressive Presidency Is Impossible for Now," *The Nation*, July 7, 2010; Eric Alterman, *Kabuki Democracy: The System vs. Barack Obama* (2011).

The Obama of Hope and Change was too tough an act for Obama, a mere chief executive, to follow. . . . As soon as Inauguration Day turned to night, the real Obama was destined to depreciate like the shiny new luxury car that starts to lose its book value the moment it's driven off the lot.*

But the sharp decline of Obama's standing in the eyes of some of his most hopeful and articulate supporters is nonetheless remarkable. "I cannot recall a president," the commentator Robert Kuttner declares, "who generated so much excitement as a candidate but who turned out to be such a political dud as chief executive."[18] According to Kuttner and like-minded left-liberals, "Obama is a disaster as a crisis president."†

A major difficulty in assessing Obama is determining his ideological coloration. Is he a liberal-leaning centrist who seduced progressives with gauzy rhetoric about "hope" and "change" (to which they ascribed undue credit partly on the basis of his race and the thrill of experiencing the first black president)? Or is Obama an ardent liberal whose progressive inclinations have been inhibited by terrible foreign and domestic circumstances (the wars and financial meltdown he inherited) and a center-right bloc of the electorate that he (and any presidential contender) must accommodate in order to claim and retain the White House?

Each of these hypotheses captures important facets of the Obama enigma. He was never as liberal as some progressives imagined him to be. Apostles have consistently given his ambiguous rhetoric more of a leftish spin than was ever warranted. A revisiting of Obama's speeches and writings reveals numerous instances

---

* Frank Rich, "Why Has He Fallen Short?," *New York Review of Books*, August 19, 2010.
† Robert Kuttner, "What Now for the Democrats?," HuffingtonPost.com, December 5, 2010. See also Katrina vanden Heuvel, "Obama: On the Way to a Failed Presidency?," *Washington Post*, December 7, 2010.

of illusory promises. Moreover, the list of his retreats from progressive commitments is considerable and will undoubtedly grow. In defense of Obama, supporters cite the need for strategic prudence and adaptability. Obama underappreciates, however, that sometimes a political leader can win in the long run by pushing a position (or an appointment) that loses in the short run. Ronald Reagan lost the battle over Robert Bork. But in waging that struggle for judicial conservatism, Reagan won a larger battle by showing fidelity to principle and loyalty to supporters. With Obama, unfortunately, his supporters on the left (champions of the poor, civil libertarians, gay rights activists, organized labor, environmentalists, antiracists) have good reason to worry about the extent to which he will fight to advance or defend their aspirations. Obama's much-vaunted pragmatism degenerates at key moments into mere expediency, facilitating default on the difficult task of promoting progressive policies and values.

A poignant example of Obama's struggle to reconcile electoral prudence and progressive idealism is framed by his reactions to antigay policies. On the one hand, Obama insistently supported the repeal of "Don't Ask, Don't Tell" (DADT). This was the policy begun during the presidency of Bill Clinton when Congress rebelled against his plan to remove all bars to service by gays and lesbians. A compromise, DADT permitted gays and lesbians to serve in the military as long as they remained closeted. Pursuant to this policy some thirteen thousand people were driven out of the military when their stigmatized orientation became known.

The repeal of DADT would never have come to fruition in December 2010 but for Obama's careful, persistent, firm, but low-key efforts. For that he is entitled to plaudits. Gay rights activists castigated Obama for declining to support their position more forcefully by, for example, refusing to defend the constitutionality of DADT. But acceding to their wishes might well have alienated the wavering and conflicted moderate and conservative senators whose votes proved decisive. Obama deserves credit for gingerly burying DADT, and a high point of his presidency occurred in the moving statement he delivered upon signing the repeal legislation. Speaking more aspirationally than descriptively, Obama declared, "We are not a nation that says 'don't ask, don't tell.' We are a nation that says 'out of many, we are one.' . . . We are a nation that believes that all men and women are created equal."[19]

On the other hand, with respect to same-sex marriage Obama's record is troubling. In 1996 as a candidate for the Illinois State Senate, Obama expressed his "unequivocal support for gay marriage." Back then he addressed the matter straightforwardly: "I favor legalizing same-sex marriages, and would fight efforts to prohibit such marriages." Subsequently, however, he changed his mind, asserting that while same-sex couples should be able to obtain civil unions, marriage itself should be reserved for only heterosexual couples. "I'm a Christian," Obama has noted. "And so, although I try not to have my religious beliefs dominate or determine my political views on this issue, I do believe that tradition and my religious beliefs say that marriage is something sanctified between a man and a woman."[20]

This is a sad spectacle: the prevarication of a decent politician impelled by his perception of electoral realities to adopt an indecent position with which he disagrees. By opposing same-sex marriage (though he simultaneously opposes legislation that prohibits same-sex marriage), Obama espouses a policy that invidiously discriminates against a vulnerable minority by wrongly preventing gays and lesbians from expressing their love for one another through matrimony.[21] By supporting the heterosexual monopoly of marriage, Obama throws his weight behind the continued oppression of gays and lesbians.

Then there is the cynical—I am tempted to say *blasphemous*—

character of Obama's cover story. It requires a suspension of disbelief to think that he is sincere when he points to "religious beliefs" (that he never identifies specifically) as the basis for his position. Much more likely is that he simply came to predict that supporting same-sex marriage would cost him too many votes as he climbed the political ladder from local to statewide to nationwide office. Obama's purported "religious beliefs" have a remarkable character: they fit almost perfectly with the political profile that, in his view, best advances his electoral ambitions. One might have thought that on some contested cultural issue—abortion, capital punishment, sexual orientation—his "religious beliefs," if authentic, would pose a problem for his politics. But that is not so. His "religious beliefs" fit with such uniform snugness into his electoral strategy that I doubt their authenticity. They are, themselves, little more than another tool.

If Obama's religious beliefs really did determine his stance on same-sex marriage, there is still the problem of retrograde religiosity. After all, religious beliefs have caused or been deployed to justify all sorts of horrible practices, including slavery and segregation.[22] Obama has repeatedly referred to the fact that when his white mother and black father gave birth to him, a score of states still criminalized marriage across the race line. It was only in 1967 that the United States Supreme Court tardily invalidated state antimiscegenation* laws. "Religious beliefs" were often cited by white supremacists as a justification for such laws. In the late 1950s, when a judge sentenced a white man and a black woman

---

* The odd term "miscegenation" itself stems from the racial history of the presidency. The word was coined during the presidential election of 1864 by opponents of Abraham Lincoln, who introduced it in a pamphlet that suggested that Lincoln encouraged interracial marriage. The term combines the Latin words *miscere* (to mix) and *genus* (race). See David Goodman Croly and George Wakeman, *Miscegenation: The Theory of Blending the Races, Applied to the American White Men and Negro* (1864); Sidney Kaplan, "The Miscegenation Issue in the Election of 1864," in Allen D. Austin, ed., *American Studies in Black and White: Selected Essays 1949–1989.*

for marrying in violation of Virginia's antimiscegenation law, he made reference to "religious beliefs," declaring:

> Almighty God created the races white, black, yellow, malay, and red, and he placed them on different continents. And but for the interference with [God's] arrangement there would be no cause for such marriages. The fact that he separated the races shows that he did not intend for the races to mix.[23]

One may safely presume that President Obama rejects *this* "religious belief." It would be good to hear him justify, or even merely clarify, the "religious beliefs" that prompt him to reject the right of same-sex couples to marry. Professor Geoffrey Stone of the University of Chicago Law School is correct in stating, "Surely, [Obama] owes the American people a candid and reasoned explanation of his position. This is, after all, one of the most profound civil rights issues [with which] our nation is grappling."[24]

Part of the problem may be that Obama does not really *feel* that gay marriage implicates a "profound" civil-rights issue—though distinguishing sincere sentiments from mere public relations, always a difficult undertaking, is especially trying here. During his campaign for the presidency, at a debate sponsored by the Human Rights Campaign (an organization advocating the legalization of same-sex marriage), Obama remarked:

> Look, when my parents got married in 1961 it would have been illegal for them to be married in a number of states in the South. So obviously, this is something that I understand intimately, it's something that I care about. But if I were advising the civil rights movement back in 1961 about its approach to civil rights, I would have probably said it's less important that we focus on an anti-miscegenation law than we focus on a voting rights law and a non-discrimination and employment law and all the legal

rights that are conferred by the state. Now, it's not for me to suggest that you shouldn't be troubled by these issues. But my job as president is going to be to make sure that the legal rights that have consequences on a day to day basis [are available] for loving same sex couples all across the country.[25]

Obama apparently does not believe that denying gay couples the validation of marriage violates their right to equality before the law so long as they have equal access to the tangible benefits of marriage "that have consequences on a day to day basis."* In saying this, Obama is reminiscent of an ambivalent defender of de jure racial segregation in its final phase, when officials, under pressure, acquiesced to putting black and white students in the same building for instruction but insisted on doing something, *anything*—for instance, assigning blacks to a certain location in a classroom—to signify the continuation of racial hierarchy.† That the nation's first black president defends separate but equal in the context of same-gender intimacy is bitterly ironic.‡

Obama has failed (thus far) to attack homophobia in law—formal invidious discriminations against gays and lesbians—with the unflinching resolve that such bigotry should attract. In positing this critique I do not measure Obama against a moral baseline outside of the domain of electoral politics. I do not reproach him because he is no Martin Luther King, Jr. Of course he isn't!§ He

* It must be recognized, however, that in February 2011 President Obama did direct the Justice Department to cease defending in litigation the constitutionality of the Federal Defense of Marriage Act. See Charlie Savage and Sheryl Gay Stolberg, "In Turnabout, U.S. Says Marriage Act Blocks Gay Rights," *New York Times,* February 24, 2011.
† See, e.g., *McLaurin v. Oklahoma State Regents,* 332 U.S. 631 (1948) (invalidating policy requiring racial separation of Negro students in classrooms, libraries, and cafeterias).
‡ See David Paul Kuhn, "Will Obama Be Truman on Civil Rights?," *Real Clear Politics,* June 9, 2009 ("If the gay rights push is akin to the civil rights era, how far and how urgently is the first black president compelled to carry on the fight?").
§ Contrasting King and Obama, but also noting problems with that endeavor, Professor Tommie Shelby observes that "because of differences in their respective voca-

is a politician seeking to lead and govern a massive, complex, dysfunctional democracy that has long suppressed the racial group with which he is affiliated. I assess Obama in terms of his role as an electoral politician. Moreover, in evaluating Obama, I keep in mind the records of his predecessors. Many comparisons have been made between Obama and Franklin Delano Roosevelt, usually at the expense of the former. When exploring that comparison, it should be recalled that FDR played a major role in the moral disaster of Japanese-American internment during World War II, tolerated Jim Crow segregation, and declined to push hard for federal antilynching legislation, fearful that doing so would put at risk reformist measures that required the support (or at least the acquiescence) of militant white supremacists. I am critical of FDR because, despite the limits within which he worked, he could have and should have done more to challenge the racist orthodoxy of his time. I am critical of Obama for the same reason: taking due account of the constraints upon him, he could and should be doing more to challenge the heterosexist orthodoxy of this era.

My claim is by no means irrefutable. Opposition to gay marriage remains widespread. It is intense, moreover, in locales such as Ohio and Florida that are pivotal in close presidential elections.* It seems, though, that excessive cautiousness has led Obama to underestimate the alacrity with which the idea of equality regardless of sexual orientation has gained ground. Obama has been more conservative than regard for public opinion requires him to be. Undue fear has inhibited him from pushing the cultural envelope as far as he could *safely* push it. Obama himself realizes this. That

---

tions . . . and because Obama is operating within a very different historical context than did King, [any] comparison is likely to be misleading and unfair. Yet . . ." "Justice and Racial Conciliation: Two Visions," *Daedalus: Journal of the American Academy of Arts and Sciences*, Winter 2011.
* See Michael Klarman, "The Political Risks of Supporting Gay Rights," *Los Angeles Times*, September 19, 2010.

is largely why, immediately after signing the bill repealing DADT, Obama indicated that his views on same-sex marriage are "evolving." He mentioned no religious epiphany, suggesting instead that he was struggling with the issue on account of his personal familiarity with and respect for same-sex couples.[26] That, too, is likely a cover story. It seems rather obvious that the evolution of his stated position is contingent upon the evolution of public opinion. As the public more fully accepts same-sex marriage, so too will Obama.

The long exclusion of blacks from positions of power has facilitated the sentimental view that, perhaps because of their long experience with victimization, African Americans will display an enhanced sensitivity to social inequity.* Unfortunately, neither an identification with blackness nor the mere experience of suffering is sufficient to generate empathy. President Obama has rightly extolled empathy as a vital trait for a judge. It is a vital trait for anyone who seeks to deploy power humanely. It is a trait that Obama needs to internalize more fully in dealing with the status of gays and lesbians. Obama should reread the apt complaints of John Lewis and other activists when they assailed President John F. Kennedy for declining to do more on behalf of African Americans who were being cruelly wronged.† To avoid replicating his prede-

---

* "[O]ne would hope that [well-educated minorities] would be more sensitive to other minorities, that is the expectation. He [Obama] should be trying harder because he is a minority." John Aravosis quoted in David Kaufman, "Will DADT's Repeal Mend Obama's Rift with LGBT Leaders?" TheRoot.com, December 22, 2010. See also Mari J. Matsuda, "Looking to the Bottom: Critical Legal Studies and Reparations," *Harvard Civil Rights–Civil Liberties Law Review* 22 (1987): 232, 346, 360.
† Having insisted during his presidential campaign that he would prohibit racial discrimination in federally supported housing projects by a stroke of the pen in an executive order, JFK took twenty months after his inauguration to see his way clear to actually signing the order. Not only did Kennedy act belatedly; when he finally did sign the order, he selected the most limited of the feasible alternatives, prompting *The Pittsburgh Courier* to declare that "Negroes are getting weary of tokenism hailed as victories." See Nick Bryant, *The Bystander: John F. Kennedy and the Struggle for Black Equality* (2006).

cessors' failings, Obama needs to do more on behalf of the just demands of gays and lesbians.

Although Obama's standing has declined substantially among some liberal activists, it has remained high among the liberal "rank and file." This is so because of the momentum generated by his two-year stint in the Senate, where he compiled one of the most liberal voting records of any member of that body. It is so because of the raw relief felt by many who remain grateful to him for delivering them from yet another round of Republican presidential ascendancy. Obama also continues to be held in high esteem by liberals in general because he initiated or crucially assisted with, among other things, the passage of the Lilly Ledbetter Fair Pay Act (which strengthened gender antidiscrimination legislation); the American Recovery and Reinvestment Act (the economic stimulus bill); the Patient Protection and Affordable Care Act (the health-care reform law dubbed Obamacare by its detractors); the repeal of Don't Ask, Don't Tell; the emancipation of government-sponsored science from religious confinements; cessation of the most abusive practices undertaken against "terrorism" on behalf of national security; and the appointment of liberal-leaning Supreme Court justices, including the first Latino justice.

Another reason for Obama's high standing is his singular prestige in an important constituency of American liberalism—the African-American community. In the hearts and minds of most black Americans—indeed, the overwhelming mass of African Americans—Barack Obama is the most admired person in the canon of black celebrity and accomplishment, surpassing Frederick Douglass, Harriet Tubman, Booker T. Washington, W. E. B. Du Bois, Jackie Robinson, Muhammad Ali, Rosa Parks, Thurgood Marshall, and even Martin Luther King, Jr. This is so not because of Obama's policies or anything in particular that he has said or written. It is primarily because Obama climbed to the top of American electoral politics, besting along the way scores of people who were seemingly better positioned than he to win the presidency. Blacks, too, are powerfully attracted to success.

Another explanation for the African-American embrace of Obama is the perception among blacks that prejudice prompts many whites to oppose him and to seek his defeat. Opposition to antiblack racism generates protectiveness. Even blacks who vehemently disagree with Obama on important matters subordinate their misgivings out of a sense that racial loyalty demands solidarity with the nation's first black president.

Obama's singular standing in the black community also stems in large part from personal characteristics. He is adored for identifying as black when he could have labeled himself something other; for marrying a black woman, unlike many high-achieving African Americans who marry outside the race; for his easy familiarity with the colloquialisms and traditions of ordinary black folk; and for being a paragon of dignity and intellectuality in a culture suffused with derogatory images of brutish black masculinity. Detractors on the right have snidely claimed that Obama is an affirmative-action candidate and president. In other contexts such a dig at a black standard-bearer might have hurt the feelings of African Americans. Obama's personal superiority to his rivals, however, has allowed blacks to scoff at the attempted denigration. What, they asked, would have been Obama's fate had his academic record been as flamboyantly mediocre as, say, John McCain's? Had his marital record been as spotted by infidelity? Had his political career been as tainted by malfeasance (as, for example, the Keating Five debacle)? Had his presidential judgment been as exposed by the selection of an incompetent running mate? Any of these or kindred missteps would have irremediably crippled Obama. That he managed to avoid such snares prompts blacks to exult pridefully. Obama has filled their hearts as he has shown himself to be the most well-spoken, informed, gracious, cosmopolitan, agile, and thoughtful politician on the American political landscape. Blacks love Obama for relieving them of the burden of making excuses for him.

Blacks also adore Obama because of the way in which he has advanced himself. He has declined to pull a Clarence Thomas.* He associates himself with blacks and the African-American struggle for liberation. He pays homage to the likes of John Lewis, Joseph Lowery, and Dorothy Height. He honors the sacrifices made at the Edmund Pettus Bridge† and other sites of racial conflict, bringing them deeper into the American national narrative, placing them alongside such revered venues as Valley Forge and Gettysburg.

Obama takes care to advance the racial integration of the American narrative in ways that are acceptable to whites—or at least to a sufficient number to maintain a winning coalition. Moreover, he goes out of his way to avoid pushing what many might see as a "black" agenda. Most African Americans, however, do not hold this against him. They adopt the attitude taken by most Catholics after JFK became the first Catholic president—an attitude of patient forbearance. A cleric noted in 1962 that most Catholics were "not troubled" by Kennedy's careful tiptoeing around "so many fragile Protestant eggs."‡ Similarly, most blacks are untroubled by Obama's careful accommodation of white racial anxieties. Indeed, many see his diffidence on racial matters as either necessary or good or both. Some do not want Obama to pay special attention to the problems of African Americans because, like many whites, they perceive such solicitude as inconsistent with what they see as his overriding duty to serve the interests of *all* Americans equally regardless of race. They view a race-transcending performance

---

* See Randall Kennedy, *Sellout: The Politics of Racial Betrayal* (2008).

† At the March 2007 commemoration of the landmark voting-rights protest at Selma, Alabama, in 1965, Obama declared, "I'm here"—running for the presidency—"because somebody marched. I'm here because y'all sacrificed for me. I stand on the shoulders of giants." Quoted in Remnick, *The Bridge*, at 21.

‡ See "Religion: Catholic View of JFK," *Time*, January 19, 1962.

on Obama's part as a great boon to black America—a living lesson in the ability of blacks to exercise authority on behalf of the whole and without racial favoritism. Other blacks think that there would be nothing wrong in principle with Obama showing special solicitude for black Americans; after all, they do have special problems, just as the elderly or veterans or residents who live near flood-prone rivers have special problems. Many who believe this, however, recognize that it is an unpopular position, at least among whites, and hold, therefore, that as a matter of electoral strategy, Obama should avoid it.

There are blacks, of course, who take a very different tack. They fault Obama for his reticence on racial matters and his preference for "universal" as opposed to race-specific responses to social inequities, including those that especially burden racial minorities. Deriding the president, Professor Michael Eric Dyson of Georgetown University quips that Obama "runs from race like a black man runs from a cop." [27]

Given Obama's role, his ambitions, and the circumstances in which he finds himself, it would be folly for him to proceed in the fashion that some on the black left suggest—to offer the country an ongoing and contentious seminar on race. Candid race talk in front of a national audience is not good for Obama. Unless very carefully scripted, it is much more likely to exacerbate anxiety than to nourish understanding. That is why some of Obama's most vocal right-wing enemies—Rush Limbaugh, Glenn Beck, Sean Hannity, the whole of Fox News—delight in associating him with racial controversy. It is their most effective way of blackening him.

Detractors on the black left express little concern about this problem as they castigate Obama for declining to make race talk a higher priority. Their critique reflects a bit of narcissism. It is not coincidental that some of the most prominent of those who demand that Obama converse more about race themselves talk about race professionally. They seem to want Obama not only to agree with them but to be like them. He has, however, chosen a different line of work. Instead of presiding over a classroom, he presides over a nation. I also suspect that they underestimate the constraints that politicians must accommodate if they are to be elected and reelected. Obama's fiercest critics on the black left are used to the politics of protest. They appreciate its etiquette, strategies, and goals. They are unused to the politics of governance and appear at times to prefer a merely theoretical progressivism that is marginal and thus insulated from the contamination of strategy and compromise.

Most African Americans eschew the demanding racial politics of Obama's detractors on the black left. Warnings that blacks had excessive expectations that would inevitably be dashed and give rise to bitter disappointment have proven to be unwarranted. Blacks have, for the most part, been remarkably savvy, patient, and loyal in terms of their relationship to the Obama administration. They appreciate that Obama must accommodate a wide range of competing demands. They expect him to do what he can, consistent with political practicalities, to push the country's agenda in a progressive direction. But they perceive, rightly, that it will always be difficult to ascertain whether Obama is doing this—or whether he is failing to push as far as he safely could. Against this backdrop of virtually impenetrable uncertainty, they defer to Obama because they trust him.

In return for their support, most blacks insist only that Obama continue to identify as black, comport himself with dignity, and refrain from engaging in racial treason. The black electorate deeply appreciates his presence in the White House alongside his family. Critics object with exasperation, contending that blacks are too easily satisfied by the vicarious pleasure of witnessing the triumph of "one of their own"—even if he takes them for granted. There is some truth in that complaint. Socialized to expect hostility or indifference, many blacks are unduly impressed when politicians show them even minimal respect, let alone affection. For merely treating blacks as peers, Bill Clinton was fondly adopted by some African Americans as an honorary "brother."* A similar but still more powerful dynamic is at hand with Obama. That is largely why blacks will continue to support him almost regardless of his policies.

Is this a shallow preference for symbolism over substance? Or is this a wise attentiveness to the substance of symbolism? Some observers demote symbolism—the realm of the psychological and spiritual—to a role secondary to tangible items of political economy, such as money, positions, and policies. But time and again people of all sorts have demonstrated the transcendent importance of symbolism in their lives: the liberty to sit anywhere on a bus unhampered by a color line or the freedom to eat a hamburger at a lunch counter unburdened by caste restrictions. Most African Americans gratefully appreciate that the simple fact of a black man occupying the presidency has irrevocably transformed the United States. For one thing, as law professor David Wilkins observes, "Obama's election, in and of itself, has changed the very idea of what is possible for every black child in America. It is one thing to *say* that every little boy or girl might grow up to be President of the United States. It is quite a different thing to *see* a black President acting on the world stage every day of the week."† Having received so little for so long, blacks are happy to have someone in the White

---

* See Dewayne Wickham, *Bill Clinton and Black America* (2002); "Bill Clinton Inducted into Arkansas Black Hall of Fame," *Jet*, November 11, 2002; and "Historically Black Fraternity [Phi Beta Sigma] Inducts Bill Clinton as Honorary Member," HuffingtonPost.com, July 7, 2009.
† David B. Wilkins, "The New Social Engineers in the Age of Obama: Black Corporate Lawyers and the Making of the First Black President," *Howard Law Journal* 53 (2010): 557, 638.

House with whom they can fully identify and who fully identifies with them, even if he is unwilling to advance any set of federal initiatives that could plausibly be labeled "a black agenda."

Aware of the president's limitations, I am yet unembarrassed to say that I admire Barack Obama. To perceive that he could actually win the White House required insight. To overtake Hillary Clinton, vanquish John McCain, and persuade a center-right country to elect a black liberal required skill and, yes, audacity. To shepherd to enactment important legislation has required perseverance. To reach the heights Obama has ascended has also demanded realism. I seek, above all, to embrace that trait in analyzing the racial issues that have surrounded Obama's election and presidency.

I

The Obama Inaugural

I attended the inauguration of Barack Obama with about two million people who created one of the largest crowds in the history of Washington, D.C. This was a first for me, although I grew up in the nation's capital. I felt compelled to be present, in part because of loved ones whom I achingly wished could have been alive to share the occasion. Others felt similarly. Irma Brown-Williams from Tuskegee, Alabama, showed up wearing a coat on which she had pinned photos of her mother, father, and siblings, all of whom were deceased. Asked to explain, she said, "I'm here for them. . . . They could not be here, so I brought them with me."*1

In my imagination I brought with me my wonderful wife, Yvedt Matory, a brilliant surgeon who died of cancer when she was only forty-eight. Yvedt was at the Democratic National Convention in 2004 when Obama delivered the speech that elevated him to political stardom. She lauded his eloquence, poise, intelligence, and vision. She also admired his evident ambition, like hers, to be free of any racially confining expectations. She would have exulted at his success in showing so many Americans, including blacks— *especially* blacks—that an African American could realistically

---

* In *The Breakthrough: Politics and Race in the Age of Obama* (2009), Gwen Ifill offers another illustration of this sentiment. She dedicates her book to her parents, "who did not live to see the day."

aspire to be the country's chief executive and then manage a winning campaign.

I also brought with me Yvedt's father, Dr. William Matory, Sr., also a surgeon, a man who devoted himself tirelessly to the elevation of Freedmen's Hospital (now the Howard University Hospital) and the National Medical Association (NMA), the organization created by black physicians as an alternative to the American Medical Association (AMA) when it excluded black doctors. Dr. Matory lay dying in the intensive care unit of the Howard University Hospital during the inaugural festivities. He held on just long enough to see on television what would have seemed inconceivable for most of his life.

I am usually dismissive of the pomp that surrounds national ceremonial occasions in Washington, D.C. Not this time. I was enthralled by the sights and sounds that marked Obama's transition to power. I was thrilled by the speeding motorcades; the squadrons of dark-suited security officials with electronic transmitters in their ears; the military officers snappily saluting the president-elect; the likeness of the Obamas on T-shirts, sweatshirts, plates, mugs, posters, newspapers, and buttons; the nonstop coverage of the incoming First Family in every medium of communication. I was on the lookout for any diminution of deference typically accorded to a new president. I wanted him to be shown every iota of respect granted to previous holders of this exalted position. I inwardly objected when folks on the street referred to him as "Barack." For me that was all too colloquial. I wanted everyone to refer to him as "Mr. Obama," or "Mr. President-elect," or, after the inauguration, "Mr. President."

I mused about the significance of Obama's triumph against the historical backdrop of the city in which I was raised.[2] Prior to the Civil War, free black Washingtonians had been subjected to all manner of demeaning supervision. In 1812 the D.C. city charter required every free Negro to register and carry on his or her person a certificate of freedom. In 1828 Congress instructed the commissioner of public buildings to bar Negroes from the grounds of the Capitol unless they were there to work. A city council ordinance in 1835 provided that Negroes could drive carts and hackneys, but could not run taverns or restaurants. A city council ordinance in 1850 required the mayor's express permission for any public gathering of Negroes.

Free blacks, of course, constituted the privileged strata of Negroes, most of whom were enslaved throughout the antebellum period. Slave labor helped to build the White House and the Capitol, and slave trading in the city was a large, lucrative, visible enterprise. Slavery in D.C. lasted until 1862, when Congress freed the slaves residing within the city (some 3,100 persons) and compensated their owners.

During Reconstruction, the fortunes of D.C. Negroes improved dramatically. Like blacks elsewhere, they received, at least formally, legal protection against racial discrimination in various realms, including voting, jury service, and places of public accommodation. During the long reaction against Reconstruction they also suffered disappointment. D.C. was not Mississippi; no lynchings occurred there and, indeed, Washington was a locale to which many blacks (like my parents) fled from Jim Crow terror further south. Still, the insults, restrictions, and deprivations that D.C. Negroes experienced between the First and the Second Reconstructions were pervasive. When the Lincoln Memorial was dedicated in May 1922 the lone black speaker was barred from sitting onstage with the white speakers, and Negroes in attendance were confined to a designated area. Public schools in D.C. were racially segregated. Restrictive covenants often excluded blacks from attractive housing stock. When Negroes bought property in defiance of such covenants they frequently found themselves sub-

ject to court-ordered eviction. Although a civil-rights statute prohibited racial discrimination in places of public accommodation,
restaurants and other businesses discriminated against Negroes
anyway. Obama briefly alluded to this in his inaugural address,
noting that his own father might well have been excluded from
restaurants in the D.C. area had he journeyed there prior to the
Civil Rights Revolution.*

President Truman's Committee on Civil Rights devoted an
entire section of its landmark 1947 report to the shame of racial
caste in Washington, D.C. "The District of Columbia," the
committee observed, "should symbolize to our own citizens and
to the people of all countries our great tradition of civil liberty.
Instead, it is a graphic illustration of a failure of democracy."[3]

For a long period the residents of Washington, D.C., were de-
prived almost wholly of a say in local governance, a circumstance
due in no small measure to the potential electoral strength of the
District's black population. Federal appointees administered the
city under the watchful oversight of a congressional committee
often chaired by white supremacists who openly expressed their
contempt for black Washingtonians. In the early 1970s, Congress
gave the District a measure of home rule, providing for an elected
city council and mayor. But the legislation passed by these authorities remains subject to the approval of Congress. Furthermore,
residents of the District of Columbia enjoy no congressional representation; they have no presence in the Senate, and their lone voice
in the House of Representatives is merely a nonvoting "delegate."

To the extent that District residents have developed self-
governance and political participation, it is a record that has been

---

* It is also true, however, that some establishments that excluded American blacks admitted African blacks, granting them status as honorary whites. See Renée Romano, "No
Diplomatic Immunity: African Diplomats, the State Department, and Civil Rights,
1961–1964," *Journal of American History* 87 (2000): 546.

notably mixed, with laudable achievements sullied by inefficiency and corruption.[4] The most influential local politician during the final quarter of the twentieth century was Marion S. Barry, Jr.— the first politician for whom I voted—a civil-rights activist and thrice-elected mayor who became a bad political joke. Imprisoned for drug offenses, vilified for blatant womanizing, lampooned for exemplifying the worst features of urban bossism, Barry depressed disastrously the political morale of Washingtonians and made many of them doubly appreciative of the well-spoken, clean-cut, family-oriented Obama. D.C. voters backed Obama overwhelmingly. Indeed, no jurisdiction came close to D.C. in the extent to which its voters supported him. Voters in Obama's home state of Illinois preferred their native son to John McCain 62 percent to 37 percent, while voters in D.C. preferred him 93 percent to 7 percent.[5]

In the days prior to the inauguration, I thought about how, at long last, a Negro would join, and thereby irrevocably change, that exclusive club of American presidents that was initially dominated by slaveholders.[6] Ten of the first fifteen presidents *owned* Negroes, including George Washington, who referred to them as a "troublesome species of property."[7] Several slaves fled the Master of Mount Vernon, including a woman named Oney Judge who ran away during the waning days of Washington's presidency, successfully eluding the enraged chief executive who tried all sorts of means, including trickery, to recapture her.[8] Like many of the Founding Fathers, Washington privately criticized slavery. Yet he personally held in bondage hundreds of men, women, and children throughout his life (though he freed posthumously, upon his wife's death, all of the slaves that he owned) and took pains to protect the interests of fellow slaveholders. After the united colonies won their independence, Washington insisted that departing British warships keep a "Book of Negroes," to facilitate claims by masters aggrieved by the loss of absconding slaves.[9]

When Thomas Jefferson was inaugurated in 1801, one out of every seven Americans was enslaved, nearly two hundred by the principal author of the Declaration of Independence. Jefferson privately fulminated against slavery, calling it an "unremitting despotism," a "moral and political depravity," an "abominable crime," and a "hideous blot."*[10] But he abhorred the presence of free blacks more than he objected to slavery and thus refrained from pursuing its abolition.†[11] Unlike Jefferson, President Andrew Jackson saw nothing wrong with owning and selling slaves.[12] The same was true of presidents James Monroe, Martin Van Buren, William Henry Harrison, Zachary Taylor, and James K. Polk, whose wife turned the White House basement into slave quarters.[13]

I delighted in anticipating the Obamas' occupying the same house that the Lincolns had occupied. By the time of the inaugural, Obama had already repeatedly invoked Lincoln as his hero, muse, and model. That he should choose Lincoln is not surprising; after all, next to Washington, the sixteenth president is probably the one most beloved and respected among Americans. Embracing Lincoln, however, is not without its complications. Imbued with the racism common to his time and region, Lincoln perceived blacks as inassimilable and inferior aliens for much of his adult life.

I am not, nor ever have been in favor of bringing about in any way the social and political equality of the white and black

---

* During his presidency, Jefferson was accused of fathering children by one of his slaves, Sally Hemings. This allegation was long viewed as a calumny concocted by political enemies. Although the charge was broadly believed in African-American intellectual circles, it was heatedly denied among leading white intellectuals. Now, however, the truth of the allegation is widely accepted, largely on account of the incisive scholarship of Annette Gordon Reed. See *The Hemingses of Monticello: An American Family* (2008) and *Thomas Jefferson and Sally Hemings: An American Controversy* (1997).

† Although Jefferson castigated slavery, he did so mainly because of what he saw as its detrimental effects on whites. He found it difficult to empathize with enslaved blacks whom he suspected of being irredeemably inferior to whites. See John Chester Miller, *The Wolf by the Ears: Thomas Jefferson and Slavery* (1991).

races [*applause*] . . . I am not nor ever have been in favor of making voters or jurors of negroes, nor of qualifying them to hold office, nor to intermarry with white people; and I will say in addition to this that there is a physical difference between the white and black races which I believe will for ever forbid the two races living together on terms of social and political equality. And inasmuch as they cannot so live, while they do remain together there must be a position of superior and inferior, and I as much as any other man am in favor of having the superior position assigned to the white race.*

Yet he did take decisive steps to end slavery, allowed his perception of African Americans to evolve, and even warmed to the idea that some blacks should be accorded civil and political rights.† Frederick Douglass once described Lincoln as "emphatically the Black man's President."[14]

Lincoln's successor, Andrew Johnson, however, was the most fervent Negrophobe ever to occupy the White House. A former slaveholder who was deeply insecure and resentful because of his own impoverished origins, Johnson opposed almost all of the post–Civil War federal constitutional and statutory provisions that sought to elevate blacks, asserting unabashedly that so long as he was president the United States would remain "a government for white men."[15]

---

* From the fourth Lincoln-Douglas debate, September 18, 1858. That so many find this extract so surprising and jarring evidences the large degree to which the race issue in American life has been marginalized and obfuscated even among the well educated.

On Lincoln's views regarding race and slavery see Eric Foner, *The Fiery Trial: Abraham Lincoln and American Slavery* (2010); John Stauffer, *Giants: The Parallel Lives of Frederick Douglass and Abraham Lincoln* (2008); George M. Frederickson, *Big Enough to Be Inconsistent: Abraham Lincoln Confronts Slavery and Race* (2008).

† A speech favorably mentioning the prospect of educated black soldiers being allowed to vote was the proverbial last straw that prompted John Wilkes Booth to assassinate Lincoln. See Eric Foner, *The Fiery Trial*, 332.

On the Sunday prior to Obama's inauguration, Harvard Law School held a brunch in honor of its first alumnus to occupy the White House since Rutherford B. Hayes, the nineteenth president. At the brunch were a wide range of people whose own lives dramatize the opening up of American society that Obama's election epitomizes. Robert Bell was there. The first black chief judge of the Court of Appeals of Maryland, Bell had been arrested as a teenager in 1965 for sitting in at a segregated restaurant in Baltimore, Maryland. In attendance as well was Terri Sewell. She whispered to me that she was thinking of running for a seat in the House of Representatives. In 2010 she did, becoming the first black female Alabamian ever elected to Congress.

Also on hand were classmates of the president-elect who should feel vindicated for their prescience in singling him out as an outstanding member of the class of 1991. They had elected him to the presidency of the *Harvard Law Review*—another black "first." They had also invited him to be the keynote speaker at the annual Conference of the Harvard Black Law Students' Association. Usually the association invites a prominent professor or judge to deliver the major speech at its banquet. That year, however, the students chose a peer—Obama—who delivered a speech, "Don't Forget Where You Come From," that prompted a standing ovation.

Hayes had ascended to the presidency after a disputed election that was resolved, at least in part, by an implicit deal that involved removing federal troops from the South. This hastened the death of the experiment with multiracial democracy in the First Reconstruction. Now a man whose election was made possible by the *Second* Reconstruction would join Hayes as a presidential alumnus of Harvard Law School.

During his campaign and in his gracious concession speech to Obama on Election Day, John McCain referred to the uproar provoked by President Theodore Roosevelt when he invited Booker T. Washington to dinner at the White House on October 16, 1901.[16] The reaction against the dinner was considerably more vicious, however, than McCain's descriptions suggested. The *Memphis* [Tennessee] *Scimitar* newspaper editorialized that by dining with "a nigger" Roosevelt had produced "the most damnable outrage that has ever been perpetrated by any citizen of the United States."[17] Similarly angered was Senator Benjamin Tillman of South Carolina who declared that "the action of President Roosevelt in entertaining that nigger will necessitate our killing a thousand niggers in the South before they will learn their place again."[18] One should not infer from this incident that TR was a racial progressive; to the contrary, he was a white supremacist. Still, TR was less detrimental to the aspirations of blacks than his successor, President Woodrow Wilson, who superintended the comprehensive racial segregation of the federal civil service and welcomed to the White House a screening of D. W. Griffith's paean to the Ku Klux Klan, the landmark film *The Birth of a Nation*.

In the days before Obama's installation, I enjoyed the thought that he would soon become president like Warren G. Harding, who, bowing to segregation, had insisted upon the "fundamental, eternal, and inescapable difference" between whites and blacks;[19] like Calvin Coolidge, who won the general election after being nominated at the 1924 Republican National Convention at which a chicken-wire screen separated white and black delegates; like Franklin Delano Roosevelt, who held press conferences from which Negro reporters were barred for most of his tenure as the chief executive;* like John F. Kennedy, who proved himself to be

---

* The exclusion, though racial, was done indirectly. The White House Correspondents' Association issued press credentials for presidential news conferences only to reporters for daily newspapers. None of the black newspapers were dailies; they were weeklies or semimonthlies. White papers offered no employment to black reporters. Although Presi-

unduly cautious in challenging segregation; like Lyndon Baines Johnson, who pushed through Congress the Civil Rights Act of 1964 and the Voting Rights Act of 1965; like Richard Milhous Nixon, who casually and repeatedly referred to blacks as "jigs";* like William Jefferson Clinton, who probably had more genuinely friendly peer relationships with blacks than any other previous commander in chief.[20]

As I sat in the frigid cold for four hours on the portico of the Capitol on January 20, 2009, awaiting Obama's oath-taking, I thought of how the pursuit of electoral office has been a frustrating, heartbreaking, often futile enterprise for African Americans.

John Mercer Langston, the son of a white man and a black woman, was likely the only African American (recognized as an African American) to be elected to public office prior to the Civil War.† In 1855 voters in Brownhelm, Ohio, elected him to be

---

dent Roosevelt's press secretary, Steve Early, claimed that he and the administration had no say over the matter of eligibility for covering press conferences, they did intercede on behalf of white journalists when doing so suited their purposes.

On a trip through Harlem during FDR's reelection campaign in 1940, Early got in a scuffle with a black police officer. He was photographed kneeing the officer in the groin. When Republicans publicized the incident, the officer announced that he still intended to vote for Roosevelt. Grateful and chastened, Early worked to obtain accreditation for *a* black reporter. In February 1944, Harry McAlpin broke a journalistic color bar by becoming the first black reporter to join the White House press corps for a news conference in the Oval Office. See Donald A. Ritchie, *Reporting from Washington: The History of the Washington Press Corps* (2005), 29–32.

* During a phone conversation, Richard Nixon calmed his national security advisor, Henry Kissinger, who was agitated about the flattering press coverage received by Secretary of State William Rogers during a trip to Africa. "Henry," Nixon declared, "let's leave the niggers to Bill and we'll take care of the rest of the world." Quoted in Kenneth O'Reilly, *Nixon's Piano: Presidents and Racial Politics from Washington to Clinton* (1995), 292.

† Some would argue that Alexander Twilight should be seen as the first African American to be elected to public office. In 1836, he was elected to the Vermont legislature. His father, Ichabod Twilight, was indisputably a man of color. Historians differ regarding the race of his mother. Some believe she was white. Alexander was light-skinned and probably passed for white. He appears to have faced no racial impediments and was listed in the 1840 federal census with "Free White Persons." See Michael T. Hahn, *Alexander Twilight: Vermont's African American Pioneer* (1998), 3–6.

the town's clerk.* That Langston's election was so extraordinary highlights the somber reality that, prior to the Civil War, blacks were widely viewed as disqualified racially for participation in government.

The Reconstruction era marked the first time in American history during which a sizable number of blacks became influential participants in government. Between 1867 and 1877, about two thousand attained public offices, many of them elected posts. Most of these positions involved the representation of localities with large black voting majorities, given that whites, regardless of their political affiliation, were typically loath to vote for black candidates. Still, during Reconstruction, appreciable numbers of blacks did play important roles in popular self-government. At the local level, they became justices of the peace, city councillors, county commissioners, election officials, sheriffs, registrars, and tax collectors.[21] At the state level, blacks became delegates to constitutional conventions, superintendents of education, and members of state legislatures.[22] John R. Lynch, a former slave, became speaker of the Mississippi State House of Representatives (and later won election to the United States House of Representatives). Jonathan J. Wright became the nation's first black state supreme court justice when the South Carolina Senate elected him to that state's high court. Six blacks served as lieutenant governors, and in 1872 P. B. S. Pinchback briefly sat as the acting governor of Louisiana.

Fourteen blacks became members of the United States House of Representatives, while two were sent by state legislatures to the United States Senate.† Hiram Rhoades Revels became the first

* Langston had the appearance of an African American and was seen to be such by those who voted him into office. He had an outstanding career as an abolitionist, attorney, diplomat (United States minister to Haiti), educator (first dean of Howard Law School), and politician (member of the House of Representatives). See William Cheek and Aimee Lee Cheek, *John Mercer Langston and the Fight for Black Freedom, 1829–65* (1989).
† For a long period, United States senators were chosen by state legislatures. The federal

African American to serve in either house of Congress. Born free in North Carolina in 1822 of white, black, and Indian ancestry, Revels became a politician in Mississippi during Reconstruction and was selected by the legislature in 1870 to fill the remainder of what had been Jefferson Davis's term in the Senate before Davis resigned to become president of the Confederacy. When Revels traveled to Washington, D.C., to represent Mississippi, "railroad conductors and steamboat captains required him—senator or not—to ride in the separate colored compartments."[23] Moreover, when Revels presented himself for admission to Congress, his way was blocked by opponents who argued that he had failed to satisfy the constitutional requirement that a person must be a citizen for at least nine years before becoming eligible to serve as a senator. They contended that blacks born in the United States had been citizens only since the promulgation of the Fourteenth Amendment in 1868. According to this view, by 1870 Revels was still years shy of the Constitution's durational requirement. Still other opponents contended that, despite the Fourteenth Amendment, Negroes were ineligible for federal citizenship and thus, by extension, ineligible for congressional officeholding. The seating of a man of color, declared Senator Willard Saulsbury of Delaware, was a "great calamity" and "damning outrage" that left him with "but little hope for the future of [the] country."[24] After three days of heated debate the Senate admitted Revels.*

White supremacists abhorred black officeholding and attacked it in every imaginable way. Consider the case of Georgia. In

---

Constitution's Seventeenth Amendment, ratified in 1913, provided for the direct election of senators.

* The first black to serve a *full* term in the Senate was Blanche Kelso Bruce. Born a slave, Bruce held several positions in Mississippi—sheriff, superintendent of schools, tax collector—before the state legislature sent him to the Senate, where he served from 1875 to 1881. See Eric Foner, *Freedom's Lawmakers: A Directory of Black Officeholders During Reconstruction* (1993), 29–30.

order to regain admission to the United States Congress, that state established a new constitution that permitted black men to vote. When blacks were elected to office in the state legislature, however, they were excluded on the grounds that while the new constitution lifted the traditional racial bar on *voting*, it did not lift the traditional racial bar on *officeholding*.[25] The United States Congress repudiated Georgia's action and compelled it to recognize the black officeholders as a condition for seating the state's congressional delegation. The fact is, however, that the prospect of black voting and officeholding was also deeply unpopular among whites in most of the non-Southern states. Many whites resisted a federal constitutional prohibition against racial discrimination in voting. When such a provision was finally promulgated as the Fifteenth Amendment, it was among the narrowest of the alternatives debated and, despite the controversy in Georgia, contained no express prohibition of racial discrimination with respect to officeholding.[26]

White supremacists unleashed a campaign of intimidation against blacks who did anything suggestive of a belief that they were entitled to participate in governance. Voters were targeted. So, too, were teachers and journalists. The most hated of all "uppity" Negroes, however, were black politicians. "It is difficult to think of any group of public officials in American history," Professor Eric Foner observes, "who faced the threat of violence as persistently as Reconstruction's black officeholders."[27] Targeted by white supremacist paramilitary organizations such as the Ku Klux Klan and the White League, forty-five black officials were driven from their homes; forty-one were shot at, stabbed, or assaulted; thirty-four were murdered. Recounting the whipping inflicted upon him by the KKK, Andrew J. Flowers, a justice of the peace in Tennessee, testified that, according to his assailants, he was targeted because he had had "the impudence to run against a white man for office, and beat him. . . . They said they had nothing in particular against me . . . but they did not intend for any nigger to hold office in the United States."[28] When Lawrence Cain, a two-term congressman for South Carolina, sought votes in 1876, he was warned that he would be killed if he continued to campaign. "If you want to rule a country," he was told, "you must go to Africa."[29]

Racist enemies of black officeholders also created derogatory myths about them—charges that they were especially ignorant, inept, arrogant, corrupt, dictatorial. From the onset of black officeholding during the 1870s until the middle of the twentieth century, journalists, cartoonists, filmmakers, novelists, historians, and other shapers of public opinion and memory repeatedly portrayed the black officials of the Reconstruction era unflatteringly. Thomas Nast lampooned them as outlandish buffoons in his drawings for *Harper's Weekly*. The journalist James S. Pike depicted them as democracy's nightmare, contending that during Reconstruction the white government of South Carolina was replaced by "the most ignorant democracy that mankind ever saw. . . . It is the dregs of the population habilitated in the robes of their intelligent predecessors, and asserting over them the rule of ignorance and corruption. . . . It is barbarism overwhelming civilization."[30] In the middle of the twentieth century, it remained widely believed among whites that the Southern experiment with black officeholding in Reconstruction had been a terrible mistake with disastrous consequences. "The Negroes," Professor E. Merton Coulter of the University of Georgia declared, "were fearfully unprepared to occupy positions of rulership." Black officeholding was thus "the most spectacular and exotic development in the history of white civilization . . . [and the] longest to be remembered, shuddered at, and execrated."[31]

An aspect of the history of black officeholding that has been largely forgotten is the struggle that was waged in the final two decades of the nineteenth century by black politicians and their allies to oppose the seating in Congress of white politicians who used or benefited from illicit means, including threats or violence, to "win" elections.[32] In 1880, for example, John R. Lynch objected to the seating of his white Democratic Party opponent, former Confederate general James Ronald Chalmers. Lynch alleged that local election officials in Mississippi had illegally eliminated large numbers of black voters and then wrongly certified Chalmers as the winner. The House of Representatives agreed, ousted Chalmers, and seated Lynch instead.* Congress, unfortunately, ceased monitoring the legitimacy of elections, contending that such a task was better left to the courts. The state and federal courts, however, showed themselves to be unwilling either to "find" racial discrimination, even when it was blatantly present, or to remedy violations, even when they were stipulated to exist. Not until the late 1960s, pursuant to the Voting Rights Act, did the Fifteenth Amendment actually come to mean something in large areas of the Deep South.

The last black in Congress in the nineteenth century was also the last former slave to serve. George Henry White, a representative from North Carolina, served two terms, from 1897 to 1901. In his valedictory address to Congress, White protested the open, illegal, but effective disenfranchisement of African Americans and concomitant deprivations imposed upon them, including lynchings. Calling his speech "the Negroes' temporary farewell to the American Congress," he insisted that "Phoenix-like [they] will rise

---

* Several years later, at the 1884 Republican National Convention in Chicago, Lynch became the first black to make a keynote address to a national political convention. See Morton Stavis, "A Century of Struggle for Black Enfranchisement in Mississippi: From the Civil War to the Congressional Challenge of 1965—and Beyond," *Mississippi Law Journal* 57: 591, 632, n. 175.

up some day and come again."[33] Not until 1973 did black congressional representation from the South resume (with the elections of Andrew Young of Georgia and Barbara Jordan of Texas).

Between 1901 and 1929 there were no blacks in Congress. That appalling absence ended with the election of Representative Oscar Stanton De Priest, the first of a series of important African-American politicians from Chicago. De Priest was succeeded in 1935 by Arthur Wergs Mitchell after a landmark election. Prior to Mitchell, all of the blacks elected to Congress had been Republicans. Mitchell was the first black *Democrat* to be elected. He won a contest that was essentially a referendum on President Franklin Roosevelt's New Deal.

Since the 1930s, the great majority of black members of Congress have been Democrats.* This is attributable to FDR's New Deal policies, which were relatively friendly to workers and the poor;[34] to President Harry S. Truman's initiatives in support of blacks' civil rights, especially his order to desegregate the armed forces;[35] and to President Lyndon Johnson's sponsorship of the major legislative achievements of the Civil Rights Revolution.[36] It is also attributable to the fact that, since the early 1960s, the Republican Party has become the main political base of opposition to policies designed to advance the interests of blacks. The presidential nominee of the Republican Party in 1964, Senator Barry Goldwater of Arizona, opposed the Civil Rights Act. And, in 1968, the victorious Republican presidential candidate, Richard Nixon, adopted a "Southern strategy" which entailed a conscious effort to harness white backlash against the Civil Rights Revolution. Nixon's Southern (white) strategy was subsequently redeployed by

---

* The exceptions are sufficiently few to name easily: Senator Edward Brooke (Massachusetts, 1967–1979); Representative Gary Franks (Connecticut, 1991–1997); Representative J. C. Watts (Oklahoma, 1995–2003); Representative Tim Scott (South Carolina, 2011–); Representative Allen West (Florida, 2011–).

presidential aspirants Ronald Reagan and George H. W. Bush.[37] The racial consequences of the two parties' political calculations and commitments are stark. While the Republican Party was the predominant home of black electoral officeholders in the nineteenth and early twentieth centuries, the Democratic Party is now their main home. After the elections of 2008, *all* of the blacks in the House of Representatives were Democrats. After the elections of 2010, all but two of the blacks in the House were Democrats.

In 1960, four members of Congress were black. In 1970, the number had increased to eleven. By 1985, the number had risen to twenty-two. After the elections of 2010, the number stood at forty-three. With only three exceptions, these officials were members of the House of Representatives. The only blacks to have been popularly elected to the United States Senate are Edward Brooke of Massachusetts (1966), Carol Moseley Braun of Illinois (1992), and Barack Obama of Illinois (2004).*

Blacks have also pursued officeholding in gubernatorial and mayoral contests. "The greatest change in twentieth century urban politics," Professor Richard Bernard observes, "has been the coming to power of blacks."[38] The first dramatic breakthroughs occurred in 1967, when Richard G. Hatcher won election as mayor of Gary, Indiana, and Carl B. Stokes won election as mayor of Cleveland, Ohio. Over the next thirty years, blacks won election as mayor in many of the nation's most populous cities: Kenneth Gibson in Newark (1970–1986); Tom Bradley in Los Angeles (1973–1993); Coleman Young in Detroit (1974–1993); Harold Washington in Chicago (1983–1987); David Dinkins in New York

---

* The black senators during Reconstruction were elected by their states' legislatures. Roland Burris was a black politician selected by Illinois's governor to fill the Senate seat vacated by Barack Obama after he won the presidency.

City (1990–1993). By 1993, blacks had been elected mayor in sixty-seven cities with populations over fifty thousand.

The first black mayoral candidates often encountered fierce resistance from whites. In contest after contest, outcomes hung on the extent to which whites abandoned their traditional voting pattern in response to the jolting presence of a black contender. When Carl Stokes faced Seth Taft in Cleveland in 1967, the latter, a Republican, won 127,328 votes even though the city had only thirty-nine thousand registered Republicans. In 1983, when Harold Washington won the Chicago Democratic primary in an overwhelmingly Democratic city, he immediately faced massive white defections to his white Republican opponent. In 1987, when the black candidate Wilson Goode won the Democratic primary in Philadelphia, fifty thousand whites defected to his opponent, the Republican former police chief Frank Rizzo.

The record of racially polarized voting in mayoral elections is striking. In Detroit in 1973, the white candidate received 91 percent of the white vote while the black candidate received 92 percent of the black vote. In Philadelphia in 1987, the white candidate received 98 percent of the white vote while the black candidate received 97 percent of the black vote. In Memphis in 1991, the white candidate received 97 percent of the white vote while the black candidate received 99 percent of the black vote.

Frequently a black candidate has only been able to prevail when black voters have constituted a majority or at least a strong plurality of the electorate. After the first wave of black mayoral competitors, however, some African Americans began to prevail in cities with predominantly white populations. When Tom Bradley became mayor of Los Angeles in 1973, blacks constituted less than 18 percent of the population. When the voters of New York City selected David Dinkins as their mayor in 1989, blacks constituted only 25 percent of the Big Apple's population. In the 1980s and

1990s, blacks were elected mayor in Charlotte, Seattle, Denver, Kansas City, and Dallas—all cities in which blacks constituted less than a third of the population.[39]

The record of black advancement at the highest levels of municipal electoral politics has not been matched at the highest levels of state electoral politics. In the history of the United States only two blacks have managed to win gubernatorial elections: Deval Patrick in 2006 and 2010 in the Commonwealth of Massachusetts and Douglas Wilder in 1989 in the Commonwealth of Virginia.[40] Wilder's experience is particularly instructive. He brought to his gubernatorial campaign a formidable profile. A decorated veteran, he was the incumbent lieutenant governor. Prior to winning election to that post, he had served as a state senator for sixteen years. Wilder received the endorsement of Virginia's outgoing governor as well as the endorsement of a former governor and sitting United States senator, Chuck Robb. In addition to these assets, Wilder also had the benefit of running against a relatively weak opponent.

Wilder's vulnerability was his race, a "problem" he energetically sought to minimize. He avoided racially tinged issues such as affirmative action or welfare policy. He pointedly requested that the then-reigning black activist, Jesse Jackson, stay away from his campaign. He denied his own activist past, portraying himself as a dutiful "son of Virginia" who was strong on law and order, supportive of capital punishment, open to the endorsement of past segregationists, and unperturbed by the display of the Confederate flag. Among whites, Wilder did best with younger, more affluent, and well-educated voters. Among blacks he did well all around. Although he refrained from outwardly courting the African-American vote, he received the bulk of its support, upwards of 95 percent, with a turnout that exceeded the white turnout by a margin of 76 percent to 65 percent.

Preelection polling pointed to a comfortable margin of victory for Wilder. The final tally, however, revealed a photo finish, with Wilder winning by the slimmest margin in Virginia history—50.1 percent to 49.8 percent. Two points about this result bear emphasizing. First, racial considerations largely explain the closeness of the vote. One-quarter of those who voted for Wilder's white opponent supported the Democratic candidate for lieutenant governor and the Democratic candidate for attorney general. Moreover, the Democratic candidate for lieutenant governor, a political neophyte, received forty thousand more votes than Wilder. Attributing a given motivation to voters is always somewhat hazardous. Even when voters explain themselves, one confronts the problem of deception and self-deception. In this case, however, circumstantial evidence, buttressed by the impressions of knowledgeable observers, provides a solid basis for concluding that voter unease with Wilder's race played a major role in the contest. Obviously that racial unease was not dispositive since Wilder ultimately prevailed. But it was an impediment around which he had to maneuver, a factor about which he was always aware, a concern that affected the subjects he magnified or avoided and the allies he publicized or obscured.

A second point has to do with the difference between the actual and projected voting returns. This was not the first time that polling data seemed to overestimate support for a black candidate. In 1982, when Tom Bradley, the black mayor of Los Angeles, sought election as California's governor, public-opinion polling showed him leading his white opponent, George Deukmejian, by a wide margin. In the actual balloting, however, Deukmejian won. The apparent gap between expressed preelection preferences and actual voting behavior became commonly known as the Bradley effect (or sometimes as the Wilder effect).[41] One explanation is that white voters, ashamed of their prejudices, falsely describe their intentions in polls. Another explanation is that white voters truthfully relate to pollsters preelection intentions that simply change in the private crucible of the voting booth.

The concept of the Bradley effect is controversial. Some observers believe that it helpfully describes American voter conduct. Others contend that while the concept of the Bradley effect may have captured a real phenomenon in the 1980s, it no longer does so. Still others argue that the concept of the Bradley effect is, and always was, misleading. They argue that the alleged disjunction between preferences expressed before an election and Election Day voting has only been an *apparent* anomaly—a function of misperceptions by analysts as opposed to the actual conduct of voters.

This debate is of more than mere academic importance, as perceptions affect expectations, which affect behavior. Belief that there really exists a Bradley effect might well discourage potential black candidates who underestimate their chances of winning. In the mid-1990s General Colin Powell was considering a run for the White House, given polls that indicated strong popular support. Powell noted, though, that friends urged him *not* to run in part because they so distrusted the polls. "Every time I see Earl Graves"—the black businessman who founded *Black Enterprise* magazine—"he says, 'Look, man, don't let them hand you no crap. When [voters] go in that booth, they ain't going to vote for you.'"[42] While Powell's decision to refrain from seeking the presidency was probably the result of several factors, one might well have been an excessive caution nourished by belief in the Bradley effect. On the other hand, belief in the Bradley effect might also spur black candidates to greater effort when, fearful of complacency, they discount favorable preelection projections. Prior to Election Day 2008, Barack Obama pushed his campaign furiously, notwithstanding an apparent lead in the polls. Successful seekers of the presidency are typically hard-charging competitors who advance their cause until the very end. But in Obama's case the specter of the Bradley effect added special urgency to his efforts and those of his supporters.

Prior to Obama, numbers of blacks had run for the presidency on the tickets of minor parties. In 1904, George Edwin Taylor ran as the nominee of the National Liberty Party. In 1964, Clifton DeBerry ran as the nominee of the Socialist Workers Party. In 1968, Eldridge Cleaver ran as the nominee of the Peace and Freedom Party, Dick Gregory as the nominee of the Freedom and Peace Party, and Charlene Mitchell as the nominee of the American Communist Party. In 1988 and 1992, Lenora Fulani ran as the nominee of the New Alliance Party. In the latter year, Ron Daniels also ran; he was the nominee of the Peace and Freedom Party. In 1996 and 2000, Monica Moorehead ran as the nominee of the Workers World Party, and in 2008, Cynthia McKinney ran as the nominee of the Green Party.

The first black to run for the nomination of a major party was Shirley Anita Chisholm, the first black woman elected to Congress.[43] She presented herself as a presidential candidate on January 25, 1972. Declaring that she sought "to repudiate the ridiculous notion that the American people will not vote for a qualified candidate simply because he is not white or she is not male," Chisholm asserted hopefully that her candidacy "can change the face and future of American politics." She also remarked resignedly, however, that "as a black person and as a female person, I do not have a chance of actually [winning] in this election year."[44]

Chisholm never posed a real threat to the Democratic Party front-runners and figured only marginally at the convention that nominated George McGovern (who went on to lose the general election to Richard Nixon). She encountered multiple difficulties. Major arbiters of public opinion simply refused to take her candidacy seriously. When the CBS television network featured a debate involving other Democratic Party candidates, it declined to invite her. She had to obtain a court order to be heard.

Although Chisholm's candidacy is now widely lauded among African Americans, the fact is that, at the time, most black politicians didn't support her. Their attitude stemmed in part from hard-boiled pragmatism. They wanted to forge alliances with the person who would be nominated by the Democratic Party and perhaps win the general election. Chisholm had no chance of prevailing on either score. Their standoffishness was also a reflection of personal frictions. Some black politicians thought that Chisholm was insufficiently collegial. While they were debating what stance to take collectively, Chisholm declared her candidacy unilaterally without consulting them. Finally, the spotty support that Chisholm received from black activists and politicians is also attributable to sexism. Some champions of black empowerment thought it preferable, if not essential, that black *men* be the leaders of African-American political advancement.

The next black to seek the Democratic Party's nomination was Jesse Louis Jackson, who ran in 1984 and 1988.[45] On both occasions, Jackson far exceeded the expectations of supporters and detractors alike. Derided in 1984 as merely a "protest" candidate, Jackson ultimately finished third in the contest for delegates behind Senator Gary Hart and the eventual nominee, former vice president Walter Mondale (who went on to lose to Ronald Reagan in the general election). Despite the absence of any governmental experience, limited financial resources, and a reputation steeped in controversy, Jackson won more than three million votes in primaries or caucuses by dint of energy, intelligence, and a populist message.

In 1988 Jackson did better still. The runner-up to Governor Michael Dukakis (who went on to lose to George Bush the

Elder), Jackson won several primaries or caucuses (including those in Michigan and South Carolina) and attracted some seven million votes. He appeared on the covers of *Time* and *Newsweek* and briefly surged to the front of the pack as a real contender. A remark made by a *New York Times* reporter in the summer of 1988 takes on new significance given Obama's triumph twenty years later. Assessing Jackson's campaign, the reporter anticipated that it would "help some other black politician finally climb the next step."[46] It did in ways that have yet to be suitably acknowledged. First, Jackson's campaigns opened imaginations more fully than ever before to the prospect of an African-American president. Second, Jackson's strong showings made it possible for him to insist that the Democratic Party change its rules in ways that increased the power of minorities in the presidential nominating process. Jackson demanded that the party move from a winner-take-all system to one of proportional representation. This and other reforms Jackson demanded helped Obama to upset the Hillary Clinton machine.[47]

Although Jackson's candidacies were important milestones, they were seriously undermined by remarks and associations that many saw as disqualifying. Early in his '84 campaign, while speaking in what he considered to be a confidential conversation with a black journalist (Jackson reportedly said to the journalist, "Let's talk some black talk"), the candidate referred to Jews as "Hymies" and to New York City as "Hymietown."[48] As if uttering those derogatory nicknames was not damning enough, Jackson compounded his delinquency by initially denying that he had made the objectionable remarks and by hesitating to apologize. Roundly criticized, Jackson saw his reputation permanently soiled. Beyond that, moreover, was a further consequence. Since Jackson had become the most prominent voice in black politics because of his quests for the nation's top electoral post, the injury his reputation suffered affected other black politicians as well. If Jesse Jackson could refer to Jews so disparagingly, what about other African-American leaders? Did they, too, speak of Jews as "Hymies" or worse when "talking black"? Jackson's "Hymie-town" remark, the reaction to it, the reaction against the reaction, and subsequent cycles of charge and countercharge have exacerbated feelings of distrust and resentment among certain circles of African-American and Jewish-American activists. The bitter memory of "Hymietown" helps to explain why some Jews needed an extra dose of persuading when Barack Obama sought their support in 2008.

An additional source of embarrassment for Jackson arose from his association with Minister Louis Farrakhan.[49] A disciple of the Honorable Elijah Muhammad, Minister Farrakhan long propagated the belief that whites are inferior to blacks and evil by nature.* He enthusiastically endorsed Jackson's candidacy, support that Jackson publicly welcomed. Despite Minister Farrakhan's prior refusal to participate in American politics, he now registered to vote and urged his followers to do so as well in order to assist Jackson.

---

* Elijah Muhammad openly expressed his belief:

> The human beast—the serpent, the dragon, the devil, and Satan—all mean one and the same: the people or race known as the white or Caucasian race. . . .

Quoted in Louis E. Lomax, *When the Word Is Given . . . : A Report on Elijah Muhammad, Malcolm X, and the Black Muslim World* (1963). See, generally, Elijah Muhammad, *Message to the Blackman in America* (1965).

Minister Farrakhan, who has resuscitated the Nation of Islam (NOI) in the wake of Elijah Muhammad's death, somewhat mutes the NOI's official racial theory but has never repudiated it. See Mattias Gardell, *In the Name of Elijah Muhammad: Louis Farrakhan and the Nation of Islam* (1996).

Under Elijah Muhammad, the NOI did not spend much effort focusing on Jews; he deemed white Jews to be evil like all whites. Minister Farrakhan, however, has singled out Jews for disparagement, using classic tropes of anti-Semitism (for example, describing Jews as "blood suckers"), all the while asserting that he is not anti-Jewish.

Minister Farrakhan probably did bring to Jackson's camp some blacks who might not otherwise have made it there. But the liabilities that Jackson reaped from the association with the minister likely outweighed the benefits bestowed. Not only did Minister Farrakhan propound an antiwhite theology, he also made statements that have been widely and rightly viewed as anti-Semitic, alarming and angering many Jews, a key component in the Democratic Party coalition.[50] That was bad enough; many Jews came to detest Jackson because of his Farrakhan connection. In the 1988 New York Democratic Party primary campaign, New York City's mayor, Ed Koch, declared bluntly that it would be crazy for any Jew to vote for Jackson. But the injury to Jackson went deeper still. People of *all* sorts lost respect for him when he failed to repudiate Farrakhan forcefully, especially when the minister publicly threatened the black journalist who revealed Jackson's "Hymietown" faux pas.

A third person in major party politics who acclimated the American mind to the idea of a black president was Colin Powell.*[51] By the late 1990s, Powell had risen to prominence on the basis of his outstanding career in the military. A general in the United States Army, he served as President Ronald Reagan's national security advisor (a black "first") and was appointed by

---

* Two other figures who bear mentioning are the Reverend Alfred Charles "Al" Sharpton, Jr., and Alan Keyes. In 2004, Reverend Sharpton announced his candidacy for the Democratic Party nomination for the presidency. He received little support, including scant black support. The high points of his campaign were the District of Columbia primary, in which he won 20 percent of the vote, and the South Carolina primary, in which he won 10 percent of the vote.

Alan Keyes ran for the presidency in 1996, 2000, and 2008. A Republican for most of his career, Keyes sought the nomination of the Constitution Party late in the 2008 electoral season and, when that bid failed, created a new organization, America's Independent Party, to sponsor his presidential ambition. Keyes is probably best known as the Illinois Republican Party nominee to the Senate whom Barack Obama defeated in 2004. In the aftermath of Obama's presidential victory, Keyes supported lawsuits challenging his eligibility on the grounds that, allegedly, he is not a natural-born citizen of the United States, as required under the Constitution.

President George H. W. Bush to serve as chairman of the Joint Chiefs of Staff (another black "first"). When he retired from the military, Powell's popularity was such that many admirers urged him to run for the presidency as a Republican. He declined. But there is evidence which suggests that he might well have won had he run.[52] Exit polling on Election Day 1996 showed him beating President-elect Bill Clinton by a comfortable margin, with more of his support coming from whites than from blacks. Among whites, Powell outpolled Clinton 53 percent to 33 percent (considerably outperforming the actual Republican nominee, Senator Bob Dole). Of course, this was merely a poll; real voting might have produced different results. Furthermore, whereas the actual candidates had suffered a year of merciless scrutiny on the campaign trail, General Powell as a hypothetical candidate had suffered from none of the wear and tear that a presidential contest exacts. Perhaps he would have seemed less attractive in the crucible of presidential competition. Still, as the political analyst Martin Plissner argues, evidence of Colin Powell's popularity does provide a basis for supposing that America's readiness to elect a black person as president has been part of the political landscape for longer than many have appreciated. Barack Obama's recognition of that feature of America's political topography set him apart and constituted a key component of his audacious exercise of ambition, will, and nerve. It prompted him to run to win and not merely to show.*

---

* Obama was adamant on this point, declaring, for instance, during the South Carolina primary:

> I'm not interested in second place. I'm not running to be Vice-President. I'm not running to be secretary of something or other. . . . I'm running to be President of the United States of America.

Quoted in David Remnick, *The Bridge: The Life and Rise of Barack Obama* (2010), 501.

Prior to Obama's campaign there had been some observers sufficiently prescient to predict the election of a black president within the foreseeable future. In 1958, Senator Jacob Javits stated that "the march of progress and world events make it quite possible that a member of the Negro race will . . . be elected to the Presidency . . . by the year 2000."[53] In 1961, Attorney General Robert F. Kennedy maintained that "there's no question that in the next thirty or forty years a Negro can also achieve the same position that my brother has as President of the United States."[54] In 1964, Martin Luther King, Jr., suggested that "we may be able to get a Negro President . . . in twenty-five years or less."[55]

Much more prevalent, however, was a resigned acceptance of the idea that for a long time to come the office of commander in chief could go only to a white person—a white woman, perhaps, or a white Jew, but someone who was seen as "white." Prior to Obama, observers imagined blacks at the highest levels of appointments—a Supreme Court justice or a secretary of state—selected by a white president. But a black president?* As late as January 2007, many people still believed what the radical activist Hubert Harrison had declared way back in the 1920s: "The only way in which a Negro could be elected President of the United States would be by virtue of the voters not knowing that the particular candidate was of Negro ancestry."[56] There will be a strong temptation to laugh at the apocalyptic pessimism expressed by the black state senator in South Carolina who, fearing the consequences of an Obama candidacy, predicted that "every Democrat running [beneath Obama] . . . would lose because he's black. . . . We'd lose the House

---

* In 1980, a researcher investigating the racial attitudes of black and white students found a notable similarity in their belief that the white electorate would find any black candidate unacceptable simply because of his race. "Eighty-eight percent of the white students and [95] percent of the black students believed that whites would not accept a black president." Charles Jarmon, "Racial Beliefs Among Blacks and Whites: An Evaluation of Perspectives," *Journal of Black Studies* 112 (1980): 235, 245.

and the Senate and the governors and everything."[57] But prior to Obama's campaign the prospect of a black president seemed dim indeed—the stuff of science fiction, or fantasy, or comedy.* Obama displayed discernment as well as bravado in perceiving that he—a black man—might well be able to prevail. William Jelani Cobb repeatedly emphasizes this point in one of the best books written about race and the Obama ascendancy. "The first and . . . greatest accomplishment of Obama and his team," Cobb notes, "was their recognition that the political climate offered a path to victory."[58]

At the inauguration, the status of the president's family as America's royalty was on full display. The event was tantamount to a democratic coronation. It was a day on which the overwhelming majority of Americans set aside political disagreements to affirm their fealty to the office of the presidency. It was a moment at which millions of Americans who voted for McCain nonetheless offered best wishes to Obama and pledged that they would recognize him as *their* president, too.

Many Americans received vicarious enjoyment as they watched the Obamas receive accolades at the various celebrations. Most blacks shared as well an unprecedented sense of validation as they witnessed "one of their own" ascend to the world's highest tier of prestige and power. After long years of degradation that gave way to ostracism that gave way to invisibility that gave way to tokenism, the emergence of a black First Family offered to black America a boost of encouragement and feeling of exhilaration.

---

* For science fiction see Philip K. Dick, *The Crack in Space* (1966), or Monteiro Lobato, *O Presidente Negro* (1926). For fantasy see the television series *24* (2001–2010), with its two black presidents. For comedy see Chris Rock as president in the film *Head of State* (2003).

Of course, not all Americans were happy to witness Obama's triumph. The owner of a convenience store in Standish, Maine, invited customers to join the "Osama Obama Shotgun Pool," in which bets were placed on when Obama would be assassinated. "Let's hope we have a winner," the store owner declared.[59] In Springfield, Massachusetts, a band of young white supremacists marked the occasion of Obama's election by torching a predominantly black church.[60] From across the country came reports of cross burnings and an uptick in the enlistment of new members in white supremacist organizations.

Some right-wing television and radio personalities—Rush Limbaugh comes immediately to mind—could barely contain their anger and disgust. And on the left, detractors began immediately to hector President Obama as well. The consumer advocate and former presidential candidate Ralph Nader asked whether Obama would act as a true agent of real change or whether the new chief executive would be a corporate Uncle Tom.[61] But immediate hostilities were marginal. For the great mass of Americans, Inauguration Day was a moment full of hope for the new president and pride in having once again nonviolently exchanged the reins of governance. Internationally, moreover, Obama's election was seen as an inspiration. "The American people gave a lesson in democracy to the whole world," a black African told a white African in Senegal. "How so?" asked the white man. "Obama," came the reply.[62]

2

Obama Courts Black America

What are the key ingredients of Barack Obama's attractiveness to black voters—the factors that have prompted them to support him in unprecedented numbers and with unparalleled enthusiasm?

First, he refers to himself as "black" or "African American."[1] He has done so throughout his adulthood, most recently when he confirmed his self-identification as "black" for the 2010 federal census.* Obama's self-labeling is noteworthy because, as is well known, his mother was a white American while his father was a black Kenyan. Millions of Americans with a black parent and a white parent have chosen to label themselves "mixed race" or "multiracial." But Obama has chosen, for the most part, to proceed otherwise. This constituted a fateful choice.† Had he decided

---

* Obama's racial self-designation for the census received a remarkable amount of attention. A report of his action on the Huffington Post blog site elicited over five thousand responses. See Mark C. Smith, "Obama Census Choice: African American," Huffington Post.com, April 2, 2010. Views, of course, varied. Compare Melissa Harris-Lacewell, "Black by Choice," *The Nation*, April 15, 2010 (admiring Obama's embrace of blackness, "with all its disprivilege, tumultuous history and disquieting symbolism"), with Abigail Thernstrom, "Obama's Census Identity," *Wall Street Journal*, April 16, 2010 (disapprovingly charging that Obama "disowned his white mother" and, contradicting his insistence upon change, "has chosen to stick with older and cruder single-race classifications, a holdover from racially ugly times").

† Obama himself has rejected the proposition that he "decided" to be black, maintaining that his appearance and people's response to it, especially prejudiced responses to it, decided the matter of his identity. A fervent Obama supporter, the writer John K. Wilson also rejects the idea that Obama had a "choice." "No one is asking Mitt Romney how he decided to be white," Wilson declares. That is true. But that shows a journalistic fault.

differently, had he acted in the manner of Tiger Woods—with
whom he was once often compared*—had he consistently labeled
himself something other than "black" or "African American," he
would not have enjoyed the overwhelming support he has received
from Negroes and would thus have been unable to win the presidency. He would have been unable to capture their affection
because many African Americans dislike practices they perceive
as being efforts to dilute or deny blackness and see labels such as
"mixed race" or "multiracial" as precisely such efforts. They are
delighted that he has wanted, in the journalist Adam Serwer's
words, "to be a part of the awesome, confusing, tragic, and trium-
phant journey of black people in America." [2]

American history is dotted with distinctions separating people
of African lineage having little or no European ancestry from
people of African lineage having substantial or even predominant
European ancestry. The former have been designated "Negroes,"
"blacks," or "African Americans," while the latter have been
labeled in terms of their perceived quotient of "colored blood"—
"mulattoes" (half colored blood), "quadroons" (one-quarter col-

---

If Obama is asked to identify himself racially and to explain his answer, Romney, and all
of the other candidates, should be asked to identify and explain themselves racially. Such
a question might provide the occasion for a productive exploration of racial identity and
racial identification. See John K. Wilson, *Barack Obama: This Improbable Quest* (2008),
53. See also Randall Kennedy, *Sellout: The Politics of Racial Betrayal* (2008), 11–31.

After having summarily rejected the notion that Obama *chose* to be black, Wilson defends him against the charge that he is not black enough by declaring (with no apparent
recognition of inconsistency), "Obama could have abandoned his 'blackness.' . . . [He]
could have *chosen* to avoid African Americans . . . to have a white family. . . . Obama's
blackness, like his religion, is all the more remarkable because it is something he *chose* to
embrace." Wilson, *Barack Obama*, at 60 (emphasis added).

* Tiger Woods famously rejected defining himself as "black" or "African American" and
instead made up a designation—"Cablinasian"—to embrace a lineage which includes
Caucasian, Black, Indian, and Asian. See Greg Couch, "Woods: I'm More Than Black,"
Chicago Sun-Times, April 22, 1997. For a defense of Tiger Woods's position see Gary
Kamiya, "Cablinasian Like Me," Salon.com, April 1997. For a critique see Leonard Pitts,
"Is There Room in This Sweet Land of Liberty for Such a Thing as 'Cablinasian'? Face
It, Tiger: If They Say You're Black, Then You're Black," *Baltimore Sun*, April 29, 1997.

Given Tiger Woods's spectacular fall from grace in a highly publicized sex scandal,
it is unlikely that he will continue to serve as a counterpoint to Obama in the future.

ored blood), and "octoroons" (one-eighth colored blood). Whites have historically, albeit unofficially, treated darker-skinned Negroes worse than lighter-skinned Negroes.* African Americans have displayed colorism as well. Lighter-skinned blacks have often tried to create a complexional aristocracy, granting privileges to those with apparently greater degrees of European ancestry. This impulse, which still exists, has prompted lighter-skinned Negroes to discriminate against darker-skinned Negroes in all sorts of ways— from the creation of clubs that exclude those deemed to be "too dark," to choices of business associates, friends, and marriage partners.[3]

The idea of the hybrid has been a gathering point for racial mythologies. Some ethnologists have asserted that mixed-race people are inferior to people of "pure" stock, because, among other things, they are more susceptible to disease and sterility. In 1843, Dr. Josiah Nott described mulattoes as "an unnatural offspring, doomed by nature to work out its own destruction."[4] Similarly, Dr. John H. Van Evrie contended that "mulattoism is an abnormality—a disease . . . mercifully doomed to final extinction."[5] This derogatory view of the mulatto long outlived slavery. In 1948, four of nine justices of the California Supreme Court unembarrassedly cited the putative inferiority of mulattoes as a justification for upholding that state's law barring interracial marriage.[6] And throughout the 1950s and 1960s, white supremacists invoked the specter of racially ambiguous "mongrels" to defend racial segregation.†

* See Jennifer Hochschild and Vesla Weaver, "The Skin Color Paradox and the American Racial Order," *Social Forces* 86 (2007): 1. See also Irene Blair, Charles Judd, and Kristine Chapleau, "The Influence of Afrocentric Facial Features in Criminal Sentencing," *Psychological Science* 15 (2004): 674; Jennifer Eberhardt, Paul Davies, Valerie Purdie-Vaughns, and Sheri Johnson, "Looking Deathworthy: Perceived Stereotypicality of Black Defendants Predicts Capital Sentencing Outcomes," *Psychological Science* 17 (2006): 383.
† In his first press conference as president-elect, Obama casually referred to himself as a "mutt," an appellation to which some listeners objected. When Obama's parents got

On the other hand, many observers have viewed mulattoes (and other multiracial people) more favorably than Negroes. The white supremacist and proslavery jurist Thomas R. R. Cobb maintained that mulattoes constituted a "superior race" to blacks that was "elevated by the mixture of blood."[7] He believed that the infusion of "white blood" enhanced the intelligence, appearance, and character of offspring of black women sired by white men. Many have agreed with Cobb that mulattoes are superior to Negroes in achievement and capability.[8]

Assessments favoring mulattoes over Negroes have long given concrete advantages to the former. Prior to the Civil War, mulattoes benefited disproportionately from private manumissions (often at the hands of masters engaged in freeing their own children). Building on the advantages they reaped from emancipation or positions as privileged slaves, mulattoes also benefited disproportionately from the new social, economic, and political opportunities that emerged after the Civil War. The first black to serve as governor of a state, P. B. S. Pinchback of Louisiana, was a mulatto. The first black to serve in the United States Senate, Hiram R. Revels of Mississippi, was a mulatto. The first black member of the House of Representatives, Joseph H. Rainey of South Carolina, was a mulatto.

Blacks with close white relatives continue to benefit from biases that favor their white lineage. Obama's light complexion and knowledge of his white relatives may well have eased the way for some voters to support him who might otherwise have been unwilling to do so. Senator Harry Reid was harshly criticized in some quarters when it surfaced after the election that he had

---

married, sixteen states still prohibited interracial marriages to discourage what they saw as dangerous "mongrelization." Only in 1967, in the most aptly titled ruling in American constitutional history—*Loving v. [the Commonwealth of] Virginia*—did the United States Supreme Court belatedly invalidate all state laws banning interracial marriages. See Peggy Pascoe, *What Comes Naturally: Miscegenation Law and the Making of Race in America* (2009).

said that, despite Obama's blackness, he might have a chance of winning in part because he was light-skinned and spoke without a Negro dialect.[9] At least with respect to skin color, however, Reid was simply making a sociological claim that has been amply substantiated. As the political scientists Jennifer Hochschild and Vesla Weaver observe in a careful and comprehensive study,

> Relative to their lighter-skinned counterparts, dark-skinned blacks have lower levels of education, income and job status. They are less likely to own homes or to marry; and dark-skinned blacks' prison sentences are longer. . . . Most Americans prefer lighter to dark skin aesthetically, normatively and culturally. Filmmakers, novelists, advertisers, modeling agencies, matchmaking websites—all demonstrate how much the power of a fair complexion, along with straight hair and Eurocentric facial features, appeals to Americans.[10]

Reid was not voicing support for this sorry reality; he was only acknowledging its existence.

Things have changed for the better since Andy Razaf plaintively asked, "What did I do to be so black and blue?"* The prospects for racial minorities have also improved since the days when, in black America, one heard the following on a regular basis:

---

* No single artwork more poignantly highlights the way in which blacks have both internalized and fought postslavery Negrophobia than Razaf's lyrics composed in 1929. Alluding to black men's preference for light-skinned Negro women, he wrote:

> Browns and yellers, all have fellers,
> Gentlemen prefer them light.
> Wish I could fade, can't make the grade,
> Nothing but dark days in sight.

See generally Barry Singer, *Black and Blue: The Life and Lyrics of Andy Razaf* (1995).

If you're white you're alright,
If you're brown stick around,
If you're black get back.

A central achievement of the Black Power Movement of the late
1960s was to remove from the minds of many Negroes the stigma
that America's white supremacist culture has heaped upon the
word "black." An important artifact of that movement was the
anthem by Soul Brother Number One, James Brown, "Say It Loud
(I'm Black and I'm Proud)." The need to insist upon that proposition was indicative of the devaluation that had long befallen blackness. Moreover, that devaluation continued, even among African
Americans. In Stevie Wonder's otherwise wonderful song "Living for the City," he writes revealingly of a girl being black "but"
pretty.* Blackness in American culture remains heavily burdened
by negative connotations and associations.

A familial tie with whites often benefits a black person. A friend
relayed the following story from North Carolina. A white volunteer
in the Obama campaign approached an elderly white woman
at her home. The woman indicated that she planned to vote for
Obama. She then leaned close to the volunteer and in a whisper
said, "He's half white, you know. That's good enough for me."
This sort of advantage sometimes generates resentment in dark-
skinned Negroes against light-skinned Negroes. But this has not
happened with Obama since he became a serious contender for the
presidency. Helping to still incipient bad feeling is Obama's clear
choice to affiliate himself racially with blacks. He acknowledges
his complicated racial lineage. He makes use occasionally of his
blood tie to whiteness. But when it comes time to check the racial

---

* His sister's black but she is sho' nuff pretty,
  Her skirt is short but Lord her legs are sturdy.

box, Obama consistently notes that he is "black" or "African American." Other blacks appreciate that constancy. It is one of the key reasons that they have rewarded him with their loyal support.

Although efforts have been made, as we have seen, to stratify the black population according to percentages of European lineage, an even more powerful tendency has been to solidify into one mass *all* persons with discernible African ancestry regardless of the extent of their European lineage. That is why Frederick Douglass, John Langston, and Booker T. Washington are almost universally seen as "black" leaders though their fathers were white, and why Walter White and W. E. B. Du Bois are seen as "black" leaders despite the conspicuousness of their European ancestries. The branch of white supremacist logic that largely prevailed held that any perceptible African ancestry made a person a Negro. This is the logic that insisted that Homer Plessy "belonged" in the car for colored people even though he was only one-eighth black.[11] This is the logic of Thomas Dixon, who proclaimed, via a character in his influential novel *The Leopard's Spots*, that a "single drop" of Negro blood "kinks the hair, flattens the nose, thickens the lips, puts out the light of intellect, and lights the fires of brutal passions."[12] This is the logic of the infamous one-drop rule: one drop of black ancestry makes you "black."

In a grand irony of American race relations, some champions of African-American collective development are now among the most fervent *supporters* of the one-drop rule. They appreciate the way it has functioned to fold into blackness people who, under different circumstances, might well have developed other racial identities and allegiances. Supporting the one-drop doctrine, law professor Christine B. Hickman writes:

The Devil fashioned [the one-drop rule] out of racism, malice, greed, lust and ignorance, but in so doing he also accomplished good: His rule created the African-American race as we know it today, and while this race had its origins in the peoples of three continents and its members can look very different from one another, over the centuries the Devil's one-drop rule united this race as a people in the fight against slavery, segregation and racial injustice.[13]

I have never heard or read Obama on the one-drop rule directly. Indirectly he has acceded to it. Asked on the television program *60 Minutes* when he had "decided" that he was black, Obama responded as if choice had nothing to do with the issue. He said that he was black because of his physiognomy, the response of onlookers to his appearance, and his shared experiences with others perceived to be "black." "If you look African American in this society," he remarked, "you're treated as an African-American."[14] In 1940, W. E. B. Du Bois observed that "the black man is a person who must ride 'Jim Crow' in Georgia."[15] Obama updated that view, noting that when he tried to hail taxis, drivers were not confused about his race. They passed him by, as they passed by other black men, out of fear or some other racially inflected calculation.*

In suggesting that choice played little or no part in his racial self-presentation, Obama is correct in a certain way, but erroneous in another. True, for many Americans his appearance does proclaim him to be black. Obama is wrong, however, in maintaining that his own choice is irrelevant. After all, despite his appearance, he could have done what Tiger Woods and others have done—opted for a designation other than "black" or "African American." That

---

* Adam Serwer suggests that Obama was using the image of racial discrimination in hailing a cab to establish racial authenticity. Serwer compares Obama's story to Walter White's dramatic, but likely fabricated, tale about guarding his home with his father and a rifle during the Atlanta race riot of 1906. "White wanted black folks to know how far he would go for the cause, and Obama wanted to make clear that he had 'lived the life of a black American.'" "He's Black, Get Over It," *American Prospect*, December 5, 2008.

he refrained from doing so was not a foregone conclusion but instead a decision.*

Some observers object to describing Obama as black. "We are racially sophisticated enough to elect a non-white president," the writer Marie Arana observes, but "are so racially backward that we insist on calling him black. Progress has outpaced vocabulary. . . . [Obama] is not our first black president. He is our first biracial, bicultural president."[16] Others, however, take umbrage at what they see as efforts to wrest Obama away from black America. They complain that the multiracialists are ignoring Obama's own will and trying to force him into racial categories of their, not his, choosing. They also perceive the effort to reclassify Obama as tantamount to a racial theft—an expropriation that would not be occurring on behalf of some less attractive figure. The journalist Jesse Washington put the point nicely: "Attempts to whiten Obama leave a bitter taste for many African Americans, who feel that at their moment of triumph, the rules are being changed to steal what once was deemed worthless—blackness itself."[17]

Critics who object to Obama's description of himself as black or African American claim that his labeling negates his maternal relatives—the very people who played the predominant role in raising him after his black Kenyan father walked out of his life when he was only a toddler.[18] But Obama has spoken movingly of his love for his white maternal relatives while also expressing his deep sense of affiliation with African Americans. Nowhere is this more evident than in this reported remark: "One of the things I

---

* I have argued elsewhere that Obama may have wanted to play down the matter of choice because of black American anxiety over racial betrayal. To have admitted that at some point he "decided" to be black Obama would have distanced himself from the majority of African Americans who do not perceive themselves as having another option. Moreover, to be able to choose to be black brings with it the possibility of changing one's mind—a prospect of potential abandonment that many African Americans find to be disturbing. See Randall Kennedy, *Sellout: The Politics of Racial Betrayal* (2008), 29–31.

loved about my mother was not only did she not feel rejected by me defining myself as African American, but she recognized that I was a black man . . . and my experiences were going to be different than hers."[19]

Obama's racial self-presentation is the most politic of the alternatives. For him to describe himself consistently as anything other than black or African-American would be perceived by most Negroes as an insulting evasion.[20] At the same time, many whites would see Obama as "black" regardless of what he called himself.

Obama occasionally makes reference to his mixedness, his hybridity, his multiraciality. In *The Audacity of Hope* he writes:

As the child of a black man and a white woman . . . with some blood relations who resemble Margaret Thatcher and others who could pass for Bernie Mac . . . I've never had the option of restricting my loyalties on the basis of race, or measuring my worth on the basis of tribe.[21]

Elsewhere he has referred to himself as a "man of mixed race without firm anchor in any particular community."[22]

Obama's references to his racial background reflect, to some degree, his long-standing struggle to create a place for himself on the American racial landscape, a struggle recounted in his memoir *Dreams from My Father* (1995), in which he explores the ambivalences and anxieties of his youth. Obama's references to his multiraciality, however, are also an effort to deploy it in advantageous ways. Obama is undoubtedly aware that he has benefited considerably from being favorably contrasted with African-American politicians such as Jesse Jackson and Al Sharpton. As the journalist Gary Younge observes, "The various ways in which so many white politicians and commentators have referred to [Obama]—the 'articulate,' 'clean,' candidate who 'transcends the racial divide'—

are all coded ways of saying he is not like the other black candidates they have had to deal with in the past."[23] That favorable comparison is mainly based on ideological and programmatic differences. But for some whites, like the elderly woman in North Carolina, an ingredient of Obama's attractiveness is his intimate connection with whiteness. For them, the whiteness in Obama's family takes the edge off his blackness. It added to white voters' level of comfort with the unprecedented prospect of a black man controlling the Oval Office.[24] Aware of the white racial anxiety he confronts, Obama says, essentially, Although I am a black man, I am a black man with close, affectionate, familial ties to white folks. To calm the nerves of whites made fearful by the idea of a black commander in chief, Obama reminded them of his white mother, white grandmother, and white grandfather.

Obama's visible and publicly invoked white relatives are not the only factor complicating his affiliation with black America; another complication is that his father, though black, was not an American but a Kenyan. In terms of his biological lineage, Obama appears to have little or no direct connection with ancestors who experienced Negro enslavement on American soil. To some observers this is a matter of importance. Writing before Obama had officially declared his candidacy, the journalist Stanley Crouch exclaimed, "When black Americans refer to Obama as 'one of us,' I do not know what they are talking about." He does not share a heritage with the majority of black Americans, who are descendants of slaves. If Obama becomes "our first black President, he will have come into the White House through a side door—which might, at this point, be the only one that's open."[25]

The writer Debra J. Dickerson made a similar point but pushed it in a somewhat different direction in an article that cast a cold, quizzical eye on the early stages of Obamamania in white America. Defining an American "black" as a person descended from Africans who were enslaved in America, Dickerson concluded (like Crouch) that Obama isn't "black." That being so, she insisted that white supporters of Obama put an end to their "paroxysm of self-congratulation."

> You're not embracing a black man, a descendant of slaves. . . . If he were Ronald Washington from Detroit, even with the same résumé, he wouldn't be getting this kind of love.[26]

In the immediate aftermath of Obama's election, the historian James Grossman echoed Dickerson. The narrative of unambiguous progress, he mused, is satisfying and irresistible but overstated and misleading. Obama, he noted, "has no roots in American slavery, the era of Jim Crow, or urban ghettoes. Is it possible that the only African-American who could cross the fragile bridge across the racial divide was a man unassociated with the great crucibles of African-American life?"*[27]

Ultimately, though, and despite the complications, Barack Obama presents himself primarily as a *black* man and thereby affiliates himself with the most stigmatized racial group in American history. That is what gave his candidacy its historic drama. In a sense, Geraldine Ferraro was correct:† if Barack Obama were

---

* Another complication is the rivalry between African-born blacks and American-born blacks. The former have equaled or forged ahead of the latter in certain settings, such as admission to highly selective schools. This has triggered accusations that African-born blacks have wrongly labeled themselves "African Americans," received favorable treatment from whites, displayed insufficient racial solidarity, and excessively exploited benefits garnered by the agitation and sacrifices of American-born blacks. See Kevin Brown and Jeannine Bell, "Demise of the Talented Tenth: Affirmative Action and the Increasing Underrepresentation of Ascendant Blacks at Selective Higher Educational Institutions," *Ohio State Law Journal* 69 (2008): 1229; Rachel Swarns, " 'African American' Becomes a Term for Debate," *New York Times*, August 29, 2004.

† For more on Ferraro see pages 145–147. See also Gary Kamiya, "It's OK to Vote for Obama Because He's Black," Salon.com, February 26, 2008 ("Obama's blackness is his indispensable asset. Without it, he would not have a snowball's chance in hell of being elected president").

white he would not occupy the exalted place he has enjoyed since February 2007, when he announced his quest for the White House. That he sought to become the first *black* president is what gave the Obama campaign its extraordinary excitement and promise.

Having decided to be black, Obama had to determine what sort of black to be. He made himself black enough to arouse the communal pride and support of African Americans but not "too black" to be accepted by whites and others.
Let's consider how he walked that tightrope.

Barack Obama worked hard to convince skeptical onlookers that he is "black enough" to warrant enthusiastic support from African Americans even in the absence of either a substantial record of participation in collective struggles for black advancement or a race-focused agenda. He had to confront the uncertainty many blacks initially felt upon learning of his upbringing in a mainly white family, his elite educational résumé, and his white support.[28] The political significance of that uncertainty showed itself vividly in 2000, when Obama, a junior state legislator, challenged Bobby Rush, a former leader of the Black Panther Party in Chicago, for his congressional seat. Rush decisively defeated Obama, in part because he and his allies framed Obama as a "white man in blackface."*[29] According to a report in the *Chicago Reader*, "There are whispers that Obama is being funded by a 'Hyde Park mafia,' a cabal of University of Chicago types, and that there's an 'Obama Project' masterminded by whites who want to push him up the political ladder."[30]
Even the ultraconservative Republican Alan Keyes attempted

* Obama's loss was a stroke of tremendous good fortune. Had he won, he would probably have had to adopt a political style attractive to the majority of his voting constituents but too liberal and too black for a presidential run.

to outflank Obama on the blackness front. During the 2004 contest for a United States Senate seat in Illinois, Keyes claimed that he, not Obama, was the authentic African American because both his parents were native-born blacks descended from slaves. Keyes's appeal was laughably ineffective. Obama won in a landslide with overwhelming black and white support. Still, Keyes's attack does highlight something that Obama has felt the need to address.*

It is easy to forget that early in the campaign for the Democratic Party nomination, Hillary Clinton attracted more support from blacks than Obama.† In the winter of 2007, one poll found that while 20 percent of black voters surveyed backed Obama, 60 percent backed Clinton.[31] Initially, she, not he, was the preferred choice of such esteemed figures as John Lewis and Andrew Young. The Clintons had long been nurturing cordial relationships with

---

* Keyes accused Obama of "wrongly claiming an African American heritage." By contrast, Keyes asserted, "My ancestors toiled in slavery in this country. My consciousness . . . has been shaped by my struggle, deeply emotional and deeply painful, with the reality of that heritage." Obama responded that he did not have "a lot of patience with identity politics, whether it's coming from the right or the left." He dismissed "self-appointed arbiters of African American culture who declare who is and who isn't black enough." Both quoted in Don Terry, "The Skin Game," *Chicago Tribune*, October 24, 2004.

   The notion that the absence of an ancestor who was enslaved in America disqualifies one from eligibility as an authentic "African American" is premised on a grossly oversimplified version of American history and a crude conception of the relationship between experience and consciousness. There were hundreds of thousands of free blacks (including some slaveholders) in the antebellum United States. Are their descendants wrong in thinking of themselves as African Americans? And why should the status or experience or self-perception of ancestors determine conclusively the racial identity of living persons? Shouldn't individual choice play at least some part in the matter?

† This may have been a benefit to him. As one student of the electoral drama observed, "It may have been the early skepticism among black voters that helped Obama gain traction with white voters. Because he was not bolstered by the overwhelming support of black America [initially], he avoided being labeled a 'black candidate.' . . . This, along with the racially innocuous tone of his campaign, allowed white voters to become comfortable with the idea of supporting [him]." Javius C. Wynn, "Assessing the Deeper Impact of the Black President" (final paper, class entitled Race and the Presidential Election of 2008, Harvard Law School, 2008).

politically influential blacks and they were undoubtedly in a position to call in political debts. Furthermore, blacks (like others) typically like siding with a winner, and early on Hillary Clinton was clearly the front-runner. In addition to these considerations, however, were others—the white mother, the Hawaiian upbringing, the elite education, the white sponsorship, the cosmopolitan aura—that made some blacks wary of Obama.

What quieted the wariness?

One signal has already been discussed: Obama identifies himself as an African American. A second signal is his marital partner, a black woman, Michelle Robinson Obama.* ³² Given the dismal state of the marriage market for black women, the shrinking number of black married couples, and the perception that successful black men often marry outside their race,† Barack Obama's marriage has won for him large amounts of goodwill among blacks. Lawrence Otis Graham, another African-American Harvard Law School alumnus, memorably highlights the importance he attaches to the marital choices of fellow blacks. Noting that he and his friends regularly engage in "race checking," Graham confides:

---

* Barack Obama married not only an African-American woman but an African-American woman with a relatively dark complexion. Accentuating this point, the journalist Allison Samuels writes that "Michelle is not only African American, but brown. Real brown." See "What Michelle Means to Us," December 1, 2008, *Newsweek.* See also Korie Edwards, Katrina Carter-Tallison, and Cedric Herring, "For Richer, For Poorer, Whether Dark or Light: Skin Tone, Marital Status, and Spouse's Earnings," in Cedric Herring, Verna Keith, and Hayward Horton, eds., *Skin Deep: How Race and Complexion Matter in the "Color Blind" Era* (2004).

† "African American men are much more likely to marry white women than white men are to marry African American women. From 1970 to 2000, black men increased their rate of marrying white women almost sixfold, so that by 2007, nearly 6 percent of black men were married to white women. Fewer than half as many . . . black women were married to white men." Elizabeth F. Emens, "Intimate Discrimination: The State's Role in the Accidents of Sex and Love," *Harvard Law Review* 122 (2009): 1307, 1320. See also R. Richard Banks, "The Aftermath of *Loving v. Virginia*: Sex Asymmetry in African American Intermarriage," *Wisconsin Law Review* (2007): 533; Ralph Richard Banks, *Is Marriage for White People? How the African American Marriage Decline Affects Everyone* (2011).

We flip through glowing profiles in *People, Ebony,* or *Business Week* quietly praising the latest black trailblazer or role model. Then we look for what we consider the final determinant of this person's black identity—that thing that will allow us to bestow our unqualified appreciation. We look for the litmus test of loyalty to the race: the photo of the person's spouse or significant other.[33]

For some blacks, nothing was more important as a clue to Obama's racial loyalty than his demonstrated commitment to "a sister." For them, few political images packed more of an emotional wallop than seeing Obama onstage in the affectionate embrace of his beautiful black wife and their two adorable children.*

A third important signal was Obama's choice of a church at which to worship. Obama grew up in a family in which he was taught about several religions but put under the discipline of none. He says that as an adult he felt a yearning for a more rooted spiritual experience and found it at the Trinity United Church of Christ in Chicago. He also acknowledges that attendance and membership at Trinity yielded significant benefits to his career. As a newcomer to the city, working as a neighborhood organizer for an outfit mainly directed by whites, Obama encountered

---

* Consider the following observations: "Why do black people love Obama? In large part, it's because of the dark-skinned woman on his arm. . . . Had Barack married a white woman, his candidacy would've never gotten off the ground with black people." Cinque Henderson, "Maybe We Can't," *The New Republic,* May 28, 2008. "He may only be half black but he is married to a black woman and his children are black. That says a lot to me because he could have married a white woman. . . ." An anonymous post in AfroChat.net, June 23, 2008. See also Vanessa Grigoriadis, "Black & Blacker: The Racial Politics of the Obama Marriage," *New York,* August 18, 2008 (quoting an Obama supporter, who states, "The fact that, as a successful black male, Barack did not choose a lighter-skinned woman, as most of them do, sends a message to me"; quoting another Obama supporter, who states, "If I want to know who you are, I look at who you sleep with and who you gave your name. When I look at Michelle, Barack doesn't have to be any blacker for me").

indifference if not skepticism from South Side Chicago blacks who questioned the depth of his commitment to their community. Active membership in Trinity helped to ease those doubts. Then, as Obama's ambitions moved to electoral politics, membership in Trinity bestowed another benefit: a far-flung network of civically active parishioners, presided over by a charismatic minister named Jeremiah Wright, Jr.[34]

I am *not* saying that every action Obama has taken is determined by careerist calculation. I am sure that he has passions and preferences that preceded his political ambitions and that exist outside of his exertions to realize those ambitions. From all that is evident, for example, it seems that the marriage of Barack Obama and Michelle Robinson contains strong elements of those mysterious, complicated, ineffable, and noninstrumental emotions that bind people who fall in love with each other. That impression, however, is consistent with the political benefits of the marriage. Regardless of what brought Barack Obama and Michelle Robinson together, the fact of their union matters to many potential voters. Obama is aware of that and, like most politicians, taps into such sentiments. In much the same way that other married politicians typically use the fact of their marriage to soothe voters who derive comfort from witnessing familial intimacy—hence the talismanic image of the candidate and his family onstage at political extravaganzas—so, too, do the Obamas use the fact of their marriage to attract blacks who derive pleasure from seeing a close-knit family of highly achieved African Americans. The same is true of Obama's relationship to the Trinity United Church of Christ. That religious devotion initially impelled him to join and contribute to the congregation is not at all inconsistent with his subsequently putting that association to political advantage.

Obama has sought to shore up his blackness in additional ways as well. Aware that some blacks found his diction to be too "white," Obama developed a folksier, "blacker" pattern of speech, especially in forums featuring predominantly African-American audiences.* Aware of a deep-seated belief in black communities that it is morally imperative to give honor to predecessors, Obama carefully and movingly pays homage to the heroes and heroines of struggles for black advancement. Aware of blacks' fear of abandonment, he continually stresses the importance of a person not forgetting his or her roots. Aware of the powerful influence of communitarian sentiments in many black precincts, Obama accentuates the obligations of "giving back" to one's neighbors.

This is not to say that Obama's gestures are all a matter of self-conscious artifice. As the writer Ta-Nehisi Coates observes:

> To say that Barack Obama is our first serious black presidential candidate drastically understates the matter. When Obama greets his political allies, he does not give a simple, firm, businesslike handshake. Instead he offers the sort of dap—a little English in the wrist and a one-armed hug—that black males spend much of their adolescence perfecting. If elected, surely Obama will be the first President to greet foreign dignitaries with a pound. Obama warms up on election morning not by running a three-miler or swimming laps but by shooting hoops. The Illinois senator sports a flawless and ever-fresh Caesar demonstrative of the razorwork native to only one side of the tracks.[35]

---

* See David Mendell, *Obama: From Promise to Power* (2007), 186–187 ("Sometimes he could work just a little too hard. When addressing African-Americans, he would drop into a Southern drawl, pepper his prose with a neatly placed 'y'all' and call up various black colloquialisms"); Todd Spivak, *Illinois Times*, March 25, 2004 ("It can be painful to hear Ivy League–bred Barack Obama talk jive. When the Democratic nominee for the U.S. Senate 'gives a shout out' to a supporter, calling him his 'homeboy,' or worse, his 'peeps,' the inflection in his voice betrays him as perhaps more vanilla than chocolate").

Still, it would be naïve to ignore the extent to which politicians and their staffs attend to all the features of a candidate's persona that might plausibly attract or repel voters. The cultural complexion of Obama's blackness has been manicured in ways that will only slowly be revealed.

Beyond racial identification and stylistic cues, Obama attracted black support by doing what most candidates do who seek enthusiastic support from the African-American electorate: he ran as a Democrat and offered a liberal domestic agenda. In addition, Obama showed through his impressive results in the Iowa caucuses and the New Hampshire and South Carolina primaries that he was a serious candidate with a real chance of prevailing.* This was absolutely essential. Regardless of his promised policies and personal attractiveness, Obama would not have elicited the support he obtained in the absence of a demonstration of electability. For many blacks the stakes were too high to allow free rein to sentimentality; realism leavened by hopefulness was the prevailing attitude of black America in 2008 as it witnessed Obama's rise.

Obama did not attract black voters on the basis of a comprehensive agenda aimed at redressing racial wrongs. He offered no such agenda. He said little about racial issues during the campaign. His "A More Perfect Union" race-relations speech was forced upon him by the uproar over his relationship with Reverend Wright. And the speech itself, while extravagantly lauded in some quarters, offered little in terms of specific programmatic initiatives. On his campaign Web site Obama chastised the Bush administration for what he termed a "tepid" commitment to civil-rights enforcement

---

* It is striking that in presidential nominations so much turns on the electoral preferences of voters in states with such racially homogeneous populations. Less than 3 percent of the Iowa population is black. In New Hampshire, blacks constitute only a little more than 1 percent of the population. Often, though, the jurisdictions most open to black advancement have been those in which populations of African Americans are relatively small.

and declared that his administration would see to it that traditional antidiscrimination laws were vigorously enforced. Even this thoroughly conventional position, however, was offered no prominence by a campaign that, with few exceptions, clearly preferred to stay clear of any sort of racial contentiousness.

Although race relations were a constant subject of public discussion during the general-election campaign, the candidates themselves never once engaged in a sustained discussion about the matter. One might have thought that at some point in the three presidential debates some questioner would have insisted that the candidates explain their position on racial affirmative action. After all, over the past quarter century, affirmative action has been hotly contested. Prior to Election Day 2008, several states (California, Washington, and Michigan) had already banned affirmative action. By the end of Election Day 2008, Nebraska had joined that list. The issue, however, was never broached in the presidential debates.

Outside of the debates what did Obama say about affirmative action? His position was studiously ambiguous—a vivid illustration of the careful way in which he walked the tightrope between being black enough but not too black. His remarks on affirmative action were (and have remained) fragmentary and elusive.[36] He devotes little attention to it in the chapter on race in his manifesto *The Audacity of Hope: Thoughts on Reclaiming the American Dream.* Indeed, he addresses the subject directly in only one sentence, a model (it could even be a caricature) of lawyerly ambiguity: "Affirmative action programs, when properly structured, can open up opportunities otherwise closed to qualified minorities without diminishing opportunities for white students."[37] In other words, Obama was willing to embrace affirmative action only to the extent that it could be rid of virtually all of its costs. In his compendium of campaign promises, *The Blueprint for Change:*

Obama and Biden's Plan for America, affirmative action does not even appear as a discrete subject. Nor does affirmative action surface for more than the merest mention in "A More Perfect Union."

When pressed, Obama said that he remained a supporter of racial affirmative action. But he emphasized that other types of policies should also be employed, such as preferences for anyone overcoming socioeconomic hardships. According to Obama, "We should take into account white kids who have been disadvantaged and have grown up in poverty and shown themselves to have what it takes to succeed." [38] Asked whether his own children should someday receive the benefit of affirmative action in college admissions, Obama remarked, "I think that my daughters should probably be treated by any admissions officer as folks who are pretty advantaged."*[39]

Affirmative action is a bad issue for Obama. He promotes himself as the candidate of change, but affirmative action is part of the status quo. He promotes himself as a uniter, but conflict over affirmative action is intense. Politically engaged blacks—the most energized sector of Obama's base—fervently embrace racial affirmative action while large percentages of white voters oppose it. No wonder Obama tries to say as little as possible about affirmative action.

There was hope in some quarters that Obama would reject racial affirmative action while embracing a class-based model. [40] Obama, however, has made no such move and is unlikely to do so. Taking that position would generate a loud, bitter rupture in his black base of support. The great mass of Obama's African-American

---

* Although Obama framed the issue as a matter of individual desert, educators who back affirmative action do so mainly on grounds of "diversity"—the idea that an educational environment will be enriched by participation of individuals from a broad array of communities. Under that rationale, the Obama children would almost certainly bring valuable diversity to a given school despite, or indeed because of, their extraordinarily privileged upbringing.

supporters permit him tremendous leeway in fashioning and refashioning himself for purposes of getting elected and governing the country. They do not begrudge his repositionings regarding campaign-finance practices, or the legitimate scope of government surveillance, or the appropriate treatment of enemy combatants, or the Bush tax cuts for the wealthy. A substantial number, however, would regard a clear jettisoning of racial affirmative action differently. They would see such a move as betrayal. That is because of what affirmative action has come to mean in black America over the past forty years. It has attained an iconic status. For many blacks, one's stance toward affirmative action is a litmus test of one's true commitment to racial fairness.[41]

Obama's status in black America has risen to unprecedented heights. But even his popularity would suffer appreciable erosion among blacks were he to repudiate affirmative action directly. Without the constraint imposed by the intense feelings of his black constituency, Obama might distance himself further from racial affirmative action. He sees it as an electoral liability. By inclination, moreover, Obama prefers policies geared toward transracial uplift as opposed to race-specific redistribution. To maintain his fractious coalition, however, Obama will continue to acquiesce to black conventional wisdom, supporting racial affirmative action, albeit in a muted fashion.

The extent of the black mobilization in support of Obama has been extraordinary. Not only did his candidacy attract the great majority of ordinary voters once it became clear that he was a serious candidate with a real chance to prevail; it also attracted the backing of a wide range of black activists, including some who, aware of their bad reputations in white America, carefully modulated their support. Early in the campaign Minister Louis Farrakhan cheered Obama's candidacy. That caused a problem for Obama insofar as journalists peppered him with demands—

often in the guise of questions—that he repudiate Farrakhan's endorsement. Obama initially tried merely to distance himself from Farrakhan's past objectionable utterances. When that failed to quell the hectoring, he proceeded to renounce the minister's support. Some black onlookers were angered by what they saw as a strategy to enlist Obama forcibly in an ongoing campaign to isolate Farrakhan. And some would have preferred Obama to offer stronger resistance to this campaign of ostracism. Yet few openly rebuked him. More to the immediate point, Farrakhan himself said hardly anything more about Obama for the remainder of the election season, even after the candidate repudiated his endorsement. Only *after* Obama had been elected did Farrakhan once again voice his support.

Even many of Minister Farrakhan's detractors give him credit for acting in a disciplined manner to avoid hurting Obama's campaign. Much the same is true for the Reverend Al Sharpton. Initially he adopted a rather dismissive or even confrontational posture toward Obama. Then, as the Obama campaign turned into a virtual crusade in black America, Sharpton's attitude changed. First, he stopped criticizing Obama's reluctance to speak out on volatile racial issues. Then he refrained from embracing the candidate in ways that might rub off negatively. Like Minister Farrakhan, Minister Sharpton adopted a posture of quiet support.

Among African Americans, blacks who were perceived as hostile or even merely indifferent to Obama's campaign became subject to communal rebuke. Consider the case of the talk-show host Tavis Smiley. Prior to the Obama campaign, Smiley enjoyed widespread respect among politically active blacks who admired his initiative in creating forums for serious discussion of political, cultural, and social issues of particular interest to African Americans. One of Smiley's forums is an annual symposium dubbed the State of the Black Union. In 2007 he invited Senator Barack Obama.

But Obama declined to appear on account of a conflict—the announcement of his campaign for the presidency. In 2008 Smiley again invited Obama. Citing the need to stay on the campaign trail, Obama again declined to appear (though Hillary Clinton attended). Michelle Robinson Obama offered to attend in place of her husband, but Smiley refused that alternative and proceeded to criticize Barack Obama's absence.[42]

Moreover, in radio commentaries on the popular *Tom Joyner Morning Show,* Smiley repeatedly voiced skepticism regarding whether blacks should back Obama. Questioning Obama's racial authenticity, Smiley remarked that "Obama has not had the quintessential black experience in America." Questioning whether Obama had paid sufficient dues for allegiance, Smiley quipped that "most black folk got to know Barack the same way white folk got to know him—two years ago when he gave that speech at the Democratic Convention." Questioning Obama's fitness as a figure around whom blacks should rally, Smiley declared that the senator from Illinois "is no Jesse Jackson. For that matter, Barack Obama is no Shirley Chisholm. When Shirley Chisholm ran in '72, when Jesse ran in '84 and '88, they had long-standing relationships with the black community. So there's some courting here that Barack is going to have to do. I don't know whether or not, after the court-ship, if black America is going to decide that we're going to date, much less be wed to him."[43] Later, acknowledging the sentimental pull of Obama's candidacy, Smiley cautioned African Americans about the perils of mixing love and politics. "You can't short-circuit the process of holding folk accountable," he warned, "just because you fall in love."[44]

The response to Smiley was intensely negative. Many African Americans had begun to insist that prominent blacks do nothing to impede Obama's progress. Smiley's complaints and warnings were seen as impediments and therefore resented.

Professor Melissa Harris-Lacewell, for example, criticized Smiley with a cold fury.[45] In "Who Died and Made Tavis King?" Harris-Lacewell scoffed at Smiley and other "self-proclaimed racial power brokers" for what she perceived as their pettiness, jealousy, and poor sense of priorities:

> Over the past two months African Americans have emerged as equal partners in a multi-racial, intergenerational, bipartisan, national coalition led by the most exciting political candidate of the past four decades, who also happens to be the first African-American presidential possibility in our history. So why is Tavis Smiley throwing a temper tantrum?*[46]

Aggressive support for Obama provoked yet another reaction: anger at what some saw as a herd mentality. Responding to Harris-

---

* In the blogosphere, many others also criticized Smiley. Consider the following: "I have yet to hear elation or praise in his voice over Barack's historic primary wins or how Barack's campaign is bringing all demographics of people together to elect a black man for president. Where is the LOVE, which he [Tavis Smiley] so often speaks of? Tavis's commentaries over the past few weeks have shown me that his helping hands have become claws, used to pull down another brutha that's trying to come-up out of the barrel. A message for Tavis: Don't be so 'crabby!'" Another respondent stated that Obama "is the one we have been waiting for, and Tavis for whatever reason, is trying his best to set him back. I believe it is finally time to check all egos at the door!" Another remarked, "Mr. Smiley, get over it. Senator Obama is running for the OFFICE OF THE PRESIDENT OF THE UNITED STATES OF AMERICA FOR ALL PEOPLE NOT JUST BLACK PEOPLE. He (Senator OBAMA) will have a place in the history books. He will be remembered for his GOOD WORKS. Question. . . . WILL YOU??? He has better things to do with his time than to come on your ONE SIDED BLACK PEOPLE ONLY SHOW. This letter was sent to you by a BLACK SISTER. . . ." Another critic of Smiley's asserted indignantly, "To think you would have him risk his presidency to kiss our ass and prove he's black enough. I'm ashamed to be in the same race as you. . . ."

Defenders of Smiley also spoke up. "So, what if he supports Hillary, why does that now all of a sudden make him a sellout? You folks are ALL unbelievable. Should we all vote for Barack because he is black and we are black? Hasn't our maker blessed us with the brains to think for ourselves and make our own decisions based on our individual perspectives and should we not respect that in everybody? Do we have to hold Obama to a different standard because he is black and say it is OK for him to pass on SOBU [the State of the Black Union symposium] because he has more important things to attend? Give me a BREAK."

Lacewell, the commentator Earl Ofari Hutchinson derided "the black Obama thought police," averring that "in their absolute, dogmatic, Obama mania, they have turned what in any other season would be a healthy give and take . . . into finger pointing . . . toward any black who disagrees that Obama is the second coming of Dr. King."[47] Backing Hutchinson were other blacks who expressed dismay at what they felt to be a naïve embrace of a candidate who had as yet done little to warrant such enthusiastic loyalty. That perspective, however, was eclipsed by the dominant mood that pervaded black America in 2008—a fierce, urgent, prayerful protectiveness toward candidate Obama.

Another offshoot of black support for Obama was a negative response to the argument that feminist imperatives counseled a preference for Hillary Clinton. Gloria Steinem voiced one version of this argument in an opinion piece in *The New York Times* entitled "Women Are Never Front-Runners."[48] Steinem posited three main points. The first was that she supported Hillary Clinton for the Democratic Party nomination. She did so, Steinem averred, because Clinton had more experience than Obama and "no masculinity to prove." Steinem made haste to say that she was not opposing Obama. "If he's the nominee," she noted, "I'll volunteer." But she preferred Clinton.

Second, Steinem criticized what she perceived as sexist double standards. Clinton "is accused of 'playing the gender card' when citing the old boys' club, while [Obama] is seen as unifying by citing civil rights confrontations."[49]

Third, Steinem related what she portrayed as the sexist mistreatment of Clinton to an ongoing story of illicit patriarchy, asserting that "gender is probably the most restricting force in American life." Sure, racism has been a terrible scourge, Steinem acknowledged. But "black men were given the vote a half century before women of any race were allowed to mark a ballot, and generally have ascended to positions of power, from the military to the boardroom, before any women (with the possible exception of obedient family members in the latter)."

It is at this point, where she compared sexism and racism, that Steinem provoked the most reaction. If Obama had been a woman, Steinem declared, alluding to his relative lack of experience, "her goose would have been cooked long ago"; in fact, she would not have been given serious consideration as a presidential contender. "Why," Steinem asked, "is the sex barrier not taken as seriously as the racial one?"[50]

Anticipating trouble, Steinem quickly interjected, "I'm not advocating a competition for who has it toughest. The caste systems of sex and race are interdependent and can only be uprooted together." But in the end Steinem did insist upon the rightness of a feminist preference for Senator Clinton. "It's time," Steinem declared, "to take equal pride in breaking all the barriers. We have to be able to say: 'I'm supporting her because she'll be a great president *and* because she's a woman.'"[51]

Some black women agreed with Steinem or for other reasons supported Clinton. Maggie Williams, who was Clinton's chief of staff when she was First Lady, became her campaign director, and Stephanie Tubbs Jones, a Democratic congresswoman from Ohio, was national cochairwoman of the Clinton campaign. They and other black women were among Clinton's fiercest partisans. At the grass roots, however, black women voters supported Obama overwhelmingly. Moreover, leading black women intellectuals and activists not only expressed support for him; some also expressed annoyance and even antagonism toward Clinton and her feminist champions.*

---

* It bears noting that those who propound a racial critique of pro-Clinton feminists hardly ever mention the black women who supported Clinton. They almost exclusively target white women.

Having lambasted Tavis Smiley, Melissa Harris-Lacewell also castigated Steinem. She charged that Steinem was "asking us to ignore the ways in which race and gender intersect," and that Steinem was "ignor[ing] an entire history in which white women have in fact been in the White House . . . as an attachment to white male patriarchal power." Decrying what she perceived as a grievous distortion, Harris-Lacewell said that for Steinem to "make an argument like black men had the right to vote long before white women is to ignore that black men were then lynched regularly for any attempt to actually exercise that right."[52]

What is one to make of the Obama feminists' racial critique of the Clinton feminists? It shows the towering importance that the election had come to have for so many African Americans. It also shows the persistence and power of racial divisions within feminist circles despite efforts over the years to avoid conflicts that had bedeviled feminism in previous eras.[53]

Was the pro-Obama racial critique of white feminists correct? Yes and no. There were undoubtedly some pro-Clinton feminists who did minimize the ongoing significance of racism, overlook the interconnectedness of gender, race, class, sexual orientation, and other vexing lines of identity and difference, exploit racial bias on behalf of the Clinton candidacy, or wrongly assert that "authentic" feminism compelled support for Clinton over Obama. Proponents of the pro-Obama racial critique misfired all too often, however, when specifically applying their general complaints. Take the case of Gloria Steinem. Detractors charged her with ignoring the ways in which race and gender intersect. Yet Steinem expressly stated that "the caste system of sex and race are interdependent and can only be uprooted together." Detractors suggested that Steinem had failed to appreciate Obama's virtues. Yet Steinem explicitly stated, "I'm not opposing Obama; if he's the nominee, I'll volunteer." Obviously, Steinem preferred Clinton. But she openly declared that if the Democratic Party selected Obama she would work to elect him.

An oft-stated criticism of Steinem was that she had organized an "oppression sweepstakes," "named sexism the greater scourge," and in so doing perpetuated a misleading, divisive, destructive strategy.[54] This complaint is mistaken. There is nothing inherently wrong with making comparisons between racism and sexism or other forms of oppression in order to better understand them individually, or collectively, or to better gauge the priority with which these social vices should be engaged depending on surrounding circumstances. Given the salience of racism as the paradigmatic form of group debasement in American life, it is virtually impossible to bring attention to any other form of group oppression without implicitly or explicitly comparing it to racism. That is why analogies between bans on same-sex marriage and bans on interracial marriage are so rife.[55] Our minds make sense of the world by making comparisons among things that are alike in certain ways and different in certain ways.

There is nothing untoward in comparing and contrasting the dynamics of sexism and racism. The underappreciated pioneer Shirley Chisholm did so. She regularly compared her experience as a victim of both racism and sexism, concluding that, for her, the latter had been more detrimental.* Such comparisons surface in the writings of those who chastise Steinem for doing this very thing. A few paragraphs after criticizing Steinem for creating a so-called oppression sweepstakes, the writer Betsy Reed herself turns to comparing sexism and racism. "While sexism may be more usually accepted," she argues, "racism is more insidious and trickier to confront."[56] Reed came to a different conclusion from

---

* "I have said many times that during twenty years in local ward politics, four as a state legislator and four as a member of Congress, I had met far more discrimination because I am a woman than because I am black." Shirley Chisholm, *The Good Fight* (1973), 32.

Steinem. But like Steinem, Reed assessed the relative oppressiveness of these prejudices in the circumstances of modern American life. To repeat: there was nothing wrong with Steinem making a comparison between racism and sexism. Arguably her conclusion was erroneous.* But there was nothing inherently bad about her methodology.

The pro-Obama black feminists and their allies were so deeply invested in Obama that they could not understand how any "true" progressive could prefer Clinton absent some misleading influence such as indebtedness, jealousy, or myopia. An illustration is Alice Walker's "Lest We Forget: An Open Letter to My Sisters Who Are Brave," in which she declared Obama to be "a remarkable human being, not perfect but humanly stunning, like King was and like Mandela is. . . . He is the change America has been trying desperately and for centuries to hide, ignore, kill. The change America must have if we are to convince the rest of the world that we care about people other than our (white) selves." After declaring that Obama "offers a rare opportunity for the country and the world to start over and do better," Walker stated that "it is a deep sadness to me that many of my feminist white friends cannot see him. Cannot see what he carries in his being. Cannot hear the fresh choices toward Movement he offers."[57] Walker's unequivocal support for Obama would simply brook no dissenting view.

Although Obama captured the hearts and minds of the great majority of black voters in 2008, he received an ambivalent, if not hostile, reception from some African Americans.

Among Obama's most relentless and vitriolic detractors were

---

* For an argument that she was wrong see Gary Kamiya, "The Race vs. Gender War," Salon.com, January 15, 2008.

black conservative commentators. Notable in this camp were Thomas Sowell, Shelby Steele, and Juan Williams. Sowell is an ultraconservative academic turned propagandist who is headquartered at the Hoover Institution. He is the dean of the black conservative commentariat, the person whose writings and counsel facilitated the ideological conversion of Supreme Court justice Clarence Thomas, who lauds Sowell as a mentor. Sowell aggressively attacked Obama's liberalism, inexperience, and associations. He assailed Obama as a seductive charlatan who was "all talk—glib talk, exciting talk, confident talk, but still just talk." He condemned Obama for associating with "people on the far left fringe . . . members of the anti-American counter-culture."[58] He asserted that Obama "has been leading as much a double life as Eliot Spitzer"— the former New York governor who was caught patronizing a prostitution ring—and charged that "while Hillary Clinton tells lies, Barack Obama is himself a lie."[59] There was little new or instructive in Sowell's commentary on Obama. It amounted to a litany of far-right talking points delivered with a sneer. More interesting were the anti-Obama musings of Shelby Steele.

Steele, like Sowell, is affiliated with the Hoover Institution. A writer whose principal focus is on what he views as the psychological pathologies of American race relations, Steele portrayed Obama as distinctly lacking in presidential stature. Obama's "extraordinary dash to the forefront of American politics," Steele argued, "is less a measure of the man than of the hunger in white America for racial innocence. . . . By the evidence of his slight political record . . . [Obama] stacks up as something of a mediocrity" who "flip-flopped on campaign financing, wire-tapping, gun control, faith-based initiatives and the terms of withdrawal from Iraq."[60]

It was regarding Obama's racial politics, however, particularly the association with Reverend Wright, that Steele was most scathing. Obama, he charged, has "fellow-traveled with a hate-filled anti-American black nationalism . . . failing to stand and challenge an ideology that would have no place for his own mother. And what portent of presidential judgment is it to have exposed his two daughters for their entire lives to what is, at the very least, a sub-text of anti-white vitriol?" Although Steele gave more credit to Obama than to Al Sharpton or Jesse Jackson, two politicians he incessantly derides, he ultimately concluded that Obama's candidacy was not "qualitatively different" from theirs. Obama's candidacy, too, he complained, was "based more on the manipulation of white guilt than on substance." The only real difference, Steele claimed, is that while Sharpton and Jackson intimidated whites, Obama flattered them, hoping "to ascend [to the White House] on the back of their gratitude."[61]

Steele was transfixed by the mistaken belief that most whites are racked by a pathological racial guilt that makes them vulnerable to black racial demagogues. He was wrong in two ways, one descriptive and one normative. Descriptively he was wrong because he exaggerated the breadth and intensity of feelings of racial guilt in white America. While *some* whites do harbor guilt and a yearning for racial redemption, most do not. Steele's analysis failed to explain rejection of demands for reparations, the pushback against affirmative action, inertia in the face of miserable social conditions that obviously stem from racial oppression in the near past, and high rates of unlawful racial discrimination in every market that has been studied, including housing markets, labor markets, and commercial transactions. The white America that Steele depicted is one which, out of racial guilt, would have overwhelmingly supported Obama—which is not what actually transpired.

Normatively Steele was wrong in his allocation of blame for America's ongoing racial conflict. In his analysis the villains were invariably those who challenge established racial hierarchies that continue to favor whites. Among those villains are those whom

Steele depicted as naïve, irresponsible white liberals who suffer from overblown feelings of racial guilt. Although Steele derided them, such whites ought to be applauded for decently acknowledging their role, albeit involuntary, as inheritors of racial privilege. And they ought to be applauded, too, for self-consciously seeking to repudiate and reform the racially deformed institutions and customs bequeathed to them, including the assumed Caucasian monopolization of the presidency. Far from condemning white racial guilt wholesale, as Steele does repeatedly, one ought to celebrate the civilizing virtue of appropriate feelings of guilt and responsibility and recognize their healthy manifestations in the presidential election of 2008. It was a wonderful thing to witness the enthusiasm with which millions of white Americans sought to redeem themselves and the country by rallying to Barack Obama. Steele, unfortunately, belittled that generous impulse.

Juan Williams is a third example of black conservative opposition to Obama. Unlike Sowell and Steele, Williams does not call himself conservative. He presents himself as nonideological. But at least during the 2008 election season he could properly be viewed as conservative regardless of his self-labeling. Although his commentaries appeared in a variety of settings, including on National Public Radio (NPR), Williams's main forum was the conservative Fox News Channel.* A stock ingredient in his commentary on racial matters is the contention that the primary impediments

---

* In October 2010, Williams was dismissed by NPR, ostensibly for remarks he made on a Fox television program hosted by Bill O'Reilly. Williams said that he felt afraid when he found himself on airplanes with passengers wearing distinctly Muslim garb. Several theories have been asserted as explanations for the firing: revulsion at what some deem to be a bigoted statement; resentment over Williams's close affiliation with Fox; anger at what some view as Williams's conservative tilt; disapproval of what some see as commentary that undermined his journalistic role. After the firing, Fox entered into a multiyear, multimillion-dollar contract with Williams. See Tobin Harshaw, "Juan Williams Offends NPR," *New York Times*, October 22, 2010, and Elizabeth Jansent, "NPR Executive Who Fired Juan Williams Resigns," *New York Times*, January 6, 2011.

to black advancement are cultural deficiencies *within* black communities.[62]

Williams's response to the Obama campaign was complicated. In November 2007 he gushed admiringly that Obama "is running an astonishing campaign."[63] "Most amazing," Williams remarked, is that Obama "has built his political base among white voters. He relies on unprecedented support among whites for a black candidate." As Williams saw it, the big problem at that stage of the campaign was the hesitance of some blacks to support Obama. "Black political and community activists still rooted in the politics of the 1960s civil rights movement are suspicious about why so many white people feel this man so acceptable." That reaction, Williams asserted, is "the latest in self-defeating black politics." What Williams found most appealing about Obama was the candidate's eschewal of such "self-defeating" politics.

> The alienation, anger, and pessimism that mark speeches from major black American leaders are missing from Mr. Obama's speeches. He talks about America as a "magical place" of diversity and immigration. He appeals to the King-like dream of getting past the racial divide to a place where the sons of slaves and the sons of slave owners can pick the best president without regard to skin color.[64]

According to Williams, Obama was thankfully "out of step with the way most black politicians approach white America," "in the vanguard of a new brand of multi-racial politics," "asking voters to move with him beyond race and beyond the civil rights movement to a politics of shared values." If voters responded to Obama's values, Williams concluded happily, "he will really have taken the nation into post-racial politics."[65]

Williams's attitude changed dramatically in the aftermath

of two developments: the publicizing of Obama's association with Reverend Wright and his subsequent difficulty in gaining support among white working-class voters in the waning stages of the nomination contest with Hillary Clinton. Williams harshly chastised Obama for his ties to Reverend Wright: "When Barack Obama . . . finds it easy to sit in Rev. Wright's pews and nod along with wacky and bitterly divisive racial rhetoric, it does call his judgment into question."[66] Williams was even more lacerating in dismissing Obama's initial unwillingness to renounce the minister unequivocally, describing the candidate's discussion of Wright in his famous race-relations speech as "a full political pander."[67]

Williams also chastised Obama for his difficulty in attracting the support of white working-class voters. Williams declared in a May 2008 New York *Daily News* column that Hillary Clinton was right in arguing that she would make the better nominee "because . . . she can win White Democrats."[68] History, he maintained, "will reflect poorly on Democrats if they believe it is virtuous to ignore race in the name of nominating the first [major party] black candidate for the White House—even if it means giving the Republicans a better chance to once again walk away with the big prize of the Presidency." Furthermore, in Williams's view, Obama's difficulty with wooing reluctant white voters did not stem only or even mainly from racial prejudice but instead from justifiable objection to a candidate besmirched by association with Reverend Wright's racial demagoguery.

After Obama secured the Democratic Party nomination, Williams continued to skewer him for failing to denounce Wright sufficiently.[69] Indeed, he not only excoriated Obama for "poor judgment in remaining a member of Rev. Wright's church" and then failing to condemn Wright with sufficient force; Williams also called into question Obama's good faith, asserting that he had failed to speak "honestly about Rev. Wright's sermons as destructive and racist." According to Williams, Obama needs to give another speech. This time he has to admit to sins of using race for political expediency—by knowingly buying into divisive, mean messages being delivered from the pulpit. . . . Only by admitting to his own sins can Mr. Obama credibly claim that he has seen the promise of our country, in which Americans of all colors work together. Only then can he convince dubious white voters that he is ready to move beyond racial antagonism and be their president.[70]

The Obama camp unsurprisingly refrained from accepting Williams's prescription for political suicide.

The Obama phenomenon generated ambivalence in left-wing black America as well as in right-wing black America. The flamboyant Christian socialist Cornel West had difficulty, for instance, calibrating his support for candidate Obama. His intermittent endorsements were qualified by expressions of sharp annoyance ("You can't take black people for granted just because you're black"),[71] as when Obama skipped Tavis Smiley's 2007 State of the Black Union conference, or even disapproval, as when Obama accepted the Democratic Party's nomination without expressly mentioning Martin Luther King, Jr., by name.[72] Maintaining that Obama had made "no mention of Martin" and "no mention of the black freedom movement," West accused the candidate of having "run from history," "and run from memory."[73]

While West evinced skepticism, others on the black left expressed derision. Notable examples were Adolph Reed, Jr., a professor of political science, and the journalists Glen Ford and Bruce Dixon. Reed disparaged "Obama's empty claims to being a candidate of progressive change," "his horribly opportunistic approach to the issues bearing on inequality," and his "style of being all things to all people." While many observers hailed Obama's famous speech on race relations, Reed dismissed it as "a string of well-crafted and coordinated platitudes and hollow images worthy of an SUV commercial."[74] Dixon scoffingly maintained that Obama was "the establishment's dream candidate, almost entirely free of obligation to African Americans and our historic agenda, but getting our votes anyway."[75] Ford lamented that Obama "steadfastly refuses to put forward any program to address the specific historical and contemporary grievances of African Americans."[76] He denounced Obama as "the NOT-Black candidate, who just looks Black, and will absolve white folks—like a priest behind a screen—of historical, present, and future sins." Obama, Ford contended, "has become a great presence that threatens the very fabric of black politics, having declared there is no such thing." Portraying Obama as potentially more damaging to blacks' proper aspirations than any white politician could ever be, Ford depicted Obama as a clear and present danger. He is, Ford concluded, "a knife in our heart."[77]

Obama's black opponents on the left were even more isolated than their right-wing counterparts. Though unpopular among African Americans, Sowell, Steele, and Williams received the amplification of a formidable conservative publicity apparatus, including Fox News and *The Wall Street Journal*. Obama's detractors on the black left, by contrast, were confined to relatively obscure forums—for instance, *The Progressive* magazine or the Web site Black Agenda Report—that rarely penetrate "mainstream" discourse. They thus wielded little influence. What, though, about the merits of their arguments? Some of their analysis was valuable. They rightly insisted on looking beneath the cosmetics of the Obama candidacy to its underlying ideological and programmatic innards. They rightly eschewed sentimental assessments, noting that, for all the talk of novelty and boldness, Obama typically ventured no further than the boundaries of conventional Democratic Party liberalism.

The big problem with Obama's opponents on the black left was that they offered so little as a plausible alternative to the incrementalism they disdained. They offered either support for utopian "revolution" with no road map for implementation within the fore-seeable future or support for abstention from voting or support for fringe candidacies (like that of Cynthia McKinney of the Green Party) that appeared to be devoid of any serious, ongoing effort toward building a credible challenge to the two-party monopoly. Obama's opponents on the black left displayed little attentiveness to the discipline of electoral politics. They showed little concern for the practicalities of winning. They acted as if Obama should have been "brave" enough to articulate a platform that would have immediately resulted in his being cripplingly attacked as an irresponsible radical. They acted as if it were wrong for him to seek election in earnest as opposed to in gesture. Perhaps they had this view because, ultimately, they thought that the presidential electoral competition was an irrelevant sham, that a ruling class controlled the presidency, that the Establishment ruthlessly screened potential contenders and only submitted to the electorate as "serious" candidates those who had been preapproved.[78] There is some truth in this critique, but its purveyors have more detachment from the here and now than I can manage when they posit that there was no "real" difference between Obama and his running mate, Senator Joseph Biden, on the one hand and McCain and his running mate, Alaska governor Sarah Palin, on the other. Convinced, apparently, that only revolution can bring appreciable relief to the people, the Reeds, Fords, and Dixons of black America condemned virtually all forms of electorally viable political engagement as "selling out." The veteran radical activist Amiri Baraka spoke aptly when he criticized his black left comrades who opposed Obama. Pleading with them to forgo "empty idealism," he maintained that "no amount of solipsistic fist-pounding about 'radical principles' will change this society as much as the election of Barack Obama."*

---

* See "Amiri Baraka Calls Out Obama Haters—Says: 'Do Something,'" HiphopNews .com, July 24, 2008.

Barack Obama's reception in black America during the election campaign of 2008 moved from ambivalence to adulation. At the outset, if polls are to be believed, he trailed Hillary Clinton. By the time of the caucuses and primaries, a massive shift had begun to occur. By the time he won the Democratic Party nomination, he had attained a status reserved only for the most revered of African Americans. By the time he walked onto the stage in Grant Park in Chicago on the evening of November 4 to acknowledge his election as president of the United States, he had achieved a singular place in the esteem of black America.

What does this trajectory reflect? It shows the magnetism of success. Obama's electoral success in Iowa attracted black voters who would otherwise have withheld their support. For many black Democratic voters (meaning the great mass of the black electorate), more important than anything else, including the race of the candidate, was the matter of ultimate electability. When Obama showed that he stood a good chance of winning a sufficient number of white votes to prevail, blacks broke toward him in a frenzy and never looked back.

Obama's ascendancy also highlights his own personal qualities. His battles with Hillary Clinton and John McCain required him repeatedly to show how he thinks and deals with victory and defeat, happiness and grief. Black Americans (like many Americans of all complexions) liked what they saw. The more familiar they became with Obama, the more they came to admire him.

Finally, the extraordinary enthusiasm with which blacks rallied around Obama reflected, sadly enough, a profound neediness. Blacks are so used to being neglected, if not mistreated, that they often tend to exaggerate the virtues of authorities that treat them with even a modicum of respect. That is largely why images of

FDR and JFK continue to adorn walls in the living spaces of blacks across the country. That is why Bill Clinton was adopted by many blacks so enthusiastically.[79] He had black friends, worshipped at black churches, knew by heart the lyrics to the "Negro national anthem," "Lift Every Voice and Sing." These signals went far toward pleasing a black population habituated to racial neglect. That pleasure, however, paled in comparison with black America's collective joy at witnessing the ascendancy of an African-American chief executive—a black president who is genuinely conversant with the African-American cultural canon (Martin Luther King, Jr., Malcolm X, Richard Pryor, Mahalia Jackson, Toni Morrison, Jay-Z) and vocally appreciative of the sacrifices made by countless Negroes who have fought for a better racial deal. By winning election to the White House, Barack Obama played the starring role in a drama that epitomized a new chapter in black Americans' relationship to the United States.

3

Obama and White America

"Why Can't They All Be Like Him?"

A key to Barack Obama's victory was his ability to attract white support. How did he do it?

Part of the answer had to do with Obama's temperament. He was cool—"no drama Obama." There is, in general, a concern that anyone with access to the force that a president has at his or her command must be even-tempered and self-disciplined. That is why John McCain's history of angry outbursts emerged as an issue. With Obama, however, there was a racial aspect to the matter. Because of the stereotype of "the angry black man" Obama had to be especially careful to express himself in a calm, measured, unthreatening fashion.*[1]

Similarly, Obama had to work hard to convince white onlookers that he harbored no racial resentment, that he loved America,

---

* The writer Brent Staples puts the point nicely:

> Mr. Obama seems to understand that he is always an utterance away from a statement . . . that could transform him in a campaign ad from the affable, rational and racially ambiguous candidate into the archetypal angry black man who scares off the white vote. His caution is evident from the way he sifts and searches the language as he speaks, stepping around words that might push him into the danger zone. These maneuvers are often painful to watch. The troubling part is that they are necessary.

"Barack Obama, John McCain and the Language of Race," *New York Times*, September 22, 2008.

and that his first and unalterable allegiance was to the nation as a whole as opposed merely to black America. That is one reason the word "reparations" never left Obama's mouth. He sought to stay clear of any conduct that would enable opponents to portray him as a latter-day Jesse Jackson. Occasionally Obama mentioned "the history of racial injustice in this country."[2] In his famous speech on race he declared that we

> need to remind ourselves that so many of the disparities that exist in the African-American community today can be directly traced to inequities passed on from an earlier generation that suffered under the brutal legacy of slavery and Jim Crow. . . . Legalized discrimination—where blacks were prevented, often through violence, from owning property, or loans were not granted to African-American business owners, or black homeowners could not access FHA mortgages, or blacks were excluded from unions, or the police force, or fire departments—meant that black families could not amass any meaningful wealth to bequeath to future generations. That history helps explain the wealth and income gap between black and white, and the concentrated pockets of poverty that persists in so many of today's urban and rural communities.[3]

Many commentators praised the speech for what they saw as its brave candor. But even the passage quoted above, the speech's most direct engagement with racial oppression, is suffused with a passive voice that obscures the participation of whites, past and present, in the making, perpetuation, and exploitation of racial subordination. Obama stated that "blacks were prevented . . . from owning property," that "loans were not granted to African-American business owners," and that "blacks were excluded from unions." But who have been the perpetrators and beneficiaries of those awful injustices? In Obama's chronicle whites are strangely absent from those roles. In his narrative, slavery and segregation happened without enslavers or segregationists. This lacuna was not inadvertent. Obama had thought long and hard about the dilemma black politicians face when addressing whites about racial problems while simultaneously seeking to avoid white backlash.

In *The Audacity of Hope*, Obama recounts an episode during his time in the Illinois legislature. He was sitting with a white senator listening to a black senator—John Doe, Obama calls him—launch into a lengthy peroration on why the elimination of a certain program was a case of blatant racism. After a few minutes, the white senator (who had one of the chamber's more liberal voting records) turned to Obama and said, "You know what the problem is with John? Whenever I hear him, he makes me feel more white."[4] Obama sought to avoid issues, positions, and rhetoric that would make whites "feel more white." He wanted whites to feel no alienation between him and them.

Some detractors have charged that Obama panders to the white electorate by, among other things, soft-pedaling white racism. They contend, for example, that racism facilitated the federal government's egregious response to Hurricane Katrina.[5] Obama asserted, by contrast, that the culprit was sheer incompetence.[6] Similarly, while many observers who champion affirmative action see white opposition as largely an outcropping of latter-day racism, Obama took a different tack. He portrayed the opposition as emanating from an understandable but misplaced resentment— the white analogue to the resentment that many blacks feel when contemplating their collective disappointments. Obama's sympathetic, indeed empathetic, understanding of whites with whom he disagrees is part of what distinguishes him, part of what elicits the gratitude of many white voters, part of what has enabled him to climb farther up the electoral mountain than any African American has climbed before.

There are other features of Obama's persona that have helped him with a hard-to-determine but appreciable number of white voters. One is his biological tie to whiteness. Some whites take comfort in viewing Obama as "half-white." Clearly, Obama and his operatives understood this. It was not accidental that during the general-election campaign they continually reminded the public of Obama's white mother and her parents, particularly the (white) grandfather who fought in Patton's army.[7]

Obama's Africanness may also have helped him. While Obama conflated the experience of his immigrant father with the experience of native-born blacks, the fact is that in many contexts whites have accorded more respect to foreign-born blacks than native-born blacks. Much was made during the campaign of how Obama's atypical family, exotic upbringing, and unusual name were impediments, distancing him from "regular folks."* Those features did have that effect for some. But they also had the effect of distancing Obama from derogatory stereotypes of black American men.

Obama's effort to assuage white racial anxieties encountered major challenges when he received expressions of support from Minister Louis Farrakhan of the Nation of Islam and when certain statements by his longtime pastor, Reverend Jeremiah Wright, Jr., became highly publicized. Journalists besieged Obama, demand-

---

* A county in New York sent absentee ballots to voters which misidentified Barack Obama as "Barack Osama." The typographical error was caught quickly, unsent ballots containing the error were shredded, and corrected ballots were sent to the approximately three hundred people who had received the erroneous ones. Throughout the campaign, people accidentally referred to Obama as Osama and, of course, there were some observers, hostile to Obama, who purposefully conflated the candidate and the terrorist. See Associated Press, "Oops! New York Ballot Drama for Obama," *Chicago Sun-Times*, October 11, 2008; Michael Luo, "Romney Makes Obama-Osama Gaffe," *New York Times*, October 23, 2007; Brian Stelter, "CNN's Obama/Osama Habit," *New York Times*, December 19, 2007.

ing responses. Curiosity was one motivation behind the questioning. More significant motivations were intentions to test Obama, to embarrass him, to force him to forswear Farrakhan and Wright in order to retain or obtain the allegiance of other supporters or potential supporters, or to enlist Obama into a campaign of ostracism. The *Washington Post* columnist Richard Cohen penned a column, "Obama's Farrakhan Test,"[8] in which he noted that Obama was a member of Reverend Jeremiah Wright's Trinity United Church of Christ, that Obama had described Wright as his spiritual adviser, and that Wright had praised Minister Louis Farrakhan's "integrity and honesty" and the depth of his analysis regarding "the racial ills of this nation." Cohen suggested that these facts gave rise to an obligation on Obama's part "to speak out" against Farrakhan. Obama, Cohen declared, "could be the next President. Where is his sense of outrage?" Of course, the world is full of things about which one can justifiably be outraged. Why should it have been a priority for Obama to express outrage against Farrakhan? Cohen seemed to believe that Farrakhan's anti-Semitism was not just any evil in a world full of vice; it was an evil within Obama's orbit and influence. What brought it there was Reverend Wright. Cohen professed to have no worry that Obama himself harbored Wright's evident liking for Farrakhan. Rather, Cohen's complaint had to do with what he suspected to be an absence of will to confront a nearby evil because doing so might entail conflict with the evildoer's followers. "The rap on Obama," said Cohen, "is that he is a fog of a man. . . . I wonder about his mettle."

Obama responded to Minister Farrakhan's expression of support by declaring, "I decry racism and anti-Semitism in every form and strongly condemn the anti-Semitic statements made by Minister Farrakhan."[9] A bit later, in a speech before a predominantly Jewish audience, Obama averred that he had consistently denounced Louis Farrakhan. Yet the issue lingered, arising again in a debate between Clinton and Obama during which the late Tim Russert of NBC repeatedly raised the Farrakhan-Wright-Obama connection.

> OBAMA: I have been very clear in my denunciation of Minister Farrakhan's anti-Semitic comments. I think they are unacceptable and reprehensible.
>   RUSSERT: Do you reject [Minister Farrakhan's] support?
>   OBAMA: Well, Tim, you know I can't say to somebody that he can't say that he thinks I'm a good guy. . . . I have been very clear in my denunciation of him and his past statements.[10]

When Russert persisted, Hillary Clinton jumped into the fray. There is a difference, she maintained, between denouncing and rejecting. At that point, Obama ended the discussion, at least with respect to Minister Farrakhan, by declaring:

> I don't see a difference between denouncing and rejecting. There's no formal offer of help from Minister Farrakhan that would involve me rejecting it. But, if the word "reject" Senator Clinton feels is stronger than the word "denounce," then I am happy to concede the point, and I would reject and denounce.[11]

Why did Obama initially refrain from categorically rejecting and denouncing Minister Farrakhan? Obama is a cautious lawyer-politician who, when confronted with a problem, typically prefers to resolve it on the narrowest available grounds. He thus addressed his Farrakhan problem first by denouncing only the minister's anti-Semitic statements, thereby leaving untouched other aspects of Farrakhan's persona. Another reason is that Minister Farrakhan is respected by a substantial number of African Americans. In October 1995 his call for black men to join him for a day in Washington, D.C., was answered by hundreds of thousands (including

Obama) in the Million Man March. Minister Farrakhan's standing has waned considerably since then. Still, he remains a figure that any candidate in need of black votes will want to treat with care.

After Obama issued his categorical denunciation, Minister Farrakhan stated that "those who have been supporting [Obama] should not allow what was said during [the debate] to lessen their support for his campaign. This is simply mischief-making intended to hurt Mr. Obama politically."[12] Blacks largely agreed with him. Even those who objected to the ostracism to which the minister had been subjected muted their voices to avoid hurting Obama. The candidate's categorical rejection of Farrakhan "wasn't his finest hour," the columnist Mary Mitchell declared, but "fortunately for Obama, most black people understand the game." The game, she averred, was to stigmatize the minister so thoroughly that any hesitancy at damning him could itself be condemned as an inadequate response to his purported antiwhite and anti-Jewish bigotry. She maintained that "Obama should have found a way to escape [the journalists'] trap without denigrating Farrakhan's legacy." But, given his predicament, she forgave him and asserted that most other blacks would as well: "We understand."[13]

The challenge posed by the Farrakhan endorsement paled in comparison with the challenge that was posed when network news shows, cable television programs, and radio talk shows began airing video and audio snippets of sermons by Obama's spiritual adviser that were soon to become notorious. Jeremiah Alvesta Wright, Jr., was born in Philadelphia in 1941 and raised in solidly middle-class surroundings by a father who was a Baptist minister and a mother who was a teacher and administrator in the city's public schools. Wright graduated from Central High School in Philadelphia before attending Virginia Union University for two years. He left college, joined the Marines, and then became a Navy corpsman, in which capacity he once assisted with the medical care of President Lyndon B. Johnson. In 1967, he returned to college at Howard University and subsequently earned a number of graduate degrees, including a doctorate from the United Theological Seminary in Dayton, Ohio. In 1972, Wright became the pastor of the Trinity United Church of Christ in Chicago. When he arrived, the church was at a low ebb, with only about ninety members regularly attending services. Thirty years later, under his vigorous leadership, Trinity had become one of the largest and most influential congregations in the city, with thousands of regularly attending parishioners.[14]

According to Obama, Reverend Wright inspired him to become a devout Christian. Wright, moreover, officiated at the Obamas' wedding, baptized their children, consecrated their home, and served as a spiritual counselor to the up-and-coming politician. Obama himself linked Wright to his presidential campaign by titling his second book *The Audacity of Hope*—a phrase taken from one of the minister's sermons.

What led to Obama's problem with Reverend Wright were audio and video tapes in which the minister was seen and heard condemning white America for its racist practices, denouncing the United States as "the U.S. of KKKA" (alluding, of course, to the notorious Ku Klux Klan), asserting that the United States had long been engaged in committing atrocities abroad, including support of "state terrorism" against black South Africans and the Palestinians, and declaring that the 9/11 attacks constituted at least in part a story of chickens coming home to roost. Appalled by policies that have led to mass incarceration in black communities, Wright was also heard to insist that it made sense for blacks to sing not "God Bless America" but "God Damn America."[15]

The storm of questions and criticisms that followed did not wholly surprise the Obama campaign. It knew, of course, the extent to which the candidate had publicized his close, twenty-year relationship with Wright. The Obama camp also knew of statements made by Reverend Wright that could be used against the candidate. That is why, from the very outset of his campaign, Obama sought delicately to distance himself from his pastor.[16] Wright had initially been invited to offer the invocation at Obama's announcement of his candidacy. On the eve of the ceremony, however, Obama revised things, and Wright merely prayed with the candidate's family in private.

Obama's hope that his pastor and his church would remain unpublicized quickly dissolved, a victim of his adversaries' watchfulness and the voraciousness of competitive news outlets. Initially attention focused on the Afrocentric ideology expressed by Reverend Wright and his church, a congregation which styled itself "Unashamedly Black and Unapologetically Christian." But soon thereafter the spotlight centered on Wright's own statements.

Obama responded to the torrent of negative publicity by suggesting first that the controversiality of Wright's statements had been exaggerated. Then he suggested that he was unfamiliar with the remarks that had given most offense. Then he likened Wright to "an old uncle who says things I don't always agree with."[17] When such ripostes failed to quell the burgeoning controversy, Obama decided to dedicate a speech to explaining his relationship to Reverend Wright and his general approach to American black-white race relations.

The speech Obama delivered on March 18, 2008, in Philadelphia's National Constitution Center, was 37 minutes long. It was the most closely watched and consequential of all of the addresses he made during the nomination ordeal. He titled it "A More Perfect Union." In it he stated that his former pastor* had

---

* By the time Obama delivered his speech, Reverend Wright had retired from his position as senior pastor of the Trinity United Church of Christ.

used "incendiary language to express views that have the potential not only to widen the racial divide, but views that denigrate both the greatness and goodness of our nation [and] that rightly offend white and black alike." Obama addressed a variety of questions that had been repeatedly raised:

> Did I know him to be an occasionally fierce critic of American domestic and foreign policy? Of course. Did I ever hear him make remarks that could be considered controversial while I sat in church? Yes. Did I strongly disagree with many of his political views? Absolutely—just as I'm sure many of you have heard remarks from your pastors, priests, or rabbis with which you strongly disagree.

Obama declared, however, that "the remarks that have caused this most recent firestorm weren't simply controversial. . . . They expressed a profoundly distorted view of this country—a view that sees white racism as endemic and that elevates what is wrong with America above all that we know is right with America. . . ." Reverend Wright's "profound mistake," Obama continued, is that "he spoke as if our society was static; as if no progress has been made; as if this country—a country that has made it possible for one of his own [congregants] to run for the highest office in the land . . . is still irrevocably bound to a tragic past." But America is not bound, Obama declared. "America can change. That is the true genius of this nation."

Still, Obama insisted that there was more to Reverend Wright than the publicized snippets of his sermons. "The man I met more than twenty years ago," Obama averred, "is a man who helped introduce me to my Christian faith, a man who spoke to me about our obligations to love one another; to care for the sick and lift up the poor. He is a man who served his country as a U.S. Marine; who has studied and lectured at some of the finest universities and seminaries in the country, and who for over thirty years led a church that serves the community by doing God's work here on Earth—by housing the homeless, ministering to the needy, providing day care services and scholarships and prison ministries and reaching out to those suffering from HIV/AIDS."

Obama also maintained that there was a context within which Wright was speaking that needed explication, particularly with respect to two points. First, Wright's anger had a basis. "For the men and women of Reverend Wright's generation," Obama noted, "the memories of humiliation and doubt and fear have not gone away." Second, Wright's sentiments and the fashion in which he expressed them are by no means idiosyncratic. "The fact that so many people are surprised to hear that anger in some of Reverend Wright's sermons simply reminds us," Obama observed, "of the old truism that the most segregated hour in American life occurs on Sunday mornings."

Obama then proceeded to critique the anger Wright expressed, asserting that "all too often it distracts attention from solving real problems." Such anger, he declared, "keeps us from squarely facing our own complicity in our condition, and prevents the African American community from forging the alliances it needs to bring about real change."

Yet Obama refrained from breaking altogether with Reverend Wright. "As imperfect as he may be," Obama averred, "he has been like family to me. . . . I can no more disown him than I can disown the black community."

Despite Obama's unwillingness at that moment to sever all ties with Reverend Wright—their complete estrangement would not come about until several more weeks had passed—influential arbiters of public opinion in white America gave the speech favorable reviews. Liberal white politicians praised it. Senator Joseph Biden described the address as "an important step forward in race relations."[18] Conservative white politicians also praised the speech. Senator John McCain described it as "excellent."[19] The former Republican speaker of the House of Representatives Newt Gingrich called it "very courageous."[20] The former Republican governor of Arkansas Mike Huckabee said that in making the speech Obama had "handled [the controversy] about as well as anybody could."[21] A similar pattern marked journalistic responses. The white conservative commentator Peggy Noonan described the speech as "strong, thoughtful, and important."[22] Charles Murray, a coauthor of the infamous *Bell Curve*, wrote that, in his view, Obama's speech was "flat-out brilliant . . . far above the standard we're used to from our pols."[23]

Liberal commentators also praised it. According to *The Washington Post*, "He used his address as a teachable moment, one in which he addressed the pain, anger, and frustration of generations of blacks and whites head on—and offered a vision of how these experiences could be surmounted, if not forgotten. It was a compelling answer both to the challenge presented by his pastor's comments and to the growing role of race in the presidential campaign."[24] George Packer, writing in *The New Yorker*, called the address "the greatest speech on race by an American politician in many decades," a performance in which Obama paid the electorate "the supreme compliment of assuming that it, too, can appreciate complexity."[25] Frank Rich, writing in *The New York Times*, announced that he shared "the general view that Mr. Obama's speech is the most remarkable utterance [on race relations] by a public figure in modern memory."[26] Nicholas Kristof, also writing in *The New York Times*, called "A More Perfect Union" "the best political speech since John F. Kennedy talked about his Catholicism in Houston in 1960. . . . It was not a sound bite but a symphony."[27] Not to be outdone, a group of progressives including Tom Hayden, Bill Fletcher, Jr., Danny Glover, and

Barbara Ehrenreich asserted that Obama's address was "as great a speech as ever given by a presidential candidate."[28]

There were, of course, observers who refused to be mollified. "Folks, don't fall for this," the conservative talk-show host Sean Hannity implored. "Most of America," he hoped, "is not going to buy this flimsy excuse."[29] According to the columnist Charles Krauthammer, "Obama's 5,000 word speech, fawned over as a great meditation on race, is little more than an elegantly crafted, brilliantly sophistic justification of . . . scandalous dereliction."[30] It voiced, he charged, "the Jesse Jackson politics of racial griev-ance . . . in Ivy League diction and Harvard Law nuance."[31] Similarly scornful was the writer Victor Davis Hanson, who main-tained that "for some bizarre reason, Obama aimed his speech at winning praise from National Public Radio, *The New York Times*, and Harvard, and solidifying an already 90 percent solid African-American base—while apparently insulting the intelligence of everyone else."[32] According to Hanson, Obama "neither explained his disastrous relationship with Wright, nor dared open up a true discussion of race. . . . Instead there were the tired platitudes, eva-sions, and politicking."[33]

What role the speech played in Obama's ultimate triumph is impossible to determine with precision. It failed to dissipate entirely the bad odor left by the Reverend Wright imbroglio.[34] The controversy undoubtedly cost him votes in primaries and probably cost him votes later in the general election as well.* There were,

---

* Newspapers and online forums received thousands of communications in which peo-ple vented their anger at Obama because of his association with Reverend Wright.

> Big mistake. I feel we have been deceived. Just words. . . . G** d*** America. . . . Just words. . . . USKKA. . . . Just words. . . . Chickens coming home to roost. . . . Just words. How do you erase all of those words from our minds and our hearts? You did not walk away. . . . That's all you had to do. . . . Walk away. Instead you donated $22,500 in just 2006 for the spread of these diseased words.
> Posted by cb, March 16, 2008, latimes.com

however, many voters who did not share the view that Obama's speech had "insulted" their intelligence and instead saw it as yet another indication of Obama's suitability as chief executive.

As a tactical intervention aimed at quelling whites' rising discomfort with Obama's long association with Reverend Wright, the speech was clearly successful. Many commentators, however, insist upon portraying the address as something far weightier and more noble than that. The journalist Joan Morgan asserts, for example, that "A More Perfect Union" stands poised "to take its rightful place in the prestigious canon of seminal American speeches— right on up there with 'I Have a Dream' and the Gettysburg Address."[35] This is a vivid example of Obamamania. Like Morgan, many observers have lauded what they see as the speech's intellectual ambitiousness. I don't see, however, what so impresses them. There is little that Obama says that would be news to anyone passably familiar with basic information about black-white race relations over the course of American history. He notes that the Constitution of 1787 "was stained by this nation's original sin of slavery," that "segregated schools were, and are, inferior schools," that "history helps explain the wealth and income gap between black and white." Although the articulation of these facts constituted a useful act of public education, the recitation of such basic

---

Obama has totally lost all credibility with his "denial" of knowledge of Wright's rants. It is totally absurd that this sophisticated, accomplished, and intelligent man could have a close association with Wright and his parishioners for two decades and not know of his hateful and racist sermons. It is like Peter denying Christ three times before the rooster crowed.
Posted by JanetP, March 16, 2008, latimes.com

Sorry, I can't hear your words. Your actions are speaking too loudly. You maintained a close relationship with Rev. Wright for 20 years. Yet, you claim to be totally unaware of his outrageous statements. Even now, you can't disavow him. Yet, your campaign has slapped down others for much less offensive statements. What have you done up to now to create this more perfect union?
WSJ.com, March 18, 2008

information should hardly qualify as a distinguished intellectual contribution. Some maintain that the speech was remarkably eloquent. I don't find in it, however, the arresting language or imagery that warrants putting this address in the same league with the most memorable utterances of King or Lincoln.

Some admire what they perceive as the speech's uncommon candor. According to blogger Andrew Sullivan it was "the most honest speech on race in America in my adult lifetime."[36] The speech, however, obscures key truths by equating the racial wrongs of whites and blacks. At each and every point at which Obama mentions failure or misconduct attributable to whites, he hastens to mention a corresponding failure or misconduct attributable to blacks. Some observers find this approach attractively evenhanded. But it is precisely the formulaic imperative to distribute plaudits and blame equally that steers the speech toward evasion. Black America and white America are not equally culpable. White America enslaved and Jim Crowed black America (*not* the other way around)—a key fact that Obama obscures even as he supposedly grapples candidly with the American Dilemma.

Obama mentions slavery and segregation in his speech but makes no mention of enslavers or segregationists. Bad things happened to blacks, but in Obama's telling of the story there are no identified perpetrators. In Obama's narrative, racial oppression is presented as if it were a force of nature without human agency. Blacks are acted upon but no one is doing the acting. Obama's use of the passive voice here is no accident. It is part of an effort to discuss racial affairs without being accusatory, without hurting feelings, without affronting the sensibilities of the white audience.

I am not deriding or condemning the speech. As I mentioned previously, it appears to have accomplished its main purpose. Eloquence and candor are not always useful qualities. The Supreme Court's opinion in *Brown v. Board of Education*, for example, is notably plain and purposefully evasive. If all one knew about segregation was what is discernible from the face of that famous ruling, one could be forgiven for wondering what was so wrong about "separate but equal." Keen to avoid accusation, Chief Justice Earl Warren produced an opinion that deliberately obscured the cruelty of the policy it invalidated.* Perhaps that was a prudent tactical decision needed to elicit unanimity within the Court and to dampen resentment among segregationists. But it is worthwhile acknowledging the limits of the opinion even while recognizing its value. The same can be said of "A More Perfect Union." Perhaps its design was prudent. Perhaps it would have been foolish for Obama to have truly been candid. But let's not delude ourselves.

In neither its rhetoric nor its analysis nor its prescriptions did the speech offer much beyond a carefully calibrated effort to defuse a public-relations crisis. "In the end," Obama declared, "what is called for is nothing more, and nothing less, than what all the world's great religions demand—that we do unto others as we would have them do unto us. Let us be our brother's keeper. . . . Let us be our sister's keeper. Let us find that common stake we all have in one another, and let our politics reflect that spirit as well." That is a fine sentiment that has been and could be voiced by a wide range of personalities, from Jesse Jackson to Glenn Beck. But that, of course, is precisely my point. Much of what Obama had to say is, frankly, banal. To speak out loud now the sentences quoted above, removed from the fears and yearnings of March 2008, is to encounter rhetoric that should be seen as notably thin. As Professor Richard Thompson Ford aptly observes, "A More Perfect Union"

---

* Warren told his colleagues that the opinions announcing the school desegregation decisions "should be short, readable by the lay public, non-rhetorical, unemotional and, above all, nonaccusatory." Quoted in Dennis J. Hutchinson, "Unanimity and Desegregating: Decisionmaking in the Supreme Court, 1948–1958," *Georgetown Law Journal* 68 (1979): 42.

"navigated the minefield of race relations . . . by employing vague generalizations and empty bromides . . . and steering safely clear of specific proposals."[37]

As is now well known, Obama's problem with Reverend Wright did not end with the speech in Philadelphia. Several weeks later, Wright decided to answer his critics and did so by restating the sentiments that had prompted the initial outcry. Moreover, in response to Obama's comments, Wright insinuated that the candidate's criticism was only expedient political posturing. Obama reacted by cutting his ties with Wright altogether, and soon thereafter resigning his membership in the Trinity Church congregation. Threatened by any continuing association with Wright, Obama did all that he could to remove the remaining linkage. Although he had previously claimed that he could no more disown Wright than he could disown the black community, Obama ultimately did disown him when the price of failing to do so became, in the candidate's view, prohibitive.

Throughout the campaign, Obama distanced himself from or outright repudiated several prominent blacks who were widely disliked among whites. In addition to denouncing and rejecting Minister Farrakhan and Reverend Wright, Obama also stayed away from Reverend Jesse Jackson. Although Jackson has long been a much-admired figure in black America, many whites loathe him. They remember his "Hymietown" remark. They recall his association with Minister Farrakhan. And they perceive that he engages in racial extortion, making allegations of racism for personal or political gain regardless of whether facts substantiate the charges.

Obama wanted to keep his distance from Jackson without appearing to be excessively deferential to the sensibilities of whites. Jackson inadvertently assisted by insulting Obama in a way that relieved the candidate of any further obligation to pay homage to the senior activist. The insult was generated by Jackson's displeasure with speeches Obama had delivered that called for greater moral responsibility in black communities. On June 15, 2008, Father's Day, for example, while addressing a black church in Chicago, Obama stated that "in the African American community . . . more than half of all black children live in single-parent households," and that "too many fathers [are] missing from too many lives and too many homes." Continuing, Obama declared that "these absent black fathers have abandoned their responsibilities, acting more like boys instead of men."[38]

Although Jackson had often made similar comments himself, he took umbrage at Obama pressing the point. Seemingly unaware that the microphone he was wearing at a Fox News television studio was active, Jackson charged Obama with "talking down" to black people and allowed as how he would like to castrate the candidate if he continued voicing this theme.[39] Jackson apologized and Obama accepted the apology. But in front of the world it was plain to see their estrangement—a development about which, on some level, Obama must have been happy. It gave him an unassailable excuse to avoid Jackson and enabled him to underscore with little effort on his own part the difference between himself and the sort of accusatory, protest-oriented, "racism is the problem" black man that many whites fear and resent.

The episode with Jackson also brought fresh attention to another facet of Obama's campaign: his lectures to black audiences on cultural values, particularly the obligations of parenthood. Some commentators abhorred this strand of the Obama campaign. They perceived Obama as using both the black targets of his criticisms and the black audiences to whom he spoke as mere props in staged events in which he could send reassuring signals to whites that at the same time reinforced stereotypes of blacks. The journalist Kevin Alexander Gray maintained disapprovingly, for instance, that Obama's Father's Day speech "was his 'Sistah Souljah' moment." Just as Bill Clinton "tried to reassure whites that he wasn't too cozy with blacks by denouncing a rapper [who was a guest of Jesse Jackson's at a public event], Obama was appealing to whites by condemning his own." Gray also contended that it was bad form for Obama to highlight black men's delinquencies on, of all days, Father's Day. "We don't honor the vets on Veterans Day by pointing out . . . the cowards." According to Gray, moreover, it was inconceivable that Obama would have gone to a white church on Father's Day (or any other holiday) and lectured whites, as he did blacks, on their parental obligations.[40]

Gray glossed over the fact that most blacks in the audiences that Obama addressed seemed to appreciate his message. It was one with which they were familiar. Personal and communal responsibility; the virtue of pulling yourself up by your own bootstraps; the futility of waiting around for deliverance by government—all of these themes have long been staples of black sermonizing and political agitation, from Booker T. Washington to Elijah Muhammad. As the writer Gary Younge observed, "Obama was not saying something new or outlandish. . . . He wasn't saying anything that wasn't being echoed in thousands of black churches around the country."[41] Another reason Obama's message was popular with black audiences is that it flattered them; by being in church pews to listen, they were, at least temporarily, doing just what Obama lauded.

Gray was correct, though, in seeing Obama's family-values homilies as principally an effort to win over white voters. Of course they were! Whites constitute three-quarters of the electorate. Any candidate seriously attempting to prevail will seek to elicit the approval of this large bloc of voters. Gray insinuated that it was wrong to attempt to do that by using blacks as "props." But virtually all electoral campaigning involves a constant use of "props"—flags, marching bands, babies waiting to be kissed, ranks of wizened veterans in VFW halls, candidates eating corn and hot dogs with everyday people at county fairs. Obama's "use" of black folks was thus nothing out of the ordinary. Perhaps it is right to object wholesale to the dramaturgy of presidential election campaigns. But it is wrong to suggest that Obama's conduct was particularly blameworthy.

In the search for votes, Obama showed himself to be a resourceful, focused, disciplined, ruthless professional politician. In facing the daunting task of winning enough white votes to become president of the United States, his guiding principle was best articulated by an American he would never have quoted during the campaign. It was Malcolm X who insisted that blacks should elevate themselves "by any means necessary."

Obama's bid for the presidency brings to mind another iconic figure from the 1960s—John F. Kennedy, the first Catholic president. From the moment Obama captured the Democratic Party nomination until Election Day, the question was whether he would go down in history as the country's new Al Smith or the country's new JFK.[42] Like Obama, Alfred Emmanuel Smith[43] was a personification of American heterogeneity, with grandparents who hailed from Germany, Italy, England, and Ireland. He was a four-term governor of New York who, in 1928, won the Democratic Party nomination for the presidency, becoming the first Catholic to reach that level of political competition. Some observers hoped that a victory by Smith would vanquish anti-Catholic prejudice. On Election Day, however, he was trounced by the Republican Herbert Hoover.

Of the factors that contributed to that outcome, one of the most important was religion, or, more specifically, anti-Catholic prejudice. Some of the religious opposition was subterranean, thinly covered by asserted differences over this or that policy. But much of the opposition also took the form of an openly stated proposition that no Catholic ought ever to occupy the presidency. Sometimes this position was advanced with civility in forums such as *The Atlantic Monthly*, where Charles C. Marshall argued that a candidate who was also a conscientious Catholic would constantly be torn by divided loyalties—the demands of the Constitution on the one hand and the demands of the Papacy on the other. But opposition on religious grounds was also expressed by hundreds of itinerant anti-Catholic lecturers who repeated age-old calumnies about priests and nuns engaging in sexual relations and molesting children, scores of newspapers that railed against purported Catholic conspiracies to subjugate America, and millions of posters and handbills warning against an international Catholic theocracy.

Although the national committee of the Republican Party promised to wage "a clean fight" for the White House, the party, or subdivisions of it, contributed to an anti-Catholic mobilization against Smith. Hoover himself never openly stoked anti-Catholic prejudice, but he also refrained from confronting his own anti-Catholic supporters.[44]

Smith rebutted allegations that his Catholicism compromised his loyalty to America. He assured audiences that he believed in the separation of church and state and desired no favoring of Catholicism over other faiths. At no point, however, did Catholics question whether Smith had gone too far to assuage the anxieties of worried non-Catholics. Never was there any fear expressed by Catholics that Smith might sell them out for the sake of getting ahead.

After Smith's resounding defeat, thirty-two years elapsed before a major party nominated another Catholic as its presidential standard-bearer. Smith had been a prototypical working-class Catholic pol who never attended high school, much less college. Kennedy was the scion of a wealthy, highly assimilated family, who attended Choate and Harvard. But despite Kennedy's wealth, education, connections, and record as a war hero, Pulitzer Prize–winning author, congressman, and senator, he still faced considerable opposition due to his religious affiliation.

Some of the resistance stemmed from rank bigotry, which, though influential, had faded from on-the-record debate. More presentable were charges that Roman Catholicism was intolerant of other religions, seeing itself as the one "true" faith; that the Catholic Church did not sincerely accept an appropriate separation of church and state; and, most important, that papal authority would constantly throw into doubt the independence and loyalty of a practicing Catholic president. Hence, the Reverend Norman Vincent Peale remarked, clearly damning Kennedy, "I don't care a bit who of the candidates is chosen except that he be an American who takes orders from no one but the American people."[45] Another influential minister, the Reverend Billy Graham, refused to sign a letter that criticized those who opposed a Catholic candidate on religious grounds alone.*

Kennedy's Republican opponent, Richard Nixon, asserted repeatedly that religion ought to play no role in the campaign or in voters' decisions about whom to support and that he would conduct his campaign accordingly.[46] Although the most comprehensive analysis of the religion issue in the election of 1960 maintains that Nixon secretly plotted with anti-Catholic operatives, the

---

* Black ministers were among the Protestant clergy who publicly rejected Kennedy's candidacy because he was Catholic. One who initially took this position was Martin Luther King, Sr., who, as a member of the Metropolitan Atlanta Baptist Ministers Union, opposed Kennedy and endorsed Richard Nixon. Later, after Kennedy attempted to assist King's famous son in fighting a trumped-up criminal charge, the elder King switched his support out of gratitude. When he did so, however, his anti-Catholic bias still revealed itself. "I'll vote for [Kennedy], even though I don't want a Catholic," he is reported to have said. "I'll take a Catholic or the Devil himself if he'll wipe the tears from my daughter-in-law's eyes." Quoted in Thomas J. Carty, *A Catholic in the White House? Religion, Politics, and John F. Kennedy's Presidential Campaign* (2004), 92.

evidence in support of that assertion is thin.[47] Incontrovertible, however, is what Nixon said in a nationally broadcast speech on the Sunday before the election. He urged voters to disregard his or Kennedy's religion in determining for whom to vote. A naïve interpretation of this statement is that Nixon was expressly repudiating religious prejudice. A realistic interpretation is that Nixon was doing precisely what he had said he would avoid doing. In desperation, at the end of a hard-fought campaign, when the outcome was too close to call, Nixon played the religion card.

How did JFK respond? He did several things that prefigured Obama's effort to minimize "otherness" and assuage anxiety about ceding presidential power to a member of a long-suppressed minority. First, Kennedy had to banish the ghost of Al Smith by convincing people that in 1960 a Catholic candidate—the *right* Catholic candidate—could indeed win. Kennedy began this process in 1956 when, seeking the vice-presidential slot under Adlai Stevenson, he planted and publicized analyses that highlighted the electoral assets of Catholic politicians. In the fight for the Democratic Party nomination, Kennedy underscored his electability by winning the West Virginia primary even though only 5 percent of the state's population was Catholic. When Kennedy prevailed there he convinced many onlookers that he just might be able to win the general election, just as Obama convinced many skeptics of his seriousness as a candidate when he won in the Iowa caucuses.

In seeking to gain the presidency in an electorate dominated by non-Catholics, including many who were prejudiced against Catholics,* Kennedy had to decide whether to avoid or confront

---

* In May 1960, George Gallup published a survey of nine thousand Americans nationwide which indicated, among other things, that 62 percent of respondents said they would vote for a well-qualified Catholic while 28 percent said that they would not. See Shaun A. Casey, *The Making of a Catholic President: Kennedy vs. Nixon 1960* (2009), 24.
Note that when pioneering "outsiders" are being considered for leadership positions,

the religion issue. He chose the latter, a tactical decision that prompted him to discuss his views on religion and politics more fully and programmatically than Obama ever discussed his views on racial policy. Accepting his party's nomination, Kennedy declared:

> I am fully aware of the fact that the Democratic Party, by nominating someone of my faith, has taken what many regard as a new and hazardous risk—new, at least, since 1928. But look at it this way: the Democratic Party has once again placed its confidence in the American people, and in their ability to render a free, fair judgment. And you have, at the same time, placed your confidence in me, and in my ability to render a free, fair judgment—to uphold the Constitution and my oath of office—and to reject any kind of religious pressure or obligation that might directly or indirectly interfere with my conduct of the Presidency in the national interest. My record of fourteen years supporting public education—supporting complete separation of church and state—and resisting pressure from any source on any issue should be clear by now to everyone.[48]

Several weeks later, Kennedy devoted an entire speech, the most important of his campaign, to the religion issue. He gave the speech in the crucial, closely contested state of Texas to the Greater Houston Ministerial Association, an organization of Protestant clergy. He made three main points. The first was that the religion issue was, in his view, of decidedly less importance than "the real issues" of the moment—the spread of communist influence, the plight of hungry children, the predicament of old people without

---

the question of their being "well qualified" arises. Insiders typically get the benefit of being presumed well qualified.

health care, and Russian superiority in the race to the moon and beyond. Second, Kennedy reiterated his belief in church-state separatism:

> I believe in an America where the separation of church and state is absolute; where no Catholic prelate would tell the President—should he be Catholic—how to act, and no Protestant minister would tell his parishioners for whom to vote; where no church or church school is granted any public funds or political preference, and where no man is denied public office merely because his religion differs from the President who might appoint him, or the people who might elect him.

Personalizing the point, Kennedy remarked:

> I am not the Catholic candidate for President. I am the Democratic Party's candidate who happens also to be Catholic. I do not speak for my church on public matters—and the church does not speak for me.[49]

Kennedy specifically noted positions that put him at odds with many Catholics, including the higher authorities in the Church. He opposed, for example, naming a United States ambassador to the Vatican. Some Catholics criticized Kennedy for ceding too much in his efforts to propitiate hostile Protestants. Some accused him of selling out his Church to advance his political fortunes. The journalist Murray Kempton quipped that Kennedy would be the "first anti-clerical President."[50] Aware of this fear of the sellout, Kennedy ended his speech in Houston on a defiant note, stating that he would resign in the highly unlikely event that carrying out the duties of his office would require him either to violate his conscience or violate the national interest. Thus, in the event of an unbridgeable conflict between his religious faith and his secular duties, Kennedy declared that he would give up the latter. Kennedy asserted, moreover, that he did not "intend to disavow either my views or my church in order to win this election. If I should lose on the real issues, I shall return to my seat in the Senate, satisfied that I had tried my best and was fairly judged. But if this election is decided on the basis that 40 million Americans lost their chance of being President on the day they were baptized, then it is the whole nation that will be the loser, in the eyes of Catholics and non-Catholics around the world, in the eyes of history, and in the eyes of our own people."[51]

Certain features of Obama's triumph in 2008 stand out more clearly against the backdrop of Kennedy's triumph in 1960. While Kennedy seized the initiative in discussing religion, Obama tried hard to avoid discussing race and only did so when cornered. When Obama did discuss race relations, it was with notable sketchiness; he never explained during the campaign exactly where he stood on racial affirmative action, or racial voting rights, or other racial subjects that any president will influence considerably, through, among other things, his superintendency of the Department of Justice and his power to nominate federal judges.

A second contrast between 1960 and 2008 has to do with the character of the prejudice that Kennedy and Obama faced. In 1960 substantial figures in academia, journalism, theology, and politics openly argued that the danger of divided loyalties should disqualify any practicing Catholic candidate. In 2008 no substantial figure would have dared suggest openly that any candidate's race should disqualify him or her from election (though some did hint that being a Muslim should result in disqualification). There were people who privately believed that whiteness should be a prerequisite for the presidency. But that belief was so discredited that they kept it to themselves, or voiced it only anonymously. Indeed, the virtual absence of openly voiced racial resistance posed a problem for Obama. Calling attention to the largely invisible but all too real presence of white racial resistance would have opened him up to the charge that he was "playing the race card," that he was invoking faux racial martyrdom, that he was seeking opportunistically to guilt-trip white folks. When Obama jokingly raised the issue even a bit, he was strenuously criticized. Kennedy was subjected to a kindred line of attack. President Dwight Eisenhower's Catholic labor secretary accused the Kennedy campaign of reprehensibly portraying JFK as a "religious underdog whom bigotry will deprive of a fair chance."[52] Similarly critical was Nixon, who later remarked that "at every possible juncture and on every possible occasion, Kennedy's key associates were pushing the religious issue, seeing to it that it stayed squarely in the center of the campaign and even accusing me of religious bigotry."[53] On another occasion, he ruefully recalled that he was ill-prepared "for the blatant and highly successful way the Kennedys repeatedly made religion an issue in the campaign even as they professed that it should not be one."[54]

To a large extent Obama succeeded, like Kennedy, in turning a social stigma into political capital. His success was predicated upon neutralizing racial resistance while keeping to a minimum complaints that he was "playing the race card"—a vice that all of the candidates in 2008 were accused of indulging at one time or another, a vice to which the next chapter is devoted.

4

The Race Card in the
Campaign of 2008

"I am not a racist."

William Jefferson Clinton[1]

"The racial fantasy factor in this presidential campaign is out of control."

Bob Herbert[2]

"Playing the race card" refers to efforts to arouse or channel racial sentiments for selfish purposes. The term has a negative connotation and it should, because it refers to a type of conduct that is manipulative. It involves something other than expressing one's views about some racial matter. It involves self-consciously tapping into the racial sentiments of others to elicit a response that will be useful to one's own purposes. It is a type of demagoguery. It is a polemical tool used to distract or derange an audience. Racial animus against minorities has historically been the racial sentiment exploited most often by race-card players. Recently, in a sign of progress, animus *against* racial bigotry has been deployed opportunistically—as when a person enlists revulsion against racism to distract attention from his or her own misdeeds. There is often controversy over whether particular statements or gestures amount to playing the race card. But there is consensus that playing the race card is something one ought not to do. It is a category of behavior penalized in the court of public opinion.

The open appeal to racial animus is the oldest of such tactics. For a long period, white politicians frankly, unapologetically, and routinely stirred racial prejudices against blacks as an electoral strategy. The election of 1864, which pitted the Republican incumbent, Abraham Lincoln, against the Democratic challenger, George McClellan, "marked the first widespread national use of racial appeals for political gain" in a presidential contest.[3] At that year's Democratic National Convention, speakers railed against the Republican "negro-worshippers" who had emancipated the slaves of the Confederacy as a means of prosecuting the Civil War. Democratic opponents of Lincoln's reelection angrily denounced what they depicted as the president's wrongful sacrifices on behalf of "flat-nosed, wooly-headed, long-heeled, cursed of God and damned of man descendants of Africa."[4]

In the late nineteenth century, in the struggle over populism, white politicians repeatedly sabotaged existing or potential interracial coalitions by appealing to white farmers to shun blacks in honor of white solidarity. In the twentieth century, in struggles over unionism, socialism, and communism, white politicians often deployed Negrophobia to distract white workers from their own socioeconomic distress. Throughout the Jim Crow era, white supremacist political rivals sought to outdo one another in harping on "the Negro menace." Bemoaning his loss in the Alabama gubernatorial election of 1958 to an "extreme" white supremacist, the then "moderate" white supremacist George Wallace vowed that "no other son-of-a-bitch will ever out-nigger me again."[5]

The Civil Rights Revolution stigmatized the *open* appeal to racial animus. By the late 1960s, politicians were no longer able to blatantly incite racial prejudice to their advantage at little or no political cost. To tap into racial resentments openly meant falling afoul of newly ascendant norms of racial etiquette and thus attracting punishing censure. So open appeals to racist animus gave way to *implicit* appeals. To avoid being branded as racist while nonetheless trafficking in racial prejudice, some politicians began to use code words to say covertly what they could no longer safely say overtly. A mark of the change wrought by the Civil Rights Revolution was that even racial demagogues perceived it to be politically necessary to conform to the new orthodoxy—though that did not keep them from disseminating their racist message.

In 1963, at his inauguration as governor of Alabama, George Wallace famously declared, "Segregation now! Segregation tomorrow! Segregation forever!" Two years later, he still publicly referred to blacks as "niggers." By 1968, however, Wallace was staying clear of explicitly racist language.[6] His underlying message remained the same, but he substantially changed his packaging. He no longer blatantly demonized African Americans or candidly championed white supremacy. Rather, he deployed an Aesopian language of racial bigotry that offered the cover of deniability. Deciphering Wallace's language, a fellow Alabamian noted that "he can use all the other issues—law and order, running your own schools, protecting property rights—and never mention race. But people will know he's telling them 'a nigger's trying to get your job, trying to move into your neighborhood.' What Wallace is doing is talking to them in a kind of shorthand, a kind of code."[7]

If the presence of racial code is a sign of the partial success of the Civil Rights Revolution, it is also a sign of partial failure. What coded language seeks to obscure, after all, is the lingering presence of racial prejudice. Since the 1960s, no politicians have tapped this vein of volatile sentiment more effectively than Republican aspirants for the White House, particularly Richard Nixon, Ronald Reagan, and George Bush the Elder. Richard Nixon's "Southern strategy" was based on promises to repress black militancy, to restrain a federal judiciary that was said to be overly permissive and activist, and to be attentive to a "silent majority" that had become fearful of progressive reform. Ronald Reagan continued Nixon's Southern strategy, kicking off his quest for the presidency in 1980 in Neshoba, Mississippi, the site of the killings of the civil-rights martyrs Andrew Goodman, Michael Schwerner, and James Chaney (though, of course, Reagan made no mention of this inconvenient fact, preferring instead to profess his allegiance to "states' rights"). "Everybody watching the 1980 campaign knew what Reagan was signaling," the *New York Times* columnist Bob Herbert later observed. "He was tapping out the code. It was understood that when politicians started chirping about 'states' rights' to white people in places like Neshoba County they were saying when it comes down to you and the blacks, we're with you."[8]

The Republican Party's use of the Willie Horton story in the presidential campaign of 1988 is probably the most infamous example of playing the race card. William Horton was a black man convicted of murder and sentenced to a life term in prison. His sentence notwithstanding, Horton got himself enrolled in a furlough program that permitted inmates to live outside of prison on weekends. While on furlough Horton kidnapped and assaulted a white couple, stabbing the man and raping the woman. The Republicans pinned the blame for this horrifying crime on the Democratic Party's presidential nominee, Michael Dukakis, the governor of the state—Massachusetts—where Horton was supposed to be incarcerated. The Republican attack portrayed Dukakis as an aloof, legalistic technocrat who was more concerned with programs for felons than protecting vulnerable citizens. A second, unspoken aim of the Willie Horton story was to stir whites' anxieties about "black crime" and to insinuate that the liberal Dukakis would be insufficiently tough on black criminality.[9]

A third variant of the race-card tactic features feigned protest against purported racial mistreatment.[10] The player of this card either knows that there has been no invidious racial discrimination in the case at issue or is unsure about the matter. But for her own benefit she makes allegations of racial mistreatment anyway. An example of this phenomenon is the Tawana Brawley incident. Brawley, a black teenager, charged a group of white men with subjecting her through threats and violence to sordid sexual and racial indignities. Subsequent investigation showed that Brawley was lying, probably in an attempt to distract attention from her own delinquencies.*[11] Another example of what many observers see as an instance of playing the race card stemmed from the prosecution of O. J. Simpson for murdering his former wife and her lover. Defense attorneys won an acquittal after claiming that Simpson was framed by racist white police, an allegation that may have distracted jurors from appropriately assessing evidence of the defendant's guilt.[12]

Throughout the presidential campaign of 2008, various camps charged one another with "playing the race card." What should one think about these allegations and their salience? The massive attention devoted to this issue is a sign that many people were determined to prevent advantage from being gained by racial opportunism. Such heightened sensitivity to the many guises of racial demagoguery is a good thing. Certainly it is an improvement over complacency. On the other hand, many of the charges and countercharges bandied about during the campaign were overblown.

Let's start with the Clintons. During the Democratic Party

* A related phenomenon involves cases in which whites charge blacks with committing crimes they themselves actually perpetrated. The accuser selects a black person as the target for the allegation, calculating that antiblack prejudice will add persuasive force to the charge. A classic instance was the allegation by Charles Stuart in Boston in 1989 that a black man had assaulted him and his pregnant wife. After a manhunt in which civil rights were violated by police on a massive scale, it became evident that Stuart himself had murdered his wife. See Fox Butterfield, "A Boston Tragedy: The Stuart Case," *New York Times*, January 15, 1990.

nomination contest, the Clintons or their allies were charged with racial misconduct on several occasions, five of which are particularly noteworthy. First, seeking to create a contrast between Barack Obama and herself, Hillary Clinton suggested that while he was an eloquent (but inexperienced) rhetorician, she was a tried, savvy, effective doer. Emphasizing that the expression of noble aspiration is itself insufficient to generate change on the ground, Clinton remarked that "Dr. King's dream began to be realized when President Johnson passed the Civil Rights Act. . . . It took a president to get it done."[13] Some people took exception to Senator Clinton's comment, complaining that it was racially offensive in that it subordinated the influence of King and the civil-rights movement to President Lyndon Johnson and a virtually all-white Washington establishment. *The New York Times* (which endorsed Clinton over Obama) complained that Senator Clinton's comment carried "the distasteful implication that a black man needed the help of a white man to effect change."[14] One might wonder what is "distasteful" about this implication; King himself emphasized the essential need for blacks to have white allies in the struggle for racial justice.[15] Clinton, however, was not attempting to make a historiographical point. Rather, she was simply arguing, albeit awkwardly, that she (a prosaic politician like Johnson) would be better able than Obama (a gifted orator like King) to effectuate reform. There is no plausibility to the claim that this statement, fairly situated in its context, reflected any hint of racial demagoguery or even "racial insensitivity." Clinton was merely asserting that she would be a more effective chief executive than Obama. Her remark was impolitic in that it made her vulnerable to costly misinterpretation. Otherwise her remark was merely an instance of routine campaign jousting. The ominous suggestion that she was attempting to inject a fell racial element into the contest is unsupportable. Those who read Clinton's King-Johnson remark as an instance of playing the race card are misreading.

Second, after it became apparent that Obama would win the South Carolina Democratic Party primary, former president Bill Clinton was asked what it said about Obama that it took the campaigning of two Clintons to try to beat him. The former president initially referred to the question laughingly as "bait." He then said, "Jesse Jackson won South Carolina twice, in '84 and '88. And he ran a good campaign. Senator Obama has run a good campaign here, he has run a good campaign everywhere. He's a good candidate with a good organization."[16]

Bill Clinton's remark provoked a blizzard of accusations that he was bringing race into the discussion by invoking Jesse Jackson in order to "blacken" Obama and marginalize him.[17] What Clinton was really saying, his detractors asserted, is that Obama, like Jackson, is only capable of being a *black* candidate, a protest candidate, and that therefore the only *real*, that is, electable, candidate among the Democrats was his wife Hillary. There was more to this complaint than the one aimed at Hillary Clinton's King-Johnson analogy. The question to which Bill Clinton responded never mentioned Jesse Jackson; the former president on his own put Jackson's name into play. The question, however, is why? That Clinton was somehow attempting to marginalize Obama is true; he was, after all, fighting *against* Obama on behalf of his wife. Not so obvious is that Clinton was engaged in a campaign of *racial* marginalization. Yes, Jesse Jackson is black. But does that mean that every time someone places Obama and Jackson in the same frame that person is engaging in racial demagoguery? While in this case there is at least some basis for charging Bill Clinton with racial impropriety, the basis is hardly conclusive. A generous reading of the conduct in dispute would offer the former president the benefit of the doubt.*

---

* This was the spirit in which Jesse Jackson himself publicly interpreted Bill Clinton's remarks. See Katharine Q. Seelye, "Jackson: Not Upset by Clinton Remarks," *New York Times*, January 28, 2008.

Third, arguing that she would be more electable than Obama in a contest against John McCain, Hillary Clinton remarked that she had "a much broader base to build a winning coalition on" and that his "support among working, hard-working Americans, white Americans, is weakening again."[18] Although a number of journalists condemned these remarks as racially objectionable, it is noteworthy how unclear they often were in explaining themselves. Writing in Salon.com in an article provocatively titled "Was Hillary Channeling George Wallace?" the journalist Joe Conason charged Clinton with having "crossed a bright white line."[19] Yet he then proceeded to back away from his claim, averring that Clinton is devoid of "even the slightest racial animus" and maintaining that the argument she voiced "could be correct. . . . Her chances to build an Electoral College majority may well be better than his owing to his difficulty in attracting white working class voters." Given Conason's extenuating observations, it was irresponsible to suggest that Clinton was acting in a fashion at all comparable to George Wallace.* The *Washington Post* columnist Eugene Robinson charged that Clinton's statement constituted "a slap in the face to . . . African Americans" and "a repudiation of principles the [Democratic] party claims to stand for." What she is really saying, he wrote, is that "there's no way that white people are going to vote for the black guy. Come November, you'll be sorry [you nominated him instead of me]." What, however, would be wrong with such a message?† Although Robinson leaves unclear the basis of

---

* Most writers typically have no control over titles that announce their handiwork. The comparison to Wallace may thus be attributable more to the editors at Salon.com than to Conason.

† Although Robinson spent the bulk of his column criticizing Clinton on the grounds that her tactics were at odds with the professed racial ideals of the Democratic Party ("I thought the Democratic Party believed in a color blind America"), he ultimately, and confusingly, absolved her of racial wrongdoing. "Clinton's sin," he wrote, "isn't racism, it's arrogance." See "The Card Clinton Is Playing," *Washington Post*, May 9, 2008.

his complaint,* an objection might be that Clinton was attempting to create a self-fulfilling prophecy. This is what Bob Herbert meant to convey when he wrote that Clinton was trying to embed a "gruesomely destructive message in the brains of white voters and superdelegates,"[20] that message being that Obama's candidacy was futile because of racial demographics. In this view, Clinton was not simply reporting the sociological fact of white working-class racial resistance to Obama; she was also eliciting and reinforcing that resistance by publicly noting it and then using it as a basis for denying him the nomination. Is that view correct? I think that it is. A seasoned politician, Hillary Clinton knew the toxicity of references to race in American electoral politics, but nonetheless expressly alluded to "hard-working . . . white Americans" without any attempt to criticize or otherwise neutralize the prejudices that undoubtedly constituted some of the opposition to Obama within that sector of the electorate. In her desperation, Clinton did play the race card on this occasion.

The fourth instance arose from a television advertisement aired in Texas in late February 2008. With a darkened home in the background a narrator intoned, "It's 3 a.m. and your children are safe and asleep." A camera took the viewer to room after room where babies, children, and a mother were sleeping. The narrator continued: "But there's a phone in the White House, and it's ringing." A phone rang repeatedly and ominously. "Who do you want answering the phone?" the narrator asked. At that point, the advertisement featured a poised, businesslike Hillary Clinton confidently answering a ringing phone.

---

* Derrick Z. Jackson criticized Clinton's remark because, to him, it maligned blacks. "There is no way you can say in the same sentence, 'hard working Americans, white Americans,' without diminishing black Americans as lazy." See "Clinton's Diminishing of Black Voters," *Boston Globe*, May 10, 2008. Of course, one could, if one was so minded, simply chalk Clinton's murky phraseology up to inadvertent awkwardness or verbal fatigue.

In many quarters the ad was interpreted as an effort by the Clinton campaign to highlight national security and to argue that, especially on that front, Clinton would be a safer, more experienced president than Obama. Obama himself responded on those terms, averring that the commercial represented a discreditable effort to frighten the electorate and that on the most important recent national-security issue—the decision to invade Iraq—Clinton, McCain, and Bush had been wrong and he had been right.

The distinguished sociologist Orlando Patterson contended, however, that the commercial was infected with a "racist sub-message."*[21] Patterson insisted that the commercial insidiously "says that Mr. Obama is himself the danger, the outsider within." What supports such an interpretation? Patterson mentions (1) intuition—"an uneasy feeling"—educated by disciplined study of racism; (2) that "for more than a century American politicians have played on racial fears to divide the electorate"; (3) that the commercial could have, but did not, include images of a black child, mother, or father, and did not state that the danger to which it alluded was "external terrorism" as opposed to an internal threat; (4) that the Clinton campaign used the ad in Texas, where polls indicated that whites favored Obama, and not in Ohio, where Clinton had a comfortable lead among whites; and (5) that during the same weekend the ad was broadcast Clinton refused to state unambiguously that Obama is a Christian and has never been a Muslim.

These dots that Professor Patterson strung together fail by a considerable margin to substantiate his claim that the advertisement contains a racist sub-message. It is true that politicians have repeatedly engaged in racial demagoguery. The question, though,

---

* Patterson was not alone in seeing the advertisement as a racial provocation. Political scientist Lawrence Bobo of Harvard also saw it as part of a pattern of "race baiting" and "manipulation of racial cues." See "Is Clinton Getting a Pass on Race?" TheRoot.com, March 24, 2008.

is whether *this* commercial is part of that baleful racist tradition or is instead an instance of conventional electioneering. Patterson stresses the absence of any black people in the sleeping household. He suggests that the presence of such figures would have negated the inference that Clinton was seeking subtly to invoke the specter of a white household menaced by a black man. Maybe. But if blacks had been included, why couldn't it be argued that the Clinton camp was simply burying its implicit racial message beneath another layer of subtlety? Patterson contended that it was significant that the commercial did not expressly state that it was focused on external rather than internal threats. I don't see the pertinency of the distinction, but in any event it is clear, given the context, that the commercial was alluding to the problem of a foreign threat. As for running the advertisement in Texas as opposed to Ohio, a plausible, respectable, nonracial reason comes immediately to mind: she aired the commercial where she was in the closest struggle with Obama. Why waste the commercial in Ohio, where she already had a comfortable lead? Patterson's final "dot"—tepid response to the whispering campaign regarding Obama's religion—is a mark against Clinton but one that has little or no relevance to the racial character of the advertisement.*

Patterson's unsubstantiated indictment of Clinton is all too characteristic of a tendency that was vividly displayed throughout

---

* Professor Bobo also objected to a Clinton fund-raising letter that solicited donations in order to "level the playing field" against Obama. See "Will Black Democrats Abandon Clinton Over Race?," TheRoot.com, March 13, 2008. According to Bobo, this letter "cleverly borrows from anti–affirmative action rhetoric. . . . Can't let that 'black' candidate have an 'unfair advantage' is the leaden implication." This letter, Bobo charged, was part of a series of gestures "straight out of the Lee Atwater playbook. . . . The signals sent by the Clinton camp are regularly about race. They scream one thing: 'Hey, I'm the white candidate over here, remember? Don't let that slick affirmative action beneficiary over there fool you.' " In my view, Bobo's claim is unpersuasive—unless one takes the position that a white candidate is committing a racial wrong anytime she speaks of "leveling the playing field" against a black candidate.

the 2008 election cycle—a tendency to make highly stigmatizing racial charges in the absence of a persuasive or even merely plausible argument. An anonymous respondent rightly criticized Patterson's analysis:

> The interpretation you suggest requires an application of the opposite of the benefit of the doubt: that is, one must apply the most sinister interpretation to each component of the ad, and eschew anything less diabolical, in order to see it in the light you suggest.
>
> . . . I'll go so far as to accuse you of practicing the same form of insinuation of which you accuse Clinton. Your invocations of D. W. Griffith and the KKK, Richard Nixon, and Willie Horton are historically accurate in their own rights, but your connection of them to the ad, even as context, is based on nothing demonstrable or concrete. You've no evidence, textual or otherwise, for raising them; you cite no common symbology, no rhetorical motifs, no definitive visual resonance to connect them to the ad. Yet by dropping them in, you yourself have manufactured a rhetorical link between Clinton and some of the most noxious, racist figures in American cultural and political history.
>
> I'm all for a close textual reading, but you don't give us one. What you give us is an "uneasy feeling." And the "uneasy feeling" you'd seem to want us to walk away from your column with is that Clinton's a racist. I would suggest that's a powerful aspersion to cast, and one that ought to have more than loose cocultural allusions to back it up.[22]

Patterson himself offered a hint of recognition that he had engaged in interpretive overreaching. In the final paragraph of his essay he wrote:

It is possible that what I saw in the ad is different from what Mrs. Clinton and her operatives saw and intended. But as I watched it again and again I could not help but think of the sorry pass to which we may have come—that someone could be trading on the darkened memories of a twisted past that Mr. Obama has struggled to transcend.

Having previously accused the Clinton campaign of delivering a "racist sub-message," Patterson ends his piece on a decidedly more ambiguous note, contending that someone "could be" engaging in a racial wrong. That last-minute qualification does not make up for Patterson's prior recklessness. As the Web site *The Daily Howler* aptly noted, "When you're making our society's most serious charge, you really can't wait till the final paragraph to say you might have it wrong."[23]

The fifth episode in which the Clinton campaign was charged with playing the race card involved a remark by Geraldine Ferraro, who was working for the Clinton campaign. "If Obama was a white man, he would not be in this position," she said. "And if he was a woman (of any color) he would not be in this position. He happens to be very lucky to be who he is. And the country is caught up in the concept."[24]

Commentators favorably inclined toward Obama denounced Ferraro. Ta-Nehisi Coates, one of the most incisive bloggers of the electoral season, called her remarks nakedly racist.*[25] Susan Rice, a senior figure in the Obama campaign, dismissed the remarks as "outrageous and offensive."[26] Obama himself stated, "I don't

---

* Many online respondents agreed. "How anyone could read her original comments and not interpret them as bigoted is beyond me." "Ms. Ferraro's comments are RAC-IST, insulting and constructed to put Obama in a bad light. To say that Obama would only be where he is because he is black discounts that he is intelligent, competent, and capable." See Comments responding to Katharine Q. Seelye, "Ferraro Quits Clinton Post," TheCaucus.blogs.nytimes.com, March 12, 2008.

think Geraldine Ferraro's comments have any place in our politics or in the Democratic Party. They are divisive. I think anybody who understands the history of this country knows they are patently absurd."[27] Hillary Clinton "rejected" the comments of her supporter and within two days of the start of the ruckus Ferraro had resigned from her position on the campaign.

Again, as in analyzing the other race-card controversies, the first task here is to determine the meaning of the statement at issue, and the second is to assess the statement. Ferraro was saying, I think, that if Obama were white he would not have been as much of a political celebrity as he became and that if he were a woman—white, black, or anything else—he would not have been permitted to be as successful.

The idea that Obama actually benefited from his blackness struck some observers as ludicrous. Lampooning Ferraro, in *The Nation*, the writer Calvin Trillin characterized her message as saying, "Just being black is what it takes. Those colored guys get all the breaks."[28] There was, however, considerable truth in Ferraro's suggestion that Obama's blackness *assisted* him in important respects. Without his blackness Obama could not have tapped nearly as effectively into the emotions of millions of African Americans who yearned for a visible, tangible indication of their status as full, first-class citizens. Without his blackness Obama could not have appealed nearly so strongly to the emotions of millions of white Americans who yearned for a moment of racial redemption. Without his blackness Obama could not have served nearly so satisfyingly as the vehicle for those who hoped that the election of an African American would transform America's international image. "What does [Obama] offer?" the journalist Andrew Sullivan asked in an essay that championed Obama early on in the campaign.[29] Among the things he offers, Sullivan responded, are "his face." Obama's brown face could create "the most effective potential re-branding of the United States since Reagan."

But what of Ferraro's intentions? Of course she was attempting to diminish Obama. After all, she was a surrogate for Hillary Clinton. But was she attempting to do so in a fashion that should be seen as racially improper? Positing that beneficiaries of affirmative action are undeserving underperformers has been a staple of white backlash politics for several decades. Ferraro, however, does not seem to have been arguing that it was *wrong* for Obama's race to be taken into account in advancing his candidacy. She simply insisted, as a matter of fact, that it was being taken into account—the same way, as she acknowledged, her gender had been taken into account in 1984, when she was chosen as Walter Mondale's vice-presidential running mate.

As we have seen, the King-Johnson remark, the Jackson-Obama analogy, the hard-working-white-people comment, the telephone advertisement, the affirmative-action-candidate insinuation, and related statements prompted many observers to conclude that the Clinton campaign and its allies were repeatedly making race an issue in a frantic, scorched-earth attempt to deprive Obama of the nomination.[30] Castigating Clinton for voicing "poisonous rhetoric," Bob Herbert accused her of trying deliberately to "wreck the presidential prospects of [her] party's likely nominee" and doing so "in a way that has the potential to undermine the substantial racial progress that has been made in this country over many years." According to Herbert, "The Clintons should be ashamed of themselves. But they long ago proved to the world that they have no shame."[31]

The racial critique of the Clintons bumped into charges that, actually, it was the Obama camp that was playing the race card. One advocate of this position was the historian Sean Wilentz.[32] "It has never been satisfactorily explained," he wrote, "why the pro-Clinton camp would want to racialize the primary and caucus campaign. . . . Playing the race card against Obama could only cost her black votes, as well as offend white liberals who normally

turn out in disproportionately large numbers for Democratic caucuses and primaries. Indeed, indulging in racial politics would be
a sure-fire way for the Clinton campaign to shatter its own coalition." By contrast, Wilentz argued, it would and did make political
sense for Obama to deploy the race card because "doing so would
help Obama secure huge black majorities . . . and enlarge his activist white base in the university communities and among affluent
liberals."

Is there something to the charge that the Obama camp, or at
least portions of it, leveled unfair allegations of racism or "racial
insensitivity" against the Clinton camp? Yes, in some instances
the charge is well taken. I have previously noted the wrong-headed
racial charges made against Gloria Steinem and other white
pro-Clinton feminists.* Another example was the remark made
by Representative Jesse Jackson, Jr., immediately after the New
Hampshire primary. Commenting on Clinton's now famous teary
episode on the eve of the crucial primary, Jackson declared:

> Those tears have to be analyzed. . . . They have to be looked at
> very, very carefully in light of Katrina, in light of other things
> that Mrs. Clinton did not cry for, particularly as we head to
> South Carolina where 45 percent of African Americans will par-
> ticipate in the Democratic contest. . . . We saw tears in response
> to her appearance, so that her appearance brought her to tears,
> but not Hurricane Katrina, not other issues.[33]

This is a good example of a bad practice: the vague insinuation of
racial wrongdoing. Jackson accused Clinton of racially selective
sympathy without offering the detail one should expect to accom-
pany such a damning charge.

Still, Jackson's remark, the racial critique of Steinem, and similar

* See pages 91–95.

episodes hardly support Wilentz's sweeping charges, which themselves are evidence of the very vices against which he railed. Wilentz was persistently tendentious, casting in the worst light the possible motives of Obama and his backers. He was not content with accusing them of merely erring; he accused them of purposeful, deceitful race-baiting. Consider Wilentz's numerous angry accusations:

- "While promoting Obama as a 'post-racial' figure, his campaign has purposefully polluted the contest with a new strain of what historically has been the most toxic poison in American politics."
- The Obama campaign "turned the primary and caucus race to their advantage when they deliberately, falsely, and successfully portrayed Clinton and her campaign as unscrupulous race-baiters."
- The Obama campaign has engaged in "the most outrageous deployment of racial politics since the Willie Horton ad campaign in 1988 and the most insidious since Ronald Reagan kicked off his 1980 campaign in Philadelphia, Mississippi, praising states' rights."

These accusations display several important faults. Wilentz attributed what he sees as the deliberate misdeeds of supporters to Obama himself—as if any major presidential candidate can reasonably be expected to control the words and deeds of the thousands of people who work on behalf of his or her campaign. It is true that certain Obama supporters did much the same thing when they sought to pin upon Clinton responsibility for unbecoming comments made by her ally Robert L. Johnson, the founder of Black Entertainment Television (BET).* But Obama

* Seeking votes in the South Carolina primary on behalf of Hillary Clinton, Johnson crassly alluded to Barack Obama's confessed adolescent experimentation with illegal drugs. Johnson later apologized to Obama for having made the remarks. See Katharine Q.

supporters who automatically beat Clinton over the head with the comments of her surrogates were wrong to do so. In the same way, Wilentz should have been far more careful in attributing to Obama the misdeeds of wayward backers.

Contrary to what Wilentz posited, moreover, there was a perfectly plausible explanation for why Clinton might have wanted to "racialize" the contest *after* black voters started migrating en masse to Obama. At that point, she was forced to argue that if Democrats wanted to win the White House they would have to be keenly aware of the proclivities of white voters who, regardless of party affiliation, would resist voting for Obama in the general election. Adding teeth to this claim would have been an incentive for Clinton to do or say things that would encourage whites to withhold their votes from her rival. Wilentz contended that behaving in this way would have been nonsensical for Clinton because of her need for black votes and the votes of white liberals. That need, however, was at least temporarily removed or attenuated when Obama captured those voting blocs. In the latter phases of the nomination contest, Clinton's imperative was to win over sufficient numbers of working-class whites to convince Democratic Party delegates that only she could hope to prevail in the general election.

Given Clinton's incentives, the intensity of her desire to win, the stakes involved, the Clintons' reputation for ruthlessness, and the racial history of electoral politics in America, there was certainly reason for Obama supporters to fear that the former front-running senator from New York would use race to best her upstart rival. That fear was further stoked by remarks by the Clintons that many observers perceived as racial jabs. Against that backdrop it

---

Seelye, "BET Founder Slams Obama in South Carolina," *New York Times,* January 13, 2008; "Bob Johnson Apologizes to Obama," First Read, MSNBC.com, January 17, 2008.

becomes all the more understandable why some Obama partisans too quickly and too heatedly charged Senator Clinton with bringing race into the campaign. They ought to have avoided doing that. At the same time, Wilentz ought to have avoided portraying them as mere demagogues with no reason for concern in assessing Clinton's willingness to exploit white racial privilege and black racial vulnerability. In the end, Wilentz went overboard in castigating the racial politics of Obama and his backers.

A similar pattern of charge and countercharge emerged in the general election. Various observers claimed that John McCain and Sarah Palin made subtle and not-so-subtle racial appeals. Nearly a month before the election, the *New York Times* editorial page insisted that McCain and Palin were "running one of the most appalling campaigns" in memory, one that had dragged the country "into the dark territory of race baiting." [34] According to the *Boston Globe* columnist Derrick Z. Jackson, McCain and Palin were "careening into George Wallace territory to destroy [Obama]." [35] Representative John Lewis accused the McCain-Palin campaign of "sowing the seeds of hatred and division." [36]

The critics were referring to two developments in particular. One was a line of attack against Obama that linked him to radicals, such as the dissident William Ayers,* who were portrayed as anti-American and dangerous. Obama, Governor Palin remarked, "is

---

* William Ayers was a former leader of the Weather Underground, a leftist organization founded in the late 1960s. An opponent of domestic and foreign policies pursued by the United States, the Weather Underground detonated bombs at the United States Capitol Building, the Pentagon, and other locations. Ayers was indicted in 1970 for conspiracy to bomb public buildings but escaped prosecution when charges were dismissed because of governmental misconduct. Ayers became a university professor, sat on the board of a philanthropic organization on which Obama also sat, and hosted a meeting at his home at which he introduced Obama to his neighbors during the candidate's campaign for a seat in the Illinois State Senate. See Larry Rohter and Michael Luo, "'60's Radicals Become Issue in Campaign of 2008," *New York Times*, April 17, 2008; Chris Fusco and Abdon M. Pallasch, "Who Is Bill Ayers?," *Chicago Sun-Times*, April 18, 2008.

someone who sees America . . . as being so imperfect that he's palling around with terrorists who would target their own country."[37] The other development was the behavior of people at McCain-Palin rallies, conduct that involved calling Obama "nigger," lampooning him as a monkey, and voicing amorphous threats of violence.[38] Some observers charged that McCain and Palin elicited racist or otherwise boorish conduct from their followers and then, when such behavior surfaced, did all too little to counteract it.

Earlier in the campaign, critics rebuked McCain for other alleged misdeeds. One was an advertisement that ridiculed Obama-mania by portraying its object of affection as a "celebrity" fit for mindless mass adulation but unfit for the presidency. The ad parodied Obama's international stardom by comparing it to the fatuous fascination that surrounds two notorious show-business celebrities—Britney Spears and Paris Hilton. The ad featured a smiling Obama in front of huge crowds. It also included, momentarily, photos of Spears and Hilton along with a brief commentary which stated, in part, "He is the biggest celebrity in the world. But is he ready to lead?" No political advertisement of the campaign received more attention, and much of it was negative. Bill Press, a liberal radio talk-show host, denounced the advertisement as "deliberately and deceptively racist." Of celebrities to whom Obama could have been compared, why did the ad's designers not choose Tom Cruise, or Arnold Schwarzenegger, or Donald Trump, or Oprah Winfrey? "Why Britney Spears and Paris Hilton? Why two white blond bimbos? Only one reason. It's a somewhat tamer version of the white bimbo ad used so successfully against Harold Ford."

In the fall of 2006 in Tennessee, a black Democrat named Harold Ford, Jr., was locked in a tight contest with a white Republican, Bob Corker, to occupy a vacant United States Senate seat. Late in the campaign the Republican National Committee aired an advertisement featuring a young, curvaceous, saucy white woman who, staring into the camera, says, "I met Harold at the Playboy party!"—meaning one at the Super Bowl. After a number of figures make negative remarks about Ford, the woman returns to the screen, winks, and coos, "Harold, call me."[39] "In juxtaposing Barack Obama with Britney Spears and Paris Hilton," Press continued, "the McCain campaign is simply trying to plant the old racist seed of black man hitting on young white woman. Not directly, but subliminally and disgracefully."[40] According to Bob Herbert, the ad was "designed to exploit the hostility, anxiety, and resentment of the many white Americans who are still freakishly hung up on the idea of black men rising above their station and becoming sexually involved with white women."[41] Hendrik Hertzberg of *The New Yorker* expressed similar outrage, asserting that the "Celebrity" advertisement was "clearly part of a concerted strategy of provocation aimed at surfacing the 'race issue.'" Scoffing at any notion that race had nothing to do with "The Celebrity," Hertzberg maintained that "it cannot have escaped the ad makers' notice" that Spears and Hilton "symbolize white, blond sexual availability."[42]

Press, Herbert, and Hertzberg go too far. Just as the racial critique of Hillary Clinton was overblown, so, too, was the racial critique of John McCain. Of course McCain and his allies tried to make Obama look bad even on the basis of evidence that was slim, irrelevant, or even spurious. But that is what is typically done in American electoral campaigns—recall the controversies over the draft status of Clinton and Bush, over Kerry's Vietnam war record, over whether Gore had inflated his contribution to the Internet, over Bush's arrest as a young man for driving under the influence. Unless *every* criticism of candidate Obama is validly to be seen as racial, some care must be taken to distinguish racial from nonracial criticism. This is, to be sure, a difficult undertaking doomed to controversy. But in all too many instances commentators peremptorily labeled certain criticisms as "racial" without adequate justification. Consider the "Celebrity" advertisement. Unlike the Harold Ford "Call Me" ad, the "Celebrity" video made no suggestion that there existed any intimacy between Obama and the featured starlets. Some critics "saw" this insinuation in the advertisement. Perhaps what they "saw," however, is more indicative of their fears than of anything actually there in the commercial. The overly aggressive interpretation that surfaced in Orlando Patterson's castigation of the 3 a.m. phone call advertisement surfaced again in denunciations of "The Celebrity." In both cases, insistence upon finding racial subtexts led commentators astray. Why pick Spears and Hilton? Perhaps because the producers of the advertisement accurately perceived that those two figures were without peer in vividly exemplifying the pathology of American celebrity culture. I am not offering a general defense of "The Celebrity." I am arguing, however, that it is susceptible to a different interpretation than that posited by Herbert and others, and that their racial critique of the ad is unduly assertive given the ambiguity of the situation.*

Later in the campaign, observers denounced as racial demagoguery another political ad aired by the McCain camp. It was the one that associated Obama with Franklin Raines, the African American former CEO of Fannie Mae who had been forced to resign amid charges that he had been negligent and self-serving in carrying out his responsibilities. According to some critics, the real aim of the ad was not to link Obama to the discredited leadership

---

* Initially I was persuaded by Herbert and other proponents of the racial critique. The students in a course on the election that I taught at Harvard Law School changed my mind. In that racially diverse, politically sophisticated class, most students, to my surprise, eschewed the view that the ad was intended to play on racial fears. They thought that Spears and Hilton were simply unexcelled as symbols of vacuous celebrity.

at Fannie Mae; after all, if that was the purpose, the ad could have featured Jim Johnson, a white former Fannie Mae official who was closely associated with Obama. Rather, these critics asserted, the real aim of the ad was to call attention to Obama's associations with a tarnished *black* official whose misdeeds were portrayed as victimizing the sort of person accentuated at the advertisement's end—an elderly, seemingly vulnerable *white* woman.

Was the Fannie Mae ad an instance of playing the race card? Former presidential aspirant Michael Dukakis thought so. He likened it to the Willie Horton ad that damaged his candidacy in 1988.[43] But why was such an analogy apt? Dukakis did not say. He offered no justification. Karen Tumulty, a correspondent for *Time* who condemned the ad as a racial provocation, stressed the absence of any mention of Johnson, though he was closer to the Obama campaign than Raines had ever been.[44] Yet soon thereafter the McCain camp unveiled an attack ad that did feature Johnson. Was the latter ad created in order to prevent the McCain campaign from being caught engaging in race-baiting? I doubt it. Given the scheduling and the time needed to produce ads, it seems unlikely that the advertisement featuring Johnson was created in response to Tumulty and like-minded critics. Here, as with other claims, denials, and cross-claims involving racial politics in the presidential campaign of 2008, the situation was murky, the context unprecedented. It is possible that McCain's ad makers were trying to play upon whites' racial anxieties by picturing Raines as the villainous *black* adviser. It is also possible, however, that Raines's blackness was immaterial to the ad makers' calculations.

How should one proceed in the face of such ambiguity? My advice is that it is usually better to be under-sensitive rather than over-sensitive when assessing potential racial misconduct—to give the benefit of the doubt rather than jump to a conclusion of racial malfeasance. This approach definitely entails a substantial price:

the cost of permitting more instances of camouflaged misconduct to proceed unchecked. This cost, however, is less than that generated by an excessively acute sense of affront and aggrievement. Mistaken allegations of racial misconduct are expensive indeed. As Richard Thompson Ford notes, they "undermine popular support for racial justice. Every person who faces an undeserved accusation of racism is a potential future skeptic of all claims of racism. If too many people come to believe . . . that the serious charge of racism has become a ploy used for undeserved advantage, the anti-racist goodwill we currently enjoy may give way to a pervasive attitude of cynical indifference."[45]

Although there is much to criticize regarding John McCain, he deserves praise for declining to pursue certain lines of attack that might have yielded electoral dividends. Most notably, McCain rejected the counsel of fellow Republicans, including Palin, to attack Obama's longtime relationship with Reverend Wright.[46] Early on McCain stated that he thought focusing on this issue would be beneath the standard that a presidential election should set. McCain not only refrained from using the issue himself; he also discouraged allies from using it. To the consternation of many of his supporters, McCain publicly rebuked the North Carolina Republican Party when, over his objection, it continued to run ads criticizing Obama because of his association with Reverend Wright. On occasion McCain wavered and seemed to be on the verge of attacking the Obama-Wright connection regardless of his previous statements.[47] But even as he saw his chance for victory receding, McCain generally held firm to his initial position.

After the election it emerged, moreover, that McCain had muzzled his propagandists even further, prohibiting them from disseminating other imagery which, to him, seemed racially inflammatory or offensive. According to Fred Davis III, one of McCain's key publicists, the senator vetoed the use of footage that featured Obama dancing with Ellen DeGeneres, vetoed ads attacking Obama's record on crime-related issues, and insisted that care be taken to avoid portraying Obama in poses or even with soundtracks that might be objected to as racist.[48] Political calculation undoubtedly affected McCain's decisions. His own "brand" stood to be tarnished if he was widely perceived as breaking a promise* or himself playing the race card.† But I suspect that there was more to it than a narrow estimation of self-interest. Despite his desire to win the presidency, McCain was simply unwilling, on grounds of political morality, to pull out all of the racial stops that were available to him.

During the general-election campaign, Obama, too, was subjected to inflated charges that he indulged in racial demagoguery. Just as detractors condemned the JFK campaign in 1960 for engaging in "reverse bigotry," detractors charged Obama and his supporters with milking the race issue. A key event was a rally on July 30, 2008, in Missouri during which Obama stated, "Nobody really thinks that Bush or McCain have a real answer for the challenges we face. So what they're going to try to do is make you scared of me. You know, he's not patriotic enough. He's got a funny name. You know, he doesn't look like all those other presidents on those dollar bills. . . . He's risky."[49] In these remarks Obama never explicitly mentioned race. On a previous occasion,

---

* Once, when McCain did briefly criticize Obama with a reference to Reverend Wright, the reaction from the Obama camp was quick and sharp. It complained that "by sinking to a level that he specifically said he'd avoid, John McCain has broken his word to the American people and rendered hollow his promise of a respectful campaign." Quoted in Michael Cooper, "McCain Criticizes Remarks by Obama's Former Pastor," *New York Times*, April 28, 2008.

† Perhaps McCain also felt inhibited by a realization that if he sought to reignite the Reverend Wright controversy, he would himself face criticism because of his courtship of Jerry Falwell and John Hagee—right-wing Christian evangelicals who made all manner of bigoted antigay, anti-Jewish, or anti-Catholic remarks. See Frank Rich, "The All-White Elephant in the Room," *New York Times*, May 4, 2008.

however, he had: "We know what kind of campaign they're going to run. They're going to try to make you afraid of me. He's young and inexperienced and he's got a funny name. And did I mention he's black?"[50] Obama was warning the public, in other words, to be prepared for a racialized line of attack from McCain.

McCain's campaign manager Rick Davis responded testily: "Barack Obama has played the race card, and he played it from the bottom of the deck. It's divisive, negative, shameful, and wrong."[51] Elaborating further, Steve Schmidt, a leading McCain operative, remarked that "the McCain campaign was compelled to respond to this outrageous attack because we will not allow John McCain to be smeared by Senator Obama as a racist for offering legitimate criticism. We have waited for months with a sick feeling knowing this moment would come because we watched it occur with President Clinton."[52] McCain himself accused Obama of stirring racial fears, a cry echoed and amplified by conservative journalists. Declaring that he had once believed that Obama would "turn the page on the guilt-tripping grievance politics of Jesse Jackson and Al Sharpton," Charles Krauthammer denounced the senator as "the one presidential candidate who has repeatedly, and indeed quite brilliantly, deployed the race card."[53]

Although Obama's detractors seemed able to detect racial demagoguery only in the ranks of Democrats, there was some merit to this particular complaint against Obama. If you are going to indict someone for the social crime of racial wrongdoing, you should be careful about doing so, which means identifying with specificity the misconduct to which you object. Obama did not do that. One might respond that he was simply seeking, somewhat lightheartededly, to allude to an ugly fact—that McCain's party, or at least a faction of it, had notoriously practiced racial demagoguery in presidential contests and might well attempt to do so in the fight for the White House in 2008. In this instance, however, Obama had been insufficiently careful. He had launched an anticipatory attack and been called on it. Stung, Obama beat a hasty retreat, with his campaign spokesman declaring, "Barack Obama in no way believes that the McCain campaign is using race as an issue."[54] Obama's staff did not really believe in the McCain camp's racial innocence. But it felt compelled to backpedal. As one reporter noted, "For Mr. Obama . . . anything that calls attention to the racial dynamics of the contest would potentially polarize voters and stir unease about his candidacy, particularly among white voters in swing states. He is, after all, a candidate who has sought to transcend his own racial heritage in appealing to the broad electorate."[55]

In retrospect, a striking feature of the campaign of 2008 was not the presence but the paucity of racial misconduct. In a nation as large, heterogeneous, and rambunctious as the United States, in a contest for the presidency involving the first black standard-bearer of a major party, there were bound to be outbreaks of social ugliness, including racist affronts. It should have come as no surprise that there were people who likened Obama to an ape, who called him "nigger," who scorned the Obamas for being "uppity," who warned of chicken bones and watermelon rinds festooning the White House, and who vowed never to vote for a black man for the presidency whatever the circumstances. Surprising to me is that there wasn't *more* of an antiblack reaction.

McCain fought Obama fiercely, sometimes using tactics that fell below the standards he initially championed. But despite, or maybe in part because of, what was at stake, McCain refused to use all of the polemical weaponry he could have deployed against his black adversary. McCain's record on racial matters is considerably less impressive than what one would like to see in a leading American statesman. He has never been in the forefront of racial egalitarianism.* Running for the presidency, however, and

---

* During his campaign for the presidency in 2000, McCain told reporters, "I hated the gooks. I will hate them as long as I live." Subsequently questioned about his use of this epithet, McCain insisted that he was referring only to his prison guards, not to the

to the dismay of allies, McCain imposed upon himself a code of conduct that precluded taking full advantage of his opponent's racial vulnerability. He acted better than his biography would have led many to anticipate, just as the electorate voted with more of an open mind than many expected.

Vietnamese in general. Journalists focused little attention on this matter. Perhaps they refrained from doing so in 2008 on the grounds that the incident had become stale news, that McCain had discontinued using the term (though he never apologized for having used it in the past), and that given McCain's horrendous experience as a prisoner of war he ought to be given extra leeway in discussing anything having to do with that experience. One wonders, however, whether the calculation would have been different had the epithet in question been used historically to stigmatize a more politically influential group, or had the epithet in question triggered the widespread alarm and disgust generated by the infamous slur "nigger," or had a candidate with lesser social prestige been identified using such language. See Irwin A. Tang, *Gook: John McCain's Racism and Why It Matters* (2008); Raymond Leon Roker, "How Come McCain's 'Gook' Slur Isn't Bigger News?," HuffingtonPost.com, October 20, 2008; Katie Hong, "John McCain's Racist Remark Very Troubling," SeattlePI.com, March 20, 2008.

5

Reverend Wright and My Father

Reflections on Blacks and Patriotism

"For the first time in my adult life I am proud of my country because it feels like hope is finally making a comeback."

Michelle Robinson Obama[1]

"I have, and always will be, proud of my country."

Cindy McCain[2]

On June 30, 2008, Barack Obama delivered an address in Independence, Missouri, entitled "The America We Love." Patriotic speeches delivered by candidates are usually unremarkable, part of the banal ritual of electoral politics. Clearly, though, Obama wanted to break out of the grip of the ordinary with this address. He wanted it to be a key statement in his campaign.

Obama offered several reasons why it was "fitting to pause for a moment and reflect on the meaning of patriotism." One was that the nation was in the midst of a controversial war in Iraq that had, at that point, claimed forty-six hundred American lives and sixty thousand wounded. "It is natural," Obama declared, "in light of such sacrifice by so many, to think more deeply about the commitments that bind us to our nation, and to each other."

Obama also noted that the country was in the midst of a presidential election campaign from which had arisen a steady stream of insinuations suggesting doubts as to whether he harbored sufficient patriotism to be entrusted with the nation's highest office. "Throughout my life," Obama averred, "I have always taken my deep and abiding love for this country as a given." But now he found his patriotism challenged, "at times as a result of my own carelessness, more often as a result of the desire by some to score political points and raise fears about who I am and what I stand for." Obama did not elaborate on what he meant by his own "carelessness." Perhaps he was referring to refraining at times from wearing an American flag lapel pin, an omission that was portrayed as an ominous signal of disloyalty by some of Obama's more paranoid detractors. Neither did he specifically name those whom he accused of wrongly challenging his fidelity to the nation. He did declare, however, that he would not question the patriotism of others during the presidential campaign and that he would "not stand idly by when I hear others question mine."

Impugning a rival's patriotism has deep roots in American political history. Obama observed that Federalists had accused Thomas Jefferson of "selling out to the French" and that anti-Federalists had accused John Adams of being "in cahoots with the British." What he did not say but what is more pertinent is that since at least the 1950s, a major Republican theme has been that Democrats cannot be trusted to govern because their ranks have been riddled with cowards and weaklings and infiltrated by agents with mixed loyalties or even by out-and-out traitors. Democrats, too, have used patriotism as a cudgel. But on this score—who can be more unequivocal, sentimental, and militant in populist displays of patriotism—Republicans have long enjoyed an edge. "It's hard to remember a time," historian David Greenberg rightly observes, "when Republicans didn't own the patriotism issue."[3]

The challenge to Obama's patriotism included novel elements— his Kenyan father, his birth outside the continental United States, his schooling as a youngster in Indonesia. For an appreciable number of Americans, Obama's unfamiliar background conjured up visions of a "Manchurian Candidate" who may have been inculcated at an early age with un-American values. Nativism, however, is not limited to people on the margins who obsessively question whether Obama was, in fact, born in America. The United States Constitution regrettably conditions eligibility for the presidency on being a natural-born citizen.* In his address, Obama declared that an "essential American idea" is the notion that "we are not constituted by the accident of birth but can make of our lives what we will." But skepticism about the reliability of Obama's patriotism was nourished, in part, by a Constitution which itself wrongly discriminates on the basis of "the accident of birth."

Another element in the campaign to question Obama's patriotism had to do with the charge that he is a Muslim. Several features of this accusation are worth noting. First, Obama identifies himself as a devout Christian. Some detractors maintain, however, that Obama's asserted devotion to Christianity is false; they claim that he is a *secret* Muslim. John F. Kennedy had to contend with a similar hostility. After he set forth his views on church-state relations, some of which diverged markedly from the doctrines of the Catholic Church, die-hard opponents maintained that the Catholic doctrine of "mental reservation" would permit him to lie, without sinning, if in so doing he was seeking to advance the cause of the Church.

Second, that Obama was "accused" of being a Muslim is itself evidence of religious bigotry, since it suggests that being a Muslim is itself dirtying, shameful, disqualifying, un-American.

---

* "No person except a natural born Citizen, or a Citizen of the United States, at the time of the Adoption of this Constitution, shall be eligible to the Office of President . . ." United States Constitution, Article Two, Section One.

There is no formal bar precluding a Muslim president and there is no formal requirement that a president adhere to any religion. Obviously, though, large numbers of Americans view adherence to some form of Judeo-Christianity as a prerequisite.

Race was another ingredient in the case against Obama's patriotism. Many Americans suspect that, in general, African Americans are less patriotic than whites. A substantial number also believe that they have reason to fear blacks who secretly hate America. Those are perceptions that fueled the charge that the Obamas are among those who harbor deep, unrelievable resentment against America because of past racial injustices. Those who subscribe to this contention concede that there is no record of Obama expressing such sentiments. But they attribute this absence of evidence to his cunning: an ambitious man, he knows better than to express his outrage openly. They maintain that evidence of Obama's concealed attitude can be gleaned from the words of his wife and his former pastor. Speaking at a rally, Michelle Obama once remarked that the positive response to her husband's candidacy had made her proud of her country for the first time in her adult life.[4] Detractors imposed upon that comment the worst possible interpretation and resisted her efforts to amend or clarify it. In their view, Michelle Obama had revealingly confessed that, except for when her husband's campaign for the presidency was going well, she felt no pride in her country despite all of the many benefits it has bestowed upon her family and the world.

In the anti-Obama narrative, Reverend Wright's "God damn America!" was similarly revealing in that it emanated from someone who was a longtime, influential adviser to the candidate. Why, the conservative journalist Andrew C. McCarthy asked, is Barack Obama "so comfortable around people who so despise America . . . ?" Maybe, McCarthy responded, "it's because they're so comfortable around him"—a person whose attachment to

America is so attenuated that he can easily stand the company of those who disparage it.[5]

The effort to portray the Obamas as unpatriotic or at least insufficiently patriotic to entrust with the presidency brings to the fore a subject that has received all too little attention: the relationship between racial conflict and patriotism. In his pioneering study *The Roots of American Loyalty*, the historian Merle Curti asked, "What can be said of [the black American's] attitude toward America, of his loyalty to the land that enslaved him?"[6] Although Curti did not offer much elaboration, he warrants commendation for at least making the inquiry. What is the answer? And how does it figure into the election of 2008 and beyond?

First, a definition. I understand "patriotism" to refer to the love that a person feels for a place he considers "home" and a people he considers "his" people. Although the object of a loving attachment to a place and people can take many forms—a household, neighborhood, state, or region—the object with which I am concerned here is the nation known as the United States of America. I am concerned with the sentiment which prompts African Americans to say that they love the United States and to express that love through sacrifice. Patriotism may include admiration. But admiration is inessential, as one may feel love even while simultaneously feeling shame, revulsion, and even fear toward the object of one's affection. The black poet, publisher, and activist Haki Madhubuti writes, "I love[ ] America, but loathe what America [has] done to me, my people, and other nonwhite citizens of this country."[7] Loyalty, however, is an essential element of the love that I am calling "patriotism." As the philosopher Alasdair MacIntyre declares:

Patriotism is one of a class of loyalty-exhibiting [traits] . . . other members of which are marital fidelity, the love of one's own family and kin, friendship, and loyalty to such institutions as schools . . . or baseball clubs. All these attitudes exhibit a peculiar action-generating regard for particular persons, institutions or groups, a regard founded upon a particular historical relationship of association between the person exhibiting the regard and the relevant person, institution, or group.[8]

Whatever the basis of the relationship that calls the affection into being—whether it be contractual (as in the process of becoming a naturalized citizen) or status-based (as in native-born citizenship)—the affection transcends one's routine assessment of the nation's virtues or vices. The patriot loves his country even if he thinks it is gravely deficient in important respects. Patriotism is thus akin to the feeling of affection that exists within many families—the love that exists at graduation when the mother looks on with pride as her son accepts his diploma and the love that exists at sentencing when the mother looks on with dismay as her son is condemned to prison for robbery.

Patriotism is often exhibited through sacrifice—the willingness of individuals to subordinate their personal interest to the interest of the nation. The most celebrated example of patriotic sacrifice is a willingness to risk one's safety, even one's life, for the perceived greater good of the state. Hence, the pageantry of Veterans Day, the respect proffered to the winners of military medals, the valorization of civic sacrifice that the society attempts to inculcate within the minds and hearts of its young people via countless rituals and perhaps, most important, public education. "Ask not what your country can do for you," President John F. Kennedy famously declared. "Ask what you can do for your country."[9]

Although American politicians typically assume that patriotism is an appropriate, indeed admirable sentiment, it has also been reproved.[10] To George Santayana, patriotism was a delusion. "It seems a dreadful indignity," he declared, "to have a soul controlled by geography."[11] Leo Tolstoy regarded patriotism with disdain, asserting that it survived mainly because governments and ruling classes "persistently excite and maintain it among the people, both by cunning and violence."[12] To George Bernard Shaw, "Patriotism is your conviction that this country is superior to all others because you were born in it."[13]

Apart from the problem of defining and assessing patriotism is the problem of distinguishing true patriotism from counterfeit. A major difficulty is isolating authentic love of country from displays of purported affection that are the consequence of coercion. Acts (including speech) deemed to be unpatriotic make one vulnerable to punishment. That being so, people watch what they do or say to avoid trouble. They say things—"I love my country"—or do things—put an American flag in the front yard—not because such acts are truly expressive of patriotic feelings but because they fear the consequences of appearing to violate heavily policed norms.

Around no subject involving patriotism is more sentimental nonsense uttered than service in the military. Joining the military is conventionally ascribed to patriotism. In reality, however, the motivations behind enlistment vary greatly. Some enlist out of a sense of obligation, loyalty, or love. But many enlist for more self-interested purposes: to escape poverty, avoid incarceration, seek thrills, obtain discipline. The draft or the threat of a draft should remind everyone of the government's unwillingness to depend on patriotism alone to generate an adequate number of personnel in a military crisis. While political candidates almost always speak of military service as a matter of voluntary sacrifice, the government relies upon the coercion of the job market or, in a pinch, the coercion of a draft to ensure an available pool of soldiers.*

---

* "Public service" is another term often surrounded by sentimental half-truths. Asked why they want to be elected president, or senator, or governor, candidates reply that they want these posts because they are solely devoted to public service. It would be refreshing to hear a candidate say just once that he relishes power, likes being a boss, enjoys

A stock trope in discussions about black patriotism is the observation that, despite racist mistreatment, blacks have shown unwavering fidelity to their homeland. "Since the time of slavery," Michael Eric Dyson writes approvingly, "blacks have actively defended the U.S. in every war it has waged, from the Civil War down to the war on terrorism."[14] Left unmentioned is that often blacks, like others, were *forced* to fight on pain of being shot or imprisoned or at the very least disgraced. Fighting to avoid retribution is very different from fighting motivated by love of nation, although from the outside the difference may be difficult to discern.

The history of the celebration of black patriotism is itself mired in prejudice, humiliation, and coercion. Consider the first account of black patriots written by a black American—William Nell's *The Colored Patriots of the American Revolution*, published in 1855. Wendell Phillips, Nell's fellow abolitionist, observes in a preface that the book was written "to stem the tide of prejudice against the colored race."*[15] Nell was seeking to use the memory of Crispus Attucks and other blacks who fought with the colonial rebels as a shield to ward off attacks by racist whites. He was not so much interested in memorializing an accurate account of what blacks did in the Revolutionary War as in creating propaganda aimed at persuading whites that they should accord some measure of decency to colored folks whose ancestors had helped the American colonies secure independence. That being his aim, it should come

---

being the center of attention, appreciates the ego gratification that comes with winning a competition.

* Throughout the age of slavery, whites, like Phillips, wrote prefaces to books by blacks to vouch for their authenticity or merit. See Frederick Douglass, *Narrative of the Life of Frederick Douglass, An American Slave, Written by Himself* (1845), which featured a preface by William Lloyd Garrison; Harriet A. Jacobs, *Incidents in the Life of a Slave Girl Written by Herself* (1861), featuring the white abolitionist Lydia Maria Child as "editor." More recently, the trend has gone the other way, with blacks writing prefaces that vouch for the handiwork of white authors. See William G. Bowen and Derek Bok, *The Shape of the River: Long Term Consequences of Considering Race in College and University Admissions* (2000), featuring a foreword by Glenn C. Loury.

as little surprise that Nell ignored the tens of thousands of blacks, mostly slaves, who fled *to* the British.[16] It was not until 1961, when Professor Benjamin Quarles published *The Negro in the American Revolution*, that academic historians began to offer a portrayal that gave substantial attention to blacks who accepted the British offer for freedom in exchange for assistance in fighting the rebellious colonists. "The Negro's role in the Revolution," Quarles observed, "can best be understood by realizing that his major loyalty was not to a place nor to a people, but to a principle. Insofar as he had freedom of choice, he was likely to join the side that made the quickest and best offer in terms of those 'unalienable rights' of which Mr. Jefferson had spoken."[17]

The pressure Nell felt in the nineteenth century continues to exist today, albeit to a lesser extent. Still very much aware of tendencies to ignore or minimize black contributions to the United States, activists, commentators, politicians, and historians insistently laud the presence of black soldiers in the "winning of the West," the "pacification" of the Philippines, or the charge up San Juan Hill without considering whether that presence should be seen as an occasion for celebration or an occasion for lament. Why, one might ask, should we celebrate blacks' participation in cruel wars of conquest or colonial misadventures? One reason is that it serves the purpose, or is at least thought to serve the purpose, of gaining inclusion into the conventional national narrative and all of the attendant privileges that come with such involvement. Frederick Douglass voiced this view when, during the Civil War, he encouraged blacks to enlist in the Union Army. The man "who fights the battles of America," he asserted, "may claim America as his country—and have that claim respected."[18]

In his contribution to the anthology *What the Negro Wants*, published in 1944, the poet Sterling Brown posited succinctly the dominant theme in African-American thought regarding blacks' relationship to the United States of America. "Negroes," Brown declared, "want to be counted in. They want to belong."[19] Most have perceived themselves as part of the American national family, sought recognition of that status, and felt and shown loyalty to the nation notwithstanding egregious mistreatment. They have denied that the United States is a white man's country and proclaimed that this land is their land too.*

In the first half of the nineteenth century, the crisis that elicited the most searching discussion among blacks about their relationship to the United States arose from the founding of the American Colonization Society (ACS). Created in 1816 by leading white American statesmen, the ACS sought to repatriate free blacks to Africa. The motives behind the ACS proposal varied. Some slaveowners wanted to get rid of free blacks who might give troubling hope to enslaved blacks. Other members saw blacks, whatever their status, as threats to the creation of a virtuous white republic and thus wanted to get rid of as many of them as possible. The ACS also included reformers who wanted to spare blacks a future doomed to permanent subordination; they hoped to purchase the liberty of slaves and send the newly emancipated back to Africa alongside blacks who had long been free. James Madison,

---

* Langston Hughes memorably crystallized this sentiment in verse:

I, too, sing America.

I am the darker brother.
They send me to eat in the kitchen
When company comes,
But I laugh,
And eat well,
And grow strong. . . .

I, too, am America.

See Langston Hughes, *Poems*, Everyman's Library Pocket Poets (1999).

the fourth president, was a member of the ACS. He supported its program because of a conviction that he shared with his friend Thomas Jefferson that blacks and whites would never be able to reside together in the same land as equals. "To be consistent with existing and probably unalterable prejudices in the United States," Madison declared, "the freed blacks ought to be permanently removed beyond the region occupied by, or allotted to, a white population. . . . The objections to a thorough incorporation of the two people are . . . insuperable."[20]

Although a few blacks initially supported the ACS program of removal, the overwhelming majority quickly and vociferously rejected it. Free blacks overwhelmingly chose to stay in America, to assert their Americanness, and to commit themselves to narrowing the gap between noble American ideals and ugly American realities, including, most urgently, the reality of racial slavery. "Let no man of us budge one step," the black abolitionist David Walker declared in his *Appeal to the Coloured Citizens of the World.* "America is more our country than it is the whites—we have enriched it with our blood and tears."[21] Railing against colonization, clergyman and former slave Richard Allen asserted, "This land, which we have watered with our tears and our blood, is now our mother country; and we are well satisfied to stay where wisdom abounds and the Gospel is free."[22] In New York City in 1831, a mass meeting of Negroes resolved, "We are content to abide where we are. We do not believe that things will always continue the same. The time must come when the Declaration of Independence will be felt in the heart, as well as uttered from the mouth, and when the rights of all shall be properly acknowledged and appreciated. God hasten that time. This is our home, and this is our country. Beneath its sod lie the bones of our fathers; for it, some of them fought, bled, and died. Here we were born, and here we will die."[23] Repudiating emigration, the abolitionist runaway slave Henry Highland

Garnet declared in 1848, "We are planted here, and we cannot as a whole people, be re-colonized back to our fatherland. It is too late to make a successful attempt to separate the blacks and white people in the New World." America, Garnet averred, "is my home, my country, and I have no other. I love whatever good there may be in her institutions. I hate her sins. I loathe her slavery, and I pray Heaven that ere long she may wash away her guilt in tears of repentance."*24

In subsequent years, blacks contributed mightily to the canon of American patriotic expression. Three items are particularly noteworthy. The first is "Lift Every Voice and Sing," written by James Weldon Johnson† in 1900. The final stanza of the song goes as follows:

> God of our weary years,
> God of our silent tears,
> Thou who has brought us thus far on the way;
> Thou who has by Thy might,
> Led us into the light,
> Keep us forever in the path, we pray.
> Lest our feet stray from the places, our God, where we met
>   Thee,
> Lest, our hearts drunk with the wine of the world, we forget
>   Thee;
> Shadowed beneath Thy hand,
> May we forever stand,

---

* It should be noted that Garnet later changed his mind about emigration. See Martin B. Pasternack, *Rise Now and Fly to Arms: The Life of Henry Highland Garnet* (1995).
† Johnson was an extraordinary person who deserves more attention than he typically receives. He was an attorney, a diplomat, a leading figure in the National Association for the Advancement of Colored People, a poet, and a novelist (*The Autobiography of an Ex-Colored Man*). See Eugene D. Levy, *James Weldon Johnson, Black Leader, Black Voice* (1973); Kenneth M. Price and Lawrence Oliver, eds., *Critical Essays on James Weldon Johnson* (1997).

True to our God,

True to our native land.

The second is a speech, "What Does American Democracy Mean to Me?" delivered in 1939 by Mary McLeod Bethune, the founder of the National Council of Black Women, in which she declared:

> Democracy is for me . . . a goal towards which our nation is marching. It is a dream and an ideal in whose ultimate realization [I] have a deep and abiding faith. . . . We are rising out of the darkness of slavery into the light of freedom. . . . As we have been extended a *measure* of democracy, we have brought to the nation rich gifts. We have helped to build America with our labor, strengthened it with our faith, and enriched it with our song. . . . But even these are only the first fruits of a rich harvest, which will be reaped when new and wider fields are opened to us.

Turning to the question of African-American loyalty, Bethune declared:

> We have always been loyal when the ideals of American democracy have been attacked. We have given our blood in its defense. . . . We have fought to preserve one nation, conceived in liberty and dedicated to the proposition that all men are created equal. Yes, we have fought for America with all her imperfections, not so much for what she is, but for what we know she can be.[25]

A third example is the 1963 "I Have a Dream" address of Martin Luther King, Jr. With its loving references to iconic locales ("Let freedom ring from Stone Mountain of Georgia"), its prayerful allusions to the Declaration of Independence and the Constitution, and its reverential recitation of "My Country 'Tis of Thee," King's epochal speech exudes patriotic fervor.

Wars have produced numerous crises in which blacks have responded in word and deed with outpourings of patriotism. In the gravest crisis to beset the United States, some blacks responded to the cause of the Union even before emancipation became one of Lincoln's weapons and even before blacks were permitted to enter the ranks of the United States armed services. Explaining why they wished to drill, a group of blacks in Cleveland, Ohio, declared, "We, as colored citizens of Cleveland, desiring to prove our loyalty to the Government, feel that we should adopt measures to put ourselves in a position to defend the Government of which we claim protection. . . . Today, as in the times of '76 and the days of 1812, we are ready to go forth and do battle in the common cause of the country."[26] Requesting permission to participate in the defense of the Union, a group of colored men in Massachusetts declared, "Your petitioners, colored citizens . . . respectfully represent . . . that they have never been wanting in patriotism, but have always exhibited the utmost loyalty to the country and to the Commonwealth, notwithstanding the great national injustice to which they are in many ways subjected on account of their complexion."[27]

In subsequent years, this pattern reappeared. During World War I, the great W. E. B. Du Bois insisted that blacks subordinate their protests against white supremacist outrages to the imperatives of the national war effort. He asked Negroes to forget their "special grievances" and close ranks during the war.*[28] Most blacks acted in

---

* Although Du Bois's position seemed to reflect only patriotism, other motives were also at work. He feared what might happen to him if he urged a continuation of protest against a government that was clearly willing to suppress dissent. He also wanted to secure for himself a post in the government. This episode did not constitute Du Bois's

accordance with Du Bois's wishes, curtailing protest, submitting to the draft, and doing all sorts of voluntary acts indicative of patriotic sentiment. "The Negroes of South Carolina are standing by," reported the white supremacist *Columbia Record.* "They are loyal, they are earnest, they are zealous. Sometimes they shame us in their exhibition of their understanding of the causes of the war and their determination to support the Government throughout."[29]

In World War II, African Americans were similarly responsive to the government's plea for patriotic support. Much has been made of blacks' "double V" campaign for victory against fascism abroad *and* against racism at home. Some observers have suggested that blacks' opposition to racism during the forties ignited the militant dissent that blazed two and three decades later.[30] As historian Harvard Sitkoff has shown, however, blacks' feelings and displays of national solidarity after the American entry into World War II were far more widespread than their feelings and displays of racial grievance.[31] After the attack on Pearl Harbor, leaders of black organizations pledged loyalty and support to the nation. Black newspapers, such as the *Norfolk Journal and Guide* (echoing Du Bois), called upon African Americans to "close ranks and join with fervent patriotism in this battle for America."[32] Many blacks volunteered for service in the armed forces, few refused to participate in the draft, and those who did were widely ostracized. When a black gardener named Winfred W. Lynn refused induction as a protest against segregation in the military, no black newspaper or pressure group defended him. Not only did the National Association for the Advancement of Colored People (NAACP) refuse to aid Lynn, but Thurgood Marshall, who at

---

finest hour. See David Levering Lewis, *W.E.B. Du Bois: Biography of a Race: 1868–1919* (1993), 555; Mark Ellis, "W.E.B. Du Bois and the Formation of Black Opinion in World War I: A Commentary on 'The Damnable Dilemma,'" *Journal of American History* 81 (1995): 1584.

the time was the NAACP's chief counsel, used his influence to dissuade the American Civil Liberties Union (ACLU) from offering assistance.*[33]

A striking episode of armed patriotism stemmed from the horrific Battle of the Bulge, where Hitler's armies made a desperate last-ditch effort to stop the Allies' advance on the Western Front. Confronting massive losses and a surprisingly effective German counteroffensive, General Dwight Eisenhower embarked upon a racial experiment: he called upon blacks to volunteer to replace white soldiers in white units who had been killed or wounded. He also stipulated that some black volunteers would have to agree to demotions in order to avoid situations in which black soldiers would outrank white ones. Notwithstanding the dangers of combat and the insulting policy of racial demotion some four thousand black soldiers volunteered.[34]

In the 1960s and 1970s, during the most militant phases of opposition to various American domestic and international policies, especially the Vietnam War, there arose among blacks more of a challenge to conventional protocols of patriotism than at any time subsequent to the Civil War. Stokely Carmichael (Kwame Ture), Huey Newton, Eldridge Cleaver, and others associated with the radical edge of the black liberation movement lauded North Vietnam, praised Communist China, and, in general, sided with the "colored" Third World against the "white" First World. Even at the acme of the Black Power initiative, however, fidelity to the nation remained the overwhelmingly dominant sentiment among the great mass of African Americans.

---

* Another black man imprisoned for resisting induction during World War II was Elijah Poole, who became better known as Elijah Muhammad, the head of the Nation of Islam. A quarter of a century later, Muhammad Ali, one of Elijah Muhammad's disciples, also refused induction. Although his religion constituted his principal basis for declining induction in the military, Ali cited the hypocritical racism of the United States as another consideration that prompted his defiance.

What should one make of African-American patriotism? First, one should recognize the excruciating circumstances in which it has arisen and been displayed, circumstances often marked by the indifference or hostility of white Americans. Consider that most holy day of American patriotic ritual—the Fourth of July commemoration of the Continental Congress's adoption of the Declaration of Independence. This holiday has long stuck in the throats of African Americans because the framers of the Declaration tolerated Negro slavery. Frederick Douglass asked:

> What, to the American Slave, is your Fourth of July? I answer; a day that reveals to him, more than all other days in the year, the gross injustice and cruelty to which he is the constant victim. To him, your celebration is a sham; your boasted liberty, an unholy license; your national greatness, swelling vanity; your sounds of rejoicing are empty and heartless; your denunciation of tyrants, brass-fronted impudence; your shout of liberty and equality, hollow mockery; your prayers and hymns, your sermons and thanksgivings, with all your religious parade and solemnity, are to him, mere bombast, fraud, deception, impiety, and hypocrisy—a thin veil to cover up crimes which would disgrace a nation of savages. . . . There is not a nation on the earth guilty of practices more shocking and bloody than are the people of the United States, at this very hour.[35]

But beyond the ideological affront afforded by the celebration lay another difficulty. The historian Leonard Sweet observes that for much of the nineteenth century, July Fourth was "one of the most menacing days of the year" for blacks.[36] That was because of the whites who took offense at the sight of blacks celebrating as if *they* were members of the American political family. On July 4, 1805, whites in Philadelphia drove blacks out of the square facing

Independence Hall. For years thereafter, blacks attended Fourth of July festivities in that city at their peril. On July 4, 1834, a white mob in New York City burned down the Broadway Tabernacle because of the antislavery and antiracist views of the church's leaders. Firefighters in sympathy with the arsonists refused to douse the conflagration. On July 4, 1835, a white mob in Canaan, New Hampshire, destroyed a school open to blacks that was run by an abolitionist. The antebellum years were liberally dotted with such episodes.

Until relatively recently, blacks faced open hostility from those with whom they sought to fight in wars on behalf of the United States. In the Revolutionary War, they were excluded from the Continental Army until perilous circumstances impelled an informal easing of the color line. Even with defeat staring them in the face, the rebel militias in Georgia and South Carolina refused to permit the arming of blacks, saying that they would rather suffer defeat by the British than imperil slavery. During the Civil War, blacks were not permitted to enlist in the United States armed forces until two years after the start of the conflict, when conditions had become more dire than anyone had initially envisioned.

In World War I, blacks were drafted alongside other Americans, but were then subjected to all manner of invidious racial discrimination. They were largely excluded from the officer corps and mainly consigned to menial duties. The French called black American soldiers *Enfants Perdus*—Lost Children—because their mother country had abandoned them. The commander of the American Expeditionary Forces (AEF), General John J. Pershing, wrote a directive to French military officials entitled "Secret Information Concerning Black American Troops." It stated that while Negroes were citizens of the United States, the black man was regarded by the white American as an inferior being, a judgment with which the general had no quarrel. "The vices of the Negro," he maintained, "are a constant menace to the American who has to repress them sternly." Regarding Negro officers, Pershing averred, "We must not eat with them, must not shake hands or seek to talk or meet with them outside of the requirements of military service. We must not commend too highly the black American troops, particularly in the presence of Americans."[37] Out of naked racism, New York's all-black National Guard regiment, among the most decorated units in the war, was denied permission to march in the Paris victory parade.

During World War II, black soldiers and sailors were constantly bombarded by racial insults. In many places in the American South, German and Italian prisoners of war received treatment that was superior to blacks'. In one revealing instance, a white officer sought to persuade a local sheriff to allow his men, black soldiers, to get off a train to purchase food: "This is a troop train of the United States Marines on [the] way to a port of disembarkment." The reply? "I don't give a good goddam if the niggers is going to Tokyo. They ain't goin' to eat in Atlanta, Georgia, with white folks."[38]

Previously I mentioned the black volunteers at the Battle of the Bulge. Although many whites praised them, some objected to their presence. One wrote a remarkable letter to the notorious race-baiter Senator Theodore Bilbo of Mississippi:

> I am a typical American, a southerner and 27 years of age. . . .
> I am loyal to my country and know but reverence to her flag,
> BUT I shall never submit to fight beneath that banner with a
> negro by my side. Rather I should die a thousand times, and see
> Old Glory tramped in the dirt never to rise again, than to see
> this beloved land of ours become degraded by race mongrels, a
> throw back to the blackest specimen from the wilds.[39]

This revealing missive was written by a man who did not even serve in the military in World War II, a man who afterward became the longest-sitting United States senator in American history—Robert Byrd of West Virginia.

A second thing to realize about the tradition of African-American patriotism is that right beside it, albeit widely over-looked, is an alternative tradition constituted by the words and acts of blacks who have either refrained from ever loving the United States or who have fallen out of love with it. Progenitors of this alternative tradition include runaways who fled the estates of Founding Fathers Americans are taught to revere—George Washington, Thomas Jefferson, Patrick Henry.[40] Their ranks also include blacks who, accepting the terms for emancipation offered by the British, took up arms against the American rebels. One of these black Tories was an enslaved New Jerseyan named Titus. When Titus heard in 1775 of the proclamation by the royalist governor of Virginia promising freedom in exchange for assistance in putting down the American rebellion, he headed south to seek liberation. Three years later Titus returned to New Jersey, now bearing the name Colonel Tye. The leader of a multiracial guer-rilla band, he had become "one of the war's most feared Loyal-ists."[41] We know next to nothing about Colonel Tye's thoughts and sentiments. It may be, however, that in addition to serving his own personal interests, he fought the Americans on ideological grounds, outraged by the perfidiousness of a Thomas Jefferson who championed "freedom" with one hand while endorsing with another legislation that paid rebel soldiers with Negro slaves.[42] Colonel Tye was not alone. Though one would never know it from the ascendant mythology that often passes for popular history in America, it is likely that more blacks fought with the British than with the American rebels.[43]

Subsequently, substantial numbers of blacks continued to create an alternative to the African-American patriotic tradition. Consider the view of the remarkable free black abolitionist, Martin R. Delany. Convinced that blacks would forever be stymied by racism in America, Delany became a leading voice of emigration in the 1850s and sought to establish himself abroad on several occasions. "We are Americans, having a birth right of citizenship," Delany declared. "We love our country, dearly love her, but she doesn't love us—she despises us, and bids us begone, driving us from her embraces." Delany wrote that he was "not in favor of caste, nor a separation of the brotherhood of mankind, and would just as willingly live among white men as black, if [he] had an equal possession and enjoyment of privileges." But, he insisted, "I shall never be reconciled to live among them subservient to their will—existing by mere sufferance, as we, the colored people, do in this country." He continued despairingly, "If there were any probability [of attaining equality in America] I should be willing to remain in this country, fighting and struggling on, the good fight of faith. But I must admit, that I have no hopes in this country—no confidence in the American people—with a few excellent exceptions."*[44]

Early in his career as an abolitionist, before he became a patriot, the fugitive slave Frederick Douglass plaintively declared, "I have no love for America. . . . I have no patriotism. . . . I desire to see [the government of the United States] overthrown as speedily as possible and its Constitution shivered in a thousand fragments."[45] Over a century later, near the high point of the Civil Rights Revolution, Malcolm X declined to join with Martin Luther King, Jr., in assuring blacks that white America would, over time,

* The American Civil War prompted Delany to change his mind. He recruited blacks to join the Union Army, became an officer himself, and then participated in the struggle over Reconstruction in South Carolina. See Robert S. Levine, *Martin Delany, Frederick Douglass, and the Policy of Representative Identity* (1997).

be persuaded to bring its conduct into line with its promises and professions. "Being born here in America doesn't make you an American," Malcolm X asserted. "I'm not an American. I'm one of the 22 million black people who are the victims of Americanism. One of the 22 million black people who are the victims of . . . nothing but disguised hypocrisy." Expressly contrasting himself with King, Malcolm X noted, "I don't see any American dream; I see an American nightmare."[46]

Two decades later, the pan-African activist Randall Robinson quit America, sprirually and physically (he moved to St. Kitts).

> America. America. Land of my birth and erstwhile distress. . . . My heart left long ago. At long last, I have followed it. Trying my very best, how could I, in good conscience, remain *for* a country that has never, ever, at home or abroad, been *for* me or *for* mine?

Echoing Delany, Robinson remarked, "I tried to love America, its credos, its ideals, its promises. . . . I have tried to love America but America would not love the ancient, full African whole of me. . . . For all of my life, I had wished only to live in an America that would but reciprocate my loyalty."[47]

I grew up in a household in which sentiments of this sort were frequently voiced. My father, Henry Harold Kennedy, Sr., never forgave American society for its racist mistreatment of him and those whom he most loved. Born in 1917 in Covington, Louisiana, my father attended segregated schools, came to learn painfully that because of his race certain options were foreclosed to him despite his intelligence, industry, and ambition, and witnessed countless incidents in which blacks were terrorized and humiliated by whites without any hint of disapproval from public authorities. He bore a special grudge against police—municipal police, state police, military police, *all* police, because, in his experience, a central function of police was to keep blacks in their "place." I saw with my own eyes why he developed such a loathing. On several occasions in the 1960s when he drove his family from Washington, D.C., to my mother's ancestral home, Columbia, South Carolina, my father was pulled over by police officers not because he had committed any legal infraction but simply because he was a black man driving a nice car. I am not making an inference here. This is what the police openly said. And then, noting his Washington, D.C., driver's license, they would go on to say that things were different in the South than Up North, and that my father should take care to behave himself. "Okay, boy?" Then there would be a pause. It seemed as though the policeman was waiting to see how my father would respond. My dad reacted in a way calculated to provide the maximum safety to himself and his family: "Yassuh," he would say with an extra dollop of deference.

Incidents of this sort profoundly alienated my father. In his view, they justified his refusal to view the United States as "his country." He felt neither that he belonged to it nor that it belonged to him. He attempted to make the best of his situation and, in the view of many, succeeded admirably. A post-office clerk married to a schoolteacher, he was often happy, had many friends, was widely respected in his neighborhood and church, and owned a home. He sent each of his three children to Princeton University, and lived to see them all become lawyers (one is a federal judge). It could be argued that my father's life is a vivid embodiment of the American Dream. But my father did not see it that way. Like Malcolm X, he believed himself to be the victim of a terrible and ongoing injustice that white America refused to acknowledge satisfactorily.

My father echewed any sentimental bond with the American government or the American nation. He rejected patriotism.* I

* Even with racialists, race is seldom the *sole* explanation for an important decision, policy, or orientation. For my father, racial feelings played a large, probably decisive, role in his refusal to be patriotic. But another ingredient that nourished this attitude was a

once asked him why he enlisted in the Army during the 1940s. His response? "I joined in order to eat." He offered no talk about wanting to serve his country. Rather, he candidly declared that the only attraction he saw in military service was refuge from want. Years later, during the Vietnam War, he maintained that any black man drafted by the United States government should go to Canada rather than risk his life for a nation that, out of racial prejudice, continued to subordinate black folk. He relished Muhammad Ali's quip that the Vietcong had never called him "nigger."

My father's alienation was such that in virtually any conflict between the United States and some other country, especially any Third World country, he sided presumptively with America's foe. In the 1980s, when American officials railed against the Ugandan head of state Idi Amin, my father defended the dictator, reasoning that any black man who got white folks that mad had to be doing something right. In the 1990s, during the first Gulf War, my father hoped for America's defeat:

> You don't see Bush pulling out all the stops for black folks catch-
> ing hell right here, do you? You don't see him going the extra
> mile to get straight with black folks after having vetoed the civil
> rights bill or having helped that racist Jesse Helms, do you? . . .
> These white people here had to be positively shamed into doing
> anything, even the least little thing, against the South African

---

deep-seated localism. He believed in being loyal to people he knew who had been loyal to him. This included whites who were racists. He had a number of friends whom he knew to be bigots. But they were good to him and his family. For my father that was suf-ficient. In the same way that his racist white friends exempted my father and our family from their generally damning view of blacks, my father exempted his racist white friends from his generally damning view of whites.

That he should be loyal to a huge nation-state (i.e., the United States of America) was a proposition that my father did not take seriously. He believed in face-to-face dealings; bureaucratic "loyalty" struck him as false, a sham that the authorities tricked the gullible masses into worshipping.

government. And when those damn South Africans whipped up on poor Angola and Mozambique, all that white officials over here could do was try to figure out how to join in. . . . And just watch what happens after the war in Kuwait. Bush will talk about helping the Kuwaitis rebuild their country, while black communities here starve for attention. . . . And watch what happens to the black soldiers coming home. Do you think they will get any special hand for "serving their country." Hell, no! They will probably get kicked in the butt like I was. . . . They'll be told that they don't qualify for this and don't qualify for that. They'll be told in so many words that all they're good for is cannon fodder, and that if they don't like it they can get in line for prison where there are already enough black veterans of Vietnam to outfit a good-sized army. . . . Boy, you just don't know how evil and nasty these white folks can be.⁴⁸

During the presidential contest of 2008, the black American who became infamous because of his castigation of the United States was Obama's former pastor, Reverend Jeremiah Wright, Jr. There is much that was objectionable in Reverend Wright's various highly publicized statements. His suggestion that a government plot is behind the AIDS catastrophe is a baseless and destructive canard, part of a community of rumors that has alienated blacks from much-needed participation in blood banking, organ donation, and medical testing. His unqualified praise of Louis Farrakhan offered support to a figure whose record includes forays into antiwhite racism, anti-Jewish bigotry, and intraracial intimidation. Reverend Wright's critique of American racism, moreover, is all too one-sided and static—as if the struggles of the Civil Rights Revolution have failed to bring about dramatic and positive changes in race relations even amid the stubborn and frustrating continuation of racial injustice.

But there is also much that is deserving of criticism in the negative reaction to Reverend Wright. First, the air of outraged wonderment that suffused many responses reflected a notable ignorance about the spectrum of belief one encounters in black communities. As journalist Gary Kamiya noted, "the great shock so many people claim to be feeling over Wright's sermons is preposterous. Anyone who is surprised and horrified that some black people feel anger at white people, and America, is living in a racial never-never land."*[49] The fact is that much of what Reverend Wright voiced strikes a chord with many black people: his contempt for American hypocrisy; his anger at American unwillingness to face squarely the two great social crimes that haunt United States history—the removal of the Indians and the enslavement of the Africans; his suspicion that white America fears the emergence of strong, autonomous racial-minority communities. This is not to say that blacks uniformly or even predominantly embraced the particulars of his message. Many of Reverend Wright's black congregants understood him to be engaged in a performance that makes liberal use of exaggeration and parody. Moreover, some of those who clapped and shouted appreciatively were expressing approval of what they saw as his courageous articulation of figurative, as opposed to literal, truths. The great mass of politically involved blacks regretted that Reverend Wright's sermons redounded to the detriment of Obama's candidacy. And most turned against Reverend Wright when he insisted upon defending himself in a fashion that seemed, at best, indifferent to the Obama campaign. But there was no

---

* It is noteworthy that candidate Obama, too, expressed shock in some of his varied responses to the Reverend Wright imbroglio. It is hard to believe, though, that he was truly unaware of the sentiment and rhetoric that generated the uproar. The claim of surprise is best understood as a strategy aimed at distancing himself from his former pastor.

groundswell in black America to repudiate the basic message of the remarks that so infuriated white America.

Second, many observers abjured Wright simply for daring to denounce the United States at all—as if that is, in and of itself, illicit—as if the governing authorities of the United States have never done anything that could possibly justify someone calling for divine retribution.* Reverend Wright's signature declaration—"God damn America!"—was part of a sermon in which he criticized various social problems, including what he views as an egregiously misdirected criminal-justice system that is excessively punitive and especially destructive in black communities. Here, as in other instances, Wright muddies his message with a distracting folktale—the myth that the United States itself is engaged in a conspiracy to use the illegal drug trade to incapacitate large swaths of its black population through addiction, disease, and imprisonment. His central claim, however, is that authorities are needlessly compounding misery through policies that have led to massive increases in rates of incarceration. This is, in his view, a baleful development that is so shameful in its production of avoidable pain that it constitutes a moral atrocity warranting God's damnation. Numerous studies offer substantial support for Wright's indictment.†

---

* Important figures in American history have contemplated with fear and awe the prospect of divine retribution for racial slavery. "I tremble for my country," Thomas Jefferson remarked, "when I reflect that God is just." Quoted in John Chester Miller, *The Wolf by the Ears: Thomas Jefferson and Slavery* (1991), 43. And then, of course, there was Abraham Lincoln's haunting second inaugural address in which he raised the possibility that the Civil War might represent God's punishment for America's iniquitous trafficking in human bondage. If God wills that the mighty scourge of war continue "until all the wealth piled by the bond-man's two hundred and fifty years of unrequited toil shall be sunk, and until every drop of blood drawn with the lash, shall be paid by another drawn with the sword . . . so it still must be said 'the judgments of the Lord are true and righteous.'"

† See, e.g., Michelle Alexander, *The New Jim Crow: Mass Incarceration in the Age of Colorblindness* (2010); Glenn C. Loury, *Race, Incarceration and American Values* (2008);

The other statement by Reverend Wright that led to the ideo-logical quarantine put upon him came in a sermon he delivered soon after the destruction of the Twin Towers in New York City on September 11, 2001. In "The Day of Jerusalem's Fall," Wright offered a variety of criticisms of American political culture. Pre-sciently anticipating the military interventions to come, especially the war in Iraq, Wright complained that "far too many people of faith in 2001 A.D. . . . have moved from the hatred of armed ene-mies to the hatred of unarmed innocents. We want revenge. We want paybacks, and we don't care who gets hurt in the process." He went on to chastise Americans for assuming what he saw as a false posture of innocence. After all, he declared, Americans have unleashed violence to accomplish their ends all over the world. "The stuff we have done overseas," he said, "has now been brought back into our own front yard! America's chickens are coming home to roost! Violence begets violence. Hatred begets hatred and ter-rorism begets terrorism."[50]

Many people, including Barack Obama, have fulminated against Wright's statement. Yet it contains a useful message that was especially important to articulate after the 9/11 attack. Rev-erend Wright's message was that the United States, too, is tainted by worldly sin—its imperialism (the Mexican-American War, the conquest of the Philippines, the occupation of Haiti and Cuba); its dispossession of the Indians; its subordination of blacks; its use of atomic weapons; its misadventures in Vietnam, Chile, and Nica-ragua; and still other misdeeds about which all too many Ameri-cans are ignorant or indifferent.

To some, Wright's interpretation of American history is an attack upon secular scripture: the conventional narrative of Amer-

Devah Pager, *Marked: Race, Crime and Finding Work in an Era of Mass Incarceration* (2007); Bruce Western, *Punishment and Inequality in America* (2006).

ican goodness. Reaction against such perceived affronts is often fervent. Recall what happened in 1995 when the curators of the National Air and Space Museum attempted to present a heterodox view of the decision to drop atom bombs on Japan during World War II, an interpretation that called into question the necessity and hence the morality of the decision. Although this argument has been advanced by serious scholars for decades, Congress put the managers of the National Air and Space Museum on notice that they would be severely penalized (i.e., lose their jobs) if they attempted—which they did not—to mount the "objectionable" exhibition.[51] A similar intolerant, parochial conformism animated much of the reaction against Reverend Wright. How could anyone, especially an American, say what he said about the United States, especially in the throes of the grief immediately following 9/11? In the eyes of many he was stepping over the ultimate line of political incorrectness—the patriotism line.

I have already noted my criticisms of Reverend Wright's remarks. They were marred by hyperbole, one-sidedness, and an irresponsible willingness to perpetuate erroneous folktales. Worse, however, is the complacent smugness from which arose the feverish anger that Wright provoked and that temporarily posed a threat to Obama's candidacy. Neither of these alternatives is inevitable. Both should be abjured. If pushed to choose, however, between Wright's excessive denigration of America and the excessive exaltation epitomized by his most severe detractors, I'll take the former. Its consequences tend to be less lethal.

To be elected president of the United States, Obama (like any other candidate) had to stay far clear of the patriotism line. He had to voice certain talismanic statements ("I love America") and bow before certain totemic emblems such as the Pledge of Allegiance, the national anthem, and the flag. During the battle with Clinton, Obama bridled when questioned about the absence of a flag pin on his suit coat. He suggested initially that he would decline to express his patriotism through such formulaic symbolism. The fervor of the backlash, however, persuaded him rather quickly to don the flag pin.

In the speech that launched him into political celebrity, his address at the Democratic National Convention in 2004, Obama spoke reverentially of America as "a magical place," gratefully recounting how it had offered sanctuary to parents who "shared not only an improbable love" but "an abiding faith in the possibilities of this nation." During his campaign for the presidency, in his most sustained performance of patriotic ritualism, his "The America We Love" speech, Obama invoked the thoroughly familiar image of the "simple band of colonists" who "took up arms against the tyranny of an Empire . . . not on behalf of a particular tribe or lineage, but on behalf of a larger idea. The idea of liberty." That claim hardly squares with the presence of slavery in all of the colonies that confederated to form the United States. Nor does it square with the fact, noted previously, that among the enslaved who joined the British were bondsmen who eagerly fled the estates of George Washington, Thomas Jefferson, and other Founding Fathers. But Obama was not about to inject such complications into his feel-good narrative of American origins. He was not wholly uncritical. He mentioned American "imperfections" and "flaws." Yet in his speech there was only one development that he labeled "a national shame." Was this a reference to the ethnic cleansing through which the bulk of North America was wrested from the Indians? Was it a reference to slavery or segregation? Was it a reference to the exclusion of the Chinese or the internment of the Japanese? No. The act Obama judged most harshly in his wide-ranging address was the failure of some Americans "to honor those veterans coming home from Vietnam, something that remains a national shame to this day." Certainly the jeering at Vietnam veterans was misdirected, especially as it targeted low-ranking soldiers as opposed to the civilian and military elite who designed the policies soldiers were forced to implement. But even at its worst, the jeering was less destructive than other actions, policies, or episodes about which Obama was mute, forgiving, or euphemistic. He did note FDR's internment of Japanese Americans in World War II. But he refrained from labeling that moral disaster a national shame and instead termed it a mere "questionable" policy. What Obama's calibration of censure reflects is a pragmatic politician's understanding of what the dominant camps in American political culture will recognize as truth and reward as wisdom. Unvarnished accounts of the American story, especially in the mouth of a politician seeking the presidency, are seen by many as neither true nor wise.

It would be unfair to neglect to acknowledge that, in his speech, Obama injected something extra into what might have been, in other hands, a wholly banal exercise of patriotic ritual. That something extra consisted of two points. One was an insistence that dissent, too, can be patriotic. Indeed, according to Obama, "when our laws, our leaders, or our government are out of alignment with our ideals, then the dissent of ordinary Americans may prove to be one of the truest expressions of patriotism." He cited as a patriot Martin Luther King, Jr., "who led a movement to help America confront our tragic history of racial injustice and live up to the meaning of our creed." He also lauded as a patriot "the young soldier who first spoke about the prisoner abuse at Abu Ghraib," the infamous prison in Iraq. The second point was that "patriotism involves not only defending the country against external threat, but also working constantly to make America a better place for future generations. . . . Just as patriotism involves each of us making a commitment to this nation that extends beyond our own immediate self-interest, so must that commitment extend beyond our own time here on earth."

These are nice touches that broadened the discourse on patriotism and offered just the sort of distinguishing flavor that elicited from supporters the enthusiasm that helped to propel Obama to victory. But Obama's gestures toward a progressive patriotism* were situated firmly within a conventional narrative that trumpeted, in his words, "the singular greatness of our ideals." This framework is sometimes referred to as American exceptionalism—a community of perceptions, ideas, intuitions, and ambitions which posits, among other things, that the United States is uniquely virtuous, uniquely powerful, uniquely destined to accomplish great things, and thus uniquely authorized to act in ways to which Americans would object if done by other nations. One hears strains of American exceptionalism in the rhetoric of politicians across the spectrum of "mainstream" politics—from the Republican president George W. Bush ("The United States has been the greatest force for good in history. [It] provides the single surviving model of human progress") to the activist Jesse Jackson ("America is God's country") to the Democratic secretary of state Madeleine Albright ("We are the indispensable nation. We stand tall. We see further into the future") to the vice-presidential candidate Sarah Palin ("America is a nation of exceptionalism") to the candidate and then president Barack Obama. This rhetoric is so routinely voiced that it has become an expected part of an American politician's repertoire.

During Obama's first trip to Europe as president, a reporter asked him specifically whether he subscribed, as many of his pre-

---

* See Jefferson Morley, "The Triumph of Blue Patriotism," *The Washington Independent*, January 20, 2009, and John Nichols, "For Progressive Patriotism," *The Nation*, January 15, 2009.

decessors had, "to the school of American exceptionalism that sees America as uniquely qualified to lead the world?"[52] He responded by stating:

> I believe in American exceptionalism, just as I suspect that the Brits believe in British exceptionalism and the Greeks believe in Greek exceptionalism. . . . The fact that I am very proud of my country and I think we've got a whole lot to offer the world does not lessen my interest in recognizing the value and wonderful qualities of other countries, or recognizing that we're not always going to be right, or that other people may have good ideas, or that in order for us to work collectively, all parties have to compromise and that includes us.

Obama's remarks were revealing. They showed his impulse toward a gracious cosmopolitanism ("recognizing the value and wonderful qualities of other countries"), realistic modesty ("we're not always going to be right"), and sensible multilateralism ("in order for us to work collectively, all parties have to compromise," including the United States). His remarks, moreover, revised the standard American claim of exceptionalism by deemphasizing ideas of American superiority and instead internationalizing what is sometimes seen disapprovingly as a peculiarly American attitude. In the end, though, Obama did what the bulk of the American electorate expects and demands of him and any other president. He stressed what he views as the beneficent specialness of America, including a core set of democratic values that, "though imperfect, are exceptional."

When Americans elected Obama to the presidency they selected him to become the head of the American political family. He is expected to do for the American political family what a decent head of any household does—love his family to the fullest twenty-four hours a day, seven days a week. He is expected to put the family's interest before his own and, if need be, to sacrifice himself for it. He is expected not only to work on behalf of the American political family, not only to lead it, but to be its very embodiment. Every American president becomes, temporarily, the father (or one day soon, the mother) of the country. That is why there is more intimate emotionality associated with the election of a president than with any other office in American politics.

By electing Obama, America made it vividly clear that, yes, indeed, certain blacks are fully included in the American polity not only as workers or athletes, soldiers or singers, but at the highest level of governmental authority. Nothing in American history has more powerfully elicited patriotism among black folk than seeing a fellow black elevated to the presidency.* The ascendant, grand story of American redemption has assimilated this development in stride. In the age of the first black president, the conventional patriotic narrative continues to hold pride of place in America's self-understanding. Obama will do nothing to subvert it. He, too, will allow Andrew Jackson's portrait to retain a place of honor in the White House and in the pantheon of the Democratic Party despite Old Hickory's aggressive defense of Negro slavery and his cruel depredations against Indians. He, too, will portray the United States as fundamentally different, better, more moral than any other nation-state—"the world's last best hope"—a country

---

* "I wasn't expecting this man. He blindsided me. I had heard back in 2004 of a black man with an African name who was putting his name on the ballot in the near future. I thought: 'so what?' . . . Four years later, I can hardly believe what's happened. I don't care what color he is, but damn if I don't have a hard time holding back tears every time I hear him speak. I can't help but to string the images of slaves, lynchings, fire hoses, and Barack Obama into a reel of silent pride that plays over and over in my mind. There is no smug. There is no gloat. Just lightness, hope, love, solidarity with ALL Americans. I have a new-found reason to be a patriot. . . . Bless you all." Anonymous respondent to Ariel Gonzalez, "Guess Who's Coming to Dinner: From Booker T. Washington to Barack Obama," HuffingtonPost.com, October 25, 2008.

enjoying divine guidance. He, too, will posit other propositions that are at once popular and misleading. When he nominated Sonia Sotomayor for a seat on the Supreme Court it was not enough to congratulate her and her family on the commendable pluck involved in her difficult journey from the South Bronx to Princeton, Yale Law School, and the most elite circles of the American legal profession. Obama also reiterated one of his favorite tropes of American exceptionalism—the vision of a "magical place" in which social confinements are no match for individuals who are sufficiently industrious. "No dream is beyond reach in the United States of America," the president intoned, obscuring with an unusual instance of social mobility the frustrating inertia that hard-working poor people know all too well.[53]

Obama's election brightens the allure of the conventional patriotic narrative. It is one of those landmark events that prompts the utterance of the congratulatory slogan: "Only in America!" It would have moved my father deeply. It would not, however, have turned him into a patriot.

6

The Racial Politics
of the Sotomayor Confirmation

On May 26, 2009, Barack Obama nominated Sonia Sotomayor to occupy the seat on the United States Supreme Court that was being vacated by the retirement of Justice David Souter. Sotomayor became the country's first Latino* justice. That she was a Latina "first" guaranteed that race talk would suffuse discussion of her background, career, and perspective. That she had taken strong, sometimes heterodox, positions on racial issues and had participated in an important race-discrimination case that was reviewed by the Supreme Court just prior to her confirmation hearing only added to the salience of race relations as an issue in the debate over her suitability.

Prior to the 1930s, racial matters hardly ever figured significantly in federal judicial politics.† A consensus reigned regarding

---

* Many people use "Latino" and "Hispanic" interchangeably. The United States Census Bureau, for instance, allows individuals to check a box labeled "Hispanic or Latino." I describe Sotomayor as Latino or as a Latina because that is how she refers to herself. For discussions contrasting "Latino" and "Hispanic" see Richard Delgado, Juan Perea, and Jean Stefancic, *Latinos and the Law: Cases and Materials* (2008), 4–5; Clara E. Rodriguez, *Changing Race: Latinos, the Census, and the History of Ethnicity in the United States* (2000); Angel R. Oquando, "Re-Imagining the Latino/a Race," *Harvard BlackLetter Journal* 12 (1995): 93.

† Anti-Semitism, however, did play a role in the fight over Louis D. Brandeis, President Woodrow Wilson's nominee in 1916, the first Jew to sit on the Supreme Court. See Melvin Urofsky, *Louis D. Brandeis: A Life* (2009).

the subordination of colored peoples throughout the nation and its colonial outposts. Since the thirties, however, controversies regarding race relations have often played a significant role in confirmation battles. The Senate in 1930 declined (by one vote) to confirm President Herbert Hoover's pick, Judge John J. Parker, partly because of opposition voiced by the NAACP. The focal point of its objection was his statement, during a gubernatorial campaign in North Carolina in 1920, that "the participation of the Negro in politics is a source of evil and danger to both races."* Revulsion against racial bigotry also contributed to the successful effort in 1970 to block one of President Richard Nixon's nominees. G. Harrold Carswell had declared in 1948, while running for a seat in the Georgia legislature, "I yield to no man . . . in the firm, vigorous belief in the principles of White Supremacy, and I shall always be so governed." †

A third candidate for the Supreme Court stymied in part due to racial concerns was Judge Robert Bork, who was nominated in 1987 by President Ronald Reagan. Bork had called into question landmark civil-rights decisions such as *Shelley v. Kraemer* and *Brown v. Board of Education* without showing much concern, if any, for the racial mistreatment these rulings sought to address. Moreover, on libertarian grounds he had opposed the public-accommodation provision of the Civil Rights Act of 1964. Viewing

---

* According to *The Chicago Defender*, President Hoover was outraged by the Senate's rejection of his candidate, declaring, "I do not know what this country is coming to when it can be run by demagogues and Negro politicians." Quoted in Henry J. Abraham, *Justices, Presidents, and Senators: A History of the U.S. Supreme Court Appointments from Washington to Bush II* (fifth edition, 2008), 332.

† Carswell, of course, disavowed his statement and the sentiments it reflected. He attributed it to the inexperience of youth; when he made the statement he was only twenty-eight. Until his nomination to the Supreme Court, however, Carswell had said or done nothing to repudiate publicly his previous allegiance to white supremacist politics. Moreover, while serving as a U.S. attorney in Florida he had participated in transforming a publicly owned golf course into a private club for the obvious purpose of circumventing desegregation. Abraham, *Justices, Presidents, and Senators*, 11.

Bork as a formidable and frightening foe, progressives uniformly and vociferously opposed his candidacy.*

Racial controversies were prominent in other confirmation battles as well.† Two instances involved Thurgood Marshall and Clarence Thomas.

In 1967, President Lyndon Baines Johnson nominated his solicitor general, Thurgood Marshall, "Mr. Civil Rights," the longtime legal director of the NAACP Legal Defense Fund. In public, Johnson refrained from saying expressly that race played a role in his decision to nominate Marshall. All Johnson would say was that Marshall was "the right man at the right time." In private, LBJ was more candid. Responding to the president's request for other persons to consider, an aide mentioned A. Leon

---

* Among those who testified against Bork were three of the most widely respected African Americans in the country: the attorney William T. Coleman, the politician Barbara Jordan, and the historian John Hope Franklin. See Norman Viera and Leonard Gross, *Supreme Court Appointments: Judge Bork and the Polarization of Senate Confirmations* (1998); Michael Pertschuk and Wendy Schaetzel, *The People Rising: The Campaign Against the Bork Nomination* (1989).

† Whether Hugo Black had been a member of the Ku Klux Klan was discussed heatedly but inconclusively during debate over his confirmation by the Senate. During the debate he never directly addressed the issue. The debate occurred in the period before nominees testified before the Senate Judiciary Committee. Soon after he was confirmed, Black admitted that he had been a member of the Klan. He noted, though, that he had resigned and subsequently had had nothing to do with the Invisible Empire. See Gerald T. Dunne, *Hugo Black and the Judicial Revolution* (1977), 41–81.

Professor Stephen L. Carter points out that "the modern tradition of routinely requiring the nominee to appear [before the Senate Judiciary Committee] began after [*Brown v. Board of Education*]. . . . For the next twelve years, every nominee appeared and every nominee was grilled about the segregation decisions." *The Confirmation Mess: Cleaning Up the Federal Appointments Process* (1994), 66–67.

During William Rehnquist's hearings for an associate justiceship in 1971 and then the chief justiceship in 1986, allegations were made that he had supported the constitutional legitimacy of racial segregation when he worked as a law clerk to Justice Robert H. Jackson in the 1950s. Rehnquist claimed that the memoranda his critics brandished meant to represent Justice Jackson's view, not his own. There is good reason to disbelieve him. See Brad Snyder and John Q. Barrett, *Citizen Dissenter from Brown: Rehnquist and the Meaning of His Lost 1955 Letter About Jackson* (forthcoming); and Richard Kluger, *Simple Justice: The History of* Brown v. Board of Education *and Black America's Struggle for Equality* (1975), 606–609.

Higginbotham, a black jurist Johnson had appointed to the federal trial bench. LBJ reportedly dismissed the suggestion: "The only two people who have ever heard of Judge Higginbotham are you and his momma. When I appoint a nigger to the [Supreme Court], I want everyone to know he's a nigger."[1]

Segregationists tried all they could to discredit Marshall. Insinuating that the nominee knew too little constitutional history to be a good justice, South Carolina's Senator Strom Thurmond peppered Marshall with all sorts of arcane questions. Seeking to impugn Marshall's fairness, Mississippi's Senator James Eastland asked whether he was prejudiced against Southern whites. In the end Marshall was confirmed by a comfortable margin, 69 to 11.

When nominating Clarence Thomas, President George Bush the Elder, like LBJ, refrained from saying publicly what was obvious—that the nominee's race had much to do with the selection.* Race, however, was central to the most embarrassing confirmation hearing in all of American history. Anita Hill, a subordinate of Thomas's at the U.S. Department of Education and the Equal Employment Opportunity Commission, alleged that he had harassed her sexually. He denied her allegation and charged that he was the victim of "a high-tech lynching." The debate surrounding the hearings revealed an intraracial dispute. Some blacks opposed Thomas, believing that he would vote against the interest of African Americans. Other blacks supported him, believing that once he gained the security afforded by confirmation he would vote "the right way" (or that, in any event, it was better to have a

---

* Writing in the immediate aftermath of Thomas's nomination, Christopher Edley, Jr., then a professor at Harvard Law School, remarked facetiously: "I give President Bush credit for taking the value of diversity into account in his selection . . . but why in heaven's name can't the president just admit it? . . . Only color could jump [Thomas] ahead of such conventionally impressive [conservative figures as Kenneth Starr and Laurence Silberman]." "Doubting Thomas: Law, Politics and Hypocrisy," *Washington Post*, July 7, 1991.

black right-wing justice than a white right-wing justice).[2] Thomas was confirmed by a narrow margin, 52 to 48.

The nomination and confirmation of Sonia Sotomayor highlighted the inspiring personal sojourn of a driven, resourceful, disciplined woman who worked her way up from working-class obscurity and, with the assistance of influential talent scouts, entered the most elite circles of the legal profession. Her elevation, however, has a wider significance. It reflects and reinforces the steadily emerging influence of Latinos in American society.[3] Just as the selection of Roger Taney, Louis Brandeis, Thurgood Marshall, and Sandra Day O'Connor signaled new levels of acceptance for Catholics, Jews, blacks, and women, the seating of Sotomayor signals a new level of prestige for Latinos.

Sotomayor's confirmation hearing, however, was hardly uplifting. To the contrary, it displayed how the confirmation ritual as currently practiced besmirches virtually everyone involved.*

Let's begin with the president. In announcing his selection, he stated that he was looking for nominees who understood "that a judge's job is to interpret, not make, law."[4] That formulation, a way of extolling so-called judicial restraint, was a sop to conservatives, a way of evincing accommodation without, in Obama's view, giving up anything of substance. The problem is that Obama did give up something of substance. By repeating the slogan that a judge's job is to interpret and not make law, Obama validated a hackneyed and hollow claim that confuses the public about the realities of judging. Of course judges "make law." Of course they make policy

---

* Then-professor Elena Kagan complained in 1995 that "when the Senate ceases to engage nominees in meaningful discussion of legal issues, the confirmation process takes on an air of vacuity and farce." "Confirmation Messes, Old and New," *University of Chicago Law Review* 62 (1995): 919, 920. Kagan's own confirmation hearing took on that very air, exhibiting several of the same serious deficiencies that characterized the Sotomayor hearing. See, e.g., Roger Simon, " 'Vapid'? 'Hollow'? Kagan Nailed It," Politico.com, June 30, 2010.

choices. Of course they make rulings that reflect and advance their ideological preferences. That is why selecting the personnel who occupy positions of judicial power matters. To suggest otherwise is simply to nourish the misleading but deep-seated mythology that Senator Jeff Sessions invoked when, while hectoring Sotomayor, he declared that "politics has no place in the courtroom."*[5] It is the mythology reflected in the widespread journalistic convention that labels the executive and legislative branches of the federal government as "political" in contrast with the "apolitical" judicial branch, or that portrays the judiciary as outside of the government altogether. It is the mythology that Chief Justice John Roberts, Jr., deployed at his confirmation hearings when he likened judges to umpires. "I will remember that it's my job [as a judge] to call balls and strikes and not to pitch or bat," Roberts vowed. "I come . . . with no agenda. I have no platform. Judges are not politicians."[6] Of course, Roberts's performance as a justice belies his claim. He is, as Professor Christopher Eisgruber notes, "an odd sort of umpire"— one who consistently calls the key pitches the conservatives' way.[7]

In announcing the Sotomayor selection, Obama echoed Roberts, saying that he sought a nominee who would "approach decisions without any particular ideology or agenda."[8] Such a claim is literally incredible. Did the president really not care whether the nominee was essentially a liberal? Of course he cared (and should have cared), which is why the only jurists he considered seriously were people who are within the liberal camp. He cared but refrained from saying so. George Bush openly said that he preferred conservative jurists. By doing so he reinforced the

---

* "There is a delicious irony in Judge Sonia Sotomayor's confirmation hearings, in which a candidate who would never have been nominated by a Republican president is being attacked by fiercely partisan Republicans and defended by fiercely partisan Democrats—all of them solemnly intoning the mantra that politics has no place in the judicial process." Professor William R. Andersen, "Letter to the Editor," *New York Times*, July 15, 2009.

legitimacy of being a conservative in the public's mind. Obama, by contrast, took care to avoid championing liberalism in the judiciary, thereby contributing to its continued marginalization and weakness.

Obama did say that he was looking for a nominee with the experience of "being tested by obstacles and barriers, by hardship and misfortune, [and] ultimately overcoming those barriers."[9] Taken literally, this criterion does little or no screening in that *everyone* is tested at some point by obstacles and misfortunes. The criterion, however, was not meant to be taken literally. It was meant to signal, without expressly saying so, that Obama was being attentive to the claims of gender, ethnic, and racial diversity. The "barriers" he had in mind were social barriers erected by sexism, racism, nativism, and class privilege.

There are a variety of problems with Obama's position. By refraining from discussing claims for gender or racial diversity openly (while responding to such claims in action), Obama left undisturbed the pall of illegitimacy that conservatives have effectively placed over systemic efforts aimed at advancing women, blacks, Latinos, and others who have long been marginalized. Noting that Obama had "shied away from stating the obvious: that Sotomayor was picked in part because she is a Hispanic woman," Jeffrey Toobin of *The New Yorker* maintained that there was "no need for such reticence. Earlier Presidents didn't apologize for preserving the geographic balance, and this one need not be reluctant to acknowledge that Hispanics, the nation's fastest-growing ethnic group . . . deserve a place at this most exclusive table for nine."[10]

Toobin was right in arguing that Obama should have been more forthright in admitting that race* and gender played a role in

---

* Considerable confusion surrounds the characterization of Latinos. The United States Census Bureau, for example, characterizes Latinos as an ethnic group. Some scholars, however, insist that Latinos should be viewed as a race. See, e.g., Ian F. Haney-Lopez,

his selection of Sotomayor. Toobin, however, is wrong in suggesting that a mere invocation of past practice regarding geographical diversity would suffice as a politically and intellectually tenable strategy. Not all discriminations are the same. Geographical discriminations are not as fraught as gender and racial discriminations. Furthermore, the representational theory to which Toobin alludes, though popular in some quarters, is not without difficulties. If Latinos "deserve" a place at the Supreme Court on account of their large numbers, are Jews and Asian Americans "undeserving" of places because of their small numbers? And what about Catholics? Six of the nine justices, including Sotomayor, are Catholic. Are six "too many" given the percentage of Catholics in the population as a whole?

Obama should have been more candid in explaining his choice. Doing so would have been politically feasible. He clearly had sufficient support in the Senate to assure Sotomayor's confirmation absent the revelation of some personal scandal or other disability. From the safety of that support he should have acknowledged that a benefit of nominating Sotomayor was that elevating her would serve to repudiate in a highly visible way the baleful notion that certain people, because of their gender or race, are less welcome than others in the higher circles of governmental authority. While doubts about this fundamental proposition exist, it will be appropriate to take special care to guarantee the presence of women and racial minorities in governing bodies that have heretofore been almost completely monopolized by white men.

"Race, Ethnicity, Erasure: The Salience of Race to LatCrit Theory," *California Law Review* 85 (1997): 1143, and "How the Census Counts Hispanics," *Daedalus* 134 (2005): 42. See generally Richard Delgado, Juan F. Perea, and Jean Stefancic, *Latinos and the Law: Cases and Materials* (2008), 110–116; Jorge J. E. Garcia, ed., *Race or Ethnicity: On Black and Latino Identity* (2007). I describe Latinos as a "race" for purposes of this discussion because it seems to be the term that best reflects the usages and sentiments on display among the contending factions that most shaped the struggle over the Sotomayor nomination.

Beyond evasiveness, another problem with Obama's stated rationale for selecting Sotomayor resides in the way in which he portrayed "experience" as one of his criteria. Obama nourished a widespread tendency to misunderstand and overvalue "experience" as a resource. According to Obama, experience "can give a person a common touch and a sense of compassion, an understanding of how the world works and how ordinary people live."[11] Yes, experience can facilitate valuable traits. But there are numerous examples of people who have suffered from deprivation and prejudice and apparently derived little useful insight from the experience. Justice Clarence Thomas famously experienced impoverishment and bigotry. But the lessons he draws hardly evince "a sense of compassion." Obama has harshly (and rightly) criticized Thomas as a jurist. But Justice Thomas has in abundance precisely the sort of experience that Obama seemed to laud in introducing Sotomayor. Thomas's career highlights the erratic relationship between experience, knowledge, perspective, and judgment. A certain experience in one person's hands can be a source of enlightenment. That same experience in another person's hands can be a source of myopia. What matters is not experience per se but what people make of whatever experience they happen to have had.

The most important thing to consider in assessing a nominee for the Supreme Court is that person's political character—the values that will guide her votes in the years to come in the cases that matter most. On the basis of her record, what knowledgeable observers have said about her, her enemies' objections, and the company she keeps, I have the impression that Sotomayor will be a dependable liberal jurist—attentive to individual rights, solicitous of redistributionist public policies, protective of federal authority vis-à-vis claims of states' rights, and supportive of groups that suffer from social prejudice. The extent to which she proves to be a consistent, thoughtful liberal jurist is the extent to which Obama ought to be praised—a judgment that will have to await Sotomayor's maturation as a justice (though the early returns seem promising).

Liberals are right to be concerned over Obama's publicly expressed minimization of ideology as an ingredient in his calculus of selection.* They can only hope that this is merely a strategic feint and not the manifestation of a silly willingness to leave to chance the likely future votes of a person who, as a justice, will represent one-ninth of the living American Constitution. Liberals pray that Obama did not make and will not make the sort of "error" that George Bush the Elder made when he elevated David Souter to the Court only to see Souter comport himself in a fashion counter to the hopes and expectations of his sponsors. Obama, unfortunately, has given liberals cause to worry insofar as he sometimes seems insufficiently committed to reclaiming the ideological ground in jurisprudential affairs that has been lost to conservatism since Richard Nixon's presidency. Even after taking into account the requirement of senatorial confirmation in a context of Republican obstructionism, Obama seems all too restrained in the exercise of his power of judicial nomination. Reagan and the two Bushes were consistently willing to reach much further to the right than Clinton or Obama have been willing to reach to the left in tapping judicial nominees. Yes, Reagan and the Bushes were occasionally defeated, as with the Senate's negative vote on Robert Bork. But even in defeat the conservatives gained ground. By going down fighting, conservative administrations lifted the morale of the conservative movement and showed everyone that they were truly committed to certain ideological tenets. Sometimes idealism is

---

* See Jeffrey Toobin, "Bench Press: Are Obama's Judges Really Liberals?," *The New Yorker*, September 21, 2009.

pragmatic. Obama could use a bit more idealism in selecting and pushing his judicial nominations.*

Sotomayor is an able, experienced jurist whose primary claim to distinction thus far resides in her "up from the barrio" biography, particularly her status as an important Latino "first." In the struggle over her confirmation, the two most consequential challenges she faced were a meritocratic critique and an ideological critique.

The meritocratic critique charged that Sotomayor did not "deserve" the post because she was merely an ordinary jurist, lacking the distinction expected of the nation's highest court. An important intervention on this front was an article by Jeffrey Rosen, the liberal legal-affairs editor of *The New Republic*. The article was written *before* Obama's nomination, when Sotomayor was widely rumored to be on the president's short list. Rosen aired complaints against her that reverberated loudly during the debate over her confirmation. He wrote:

> There are . . . many reservations about Sotomayor. Over the past few weeks, I've been talking to a range of people who have worked with her, nearly all of them former law clerks for other judges on the Second Circuit or former federal prosecutors in New York. Most are Democrats and all of them want President Obama to appoint a judicial star of the highest intellectual caliber who has the potential to change the direction of the court. . . . They expressed questions about her temperament, her judicial craftsmanship, and most of all, her ability to provide an intellectual counterweight to the conservative justices, as well as a clear liberal alternative.

---

* See the open letter to President Obama written by Professor Geoffrey Stone of the University of Chicago Law School, which requested that the administration "act with far more energy and dispatch in the vitally important task of nominating and confirming federal judges and that he select judges that would counteract the conservatism of Republican appointees." "Obama's Judges," HuffingtonPost.com, March 2, 2010.

The most consistent concern was that Sotomayor, although an able lawyer, was "not that smart."*[12]

There is a big difference between what Rosen actually said in his article and what combatants in the looming confirmation battle stated that he said. For one thing, although his article was entitled "The Case Against Sotomayor"—a title that he did not choose—Rosen took no definitive position and drew attention to the tentativeness of his impressions. "I haven't read enough of Sotomayor's opinions," he wrote, "to have a confident sense of them, nor have I talked to enough of Sotomayor's detractors and supporters to get a fully balanced picture of her strengths."[13] These caveats, however, did not stop conservative opponents of the nomination from using Rosen's article as a weapon of discreditation. A blogger at *The National Review* posted segments of the Rosen piece and then added, "Oof. So she's dumb and obnoxious. Got it."[14] A fellow *National Review* blogger joined in: "Judge Sotomayor may indeed be dumb and obnoxious; but she's also female and Hispanic, and those are things that count nowadays."[15]

Rosen's intention was far different from that of the right-wing polemicists who cited him. His aim was to question whether the administration could nominate a candidate better able than Sotomayor to advance a liberal judicial philosophy. Their aim was to stop or hobble Sotomayor by any means, fair or foul, because they perceived her to be a liberal. Rosen never said that Sotomayor was unqualified to be a justice. He did indicate, though, that in his view she was not as able as other potential candidates to be a stirring,

---

* That criticisms similar to those aired by Rosen were believed by influential liberals and conveyed to Obama directly is demonstrated by a letter written to the president by Harvard law professor Lawrence Tribe. Seeking to dissuade Obama from nominating Sotomayor, Tribe remarked that "she's not nearly as smart as she seems to think she is" and that "her reputation for being something of a bully could well make her liberal impulses backfire." See Al Kamen, "Lawrence Tribe Unfiltered on Sonia Sotomayor," *Washington Post*, October 28, 2010.

influential, crusading liberal justice. If forced to choose between a liberal-leaning centrist with moderate talent who happened to be a Latina, and a robust liberal with greater talent who happened to be a white man or white woman, Rosen favored the latter. But that discussion is not the one that burst into public notice in the spring and summer of 2009. It was cut off when Obama made his choice. Once he selected Sotomayor, most liberals, including Rosen, supported her against right-wing assault.

Right-wing polemicists typically omitted Rosen's complaint that Sotomayor was less demonstrably liberal than other potential nominees; that criticism would have undercut their claim that Sotomayor was a far-left judicial activist. Instead, they portrayed Rosen as having questioned her competence for a Supreme Court appointment. At the same time, they used Rosen's ideological affiliation to add weight to the charges against Sotomayor, arguing essentially that doubts about her fitness *must* have a substantial basis if a liberal like Rosen was saying as much.

The insinuation was preposterous that intellectual standards would be lowered if Sotomayor was elevated to the Supreme Court.* She did not merely attend elite schools for her undergraduate and legal educations; she *excelled* at them. In college she was inducted into Phi Beta Kappa, graduated summa cum laude, and awarded the Pyne Prize, the most prestigious award that Princeton University bestows upon an undergraduate. At Yale Law School she served as an officer on the editorial board of the

---

* Refuting "the whispers of intellectual inadequacy" directed against Sotomayor, Ellis Cose observed that "it's a sure bet that Ivy League recruiters would have coveted even a white male who had overcome what she had (childhood diabetes, a father's death, life in the projects and a childhood spent speaking a foreign language) and gone on to compile a brilliant academic record at a competitive high school. And had that male graduated summa [from Princeton], his accomplishments would have been celebrated not questioned." See Ellis Cose, "Caricature Witness: The Ugly Assumptions Behind the Case Against Judge Sotomayor," *Newsweek*, June 8, 2009.

Yale Law Journal. She served as a prosecutor in the Manhattan District Attorney's Office, a shop known for its exacting standards and outstanding alumni. She then attained partnership in a firm before being named to the United States District Court by President Bush, and to the U.S. Court of Appeals by President Clinton. Sotomayor's scholastic and professional record is admirable by any measure. It surely signaled that she possesses abundantly the requisite intellectual strength to carry out the duties of a justice. It was fully as impressive as the records of most of the sitting justices' when they showed up for their confirmation hearings.

In defending Sotomayor against wrongful attacks I want to avoid the all-too-common habit of mythologizing the justices, acting as if appointment to the Supreme Court stems from some sort of meritocratic contest, the winners of which are awarded seats. That is not the way it works. With few exceptions (Oliver Wendell Holmes, Jr., Louis Brandeis, and Benjamin Cardozo come to mind) justices are not the most (or even among the most) learned or brilliant jurists in the country. They are simply the most powerful. Their power elicits sycophancy that bestows upon them unearned intellectual honor. Lawyers or judges who merely had thoughts one day have a "jurisprudence" the day after they assume office as justices. I am not claiming, then, that Sotomayor is a legal philosopher or technician of the first rank. I am merely contending that, in terms of professional accomplishment, she was fully as qualified for a seat on the Court as, say, John Roberts, Anthony Kennedy, Antonin Scalia, or Samuel Alito.

The white male justices, however, have the benefit of something often denied to Sotomayor. Because of gender and racial privilege, the white men reap the benefit of an assumption of merit conferred by their certifications and positions, an assumption that hardly anyone questioned during their confirmation proceedings. By contrast, hostile observers insistently questioned the bona fides of Sotomayor's badges of merit. A reason given for doing so was affirmative action, the likelihood that, because of her race and gender, she had received preferential treatment in competition for educational and professional advancement, thereby inflating her real standing among peers.

Although gender has long been part of many affirmative-action programs, positive discrimination on a gender basis typically creates less controversy than positive discrimination on a racial basis. In 1980, candidate Ronald Reagan promised that if elected president, "one of the first Supreme Court vacancies in [his] administration [would] be filled by the most qualified woman [he could] find."[16] When Reagan won he fulfilled his pledge, nominating Sandra Day O'Connor, who became the first female justice. Announcing his nomination, Reagan said that he had "long believed that the time has come for the highest court in our land to include not only distinguished men but distinguished women as well."[17] This was an explicit set-aside on the basis of gender for one of the most coveted positions in American government. Few objected, however, to Reagan's promise or to his fulfillment of it. I suspect that the reaction would have been different, more skeptical, if not hostile, had race been the basis of the preference. There were, to be sure, some observers who grumbled about Reagan's quota. Asked about Reagan's pledge, retiring justice Potter Stewart remarked that it would be an "insult to the Court and to the appointee and to the American public to appoint someone just because he or she is not a white male."[18] The progressive magazine *The Nation* also cast aspersions upon Reagan's choice:

> In the general satisfaction—which we share—over the selection of a woman, no one seems to have noticed that in choosing Judge O'Connor, President Reagan has overridden some fundamental conservative principles and basic policy of his

administration: for the highest Court in the land he has picked a person barely qualified for the post, almost entirely because of her sex and not on the basis of individual merit.[19]

Sotomayor, then, wasn't the first woman to be deprecated as an affirmative-action nominee. She was considerably more harried on this front than O'Connor, however, and in contrast to O'Connor, it was Sotomayor's race rather than her gender that proved to be the focal point of debate.

Anti-affirmation-action skeptics contend that it would be naïve to give Sotomayor's credentials full credit. For the sake of realism, they argue, her credentials ought to be discounted to take into account affirmative-action inflation. This belief prompted Rush Limbaugh to refer to Sotomayor sneeringly as "an affirmative action case extraordinaire,"[20] provoked Patrick J. Buchanan to call her dismissively "a quota queen,"[21] prodded Fred Barnes into saying disparagingly that "she's one of those who has benefited from affirmative action over the years tremendously."[22] Asserting that her selection was "a bad mistake," Robert Bork averred that "her record is not particularly distinguished. Far from it. And it is unusual to nominate somebody who states flatly that she was the beneficiary of affirmative action."*[23]

What should one make of the negative labeling of Sotomayor as an affirmative-action nominee?

First, it bears recalling that there is nothing new about charges of inferiority being flung at people of color; the practice long predates affirmative action. Rumors of inferiority were used to

---

* Judge Bork is dyspeptic when it comes to assessing candidates for the Supreme Court—a characteristic that probably stems, at least in part, from his own unhappy experience as a rejected nominee. After having ridiculed Sotomayor, Bork added, "But I can't believe she will be any worse than some recent white male appointees." See Stuart Taylor, "The View from 1987," *Newsweek*, June 20, 2009.

justify slavery and segregation. They have also been used to fight rearguard actions against every advance made by colored people in America. Two egregious examples should suffice to anchor the point. When black baseball players, such as the extraordinary Satchel Paige, were barred from the white major leagues, one of the rationales used to defend the exclusion was that black players simply weren't good enough. When Thurgood Marshall, one of the greatest lawyers in all of American history, was nominated for a seat on the Supreme Court by President Lyndon Johnson in 1967, segregationists maintained that he lacked the knowledge and skill to be a justice.

Second, cries of "reverse discrimination" have a long, discreditable history. Long before the arrival of affirmative action, the ideological ancestors of Rush Limbaugh and Pat Buchanan complained loudly about what they saw as the chilling prospect of a racial reversal if whites did not carefully maintain their dominance. Consider the rhetoric and logic of President Andrew Johnson, who vetoed the nation's first federal civil-rights law, the Civil Rights Act of 1866. This law made citizens of anyone born in the United States and required states to grant to all persons the same rights that whites possessed to sue, testify, enter into contracts, or own property. Such provisions, according to Johnson, were tantamount to discrimination *against* whites. After all, he reasoned, whites had never been the beneficiaries of a federal law of this sort.* Or consider the language of the Supreme Court when it

---

* By according citizenship to all persons, including former slaves, born in the United States, the Civil Rights Act, President Johnson complained, constituted a discrimination against foreign-born immigrants who faced a probationary period before becoming eligible for naturalization. The new law, he wrote, "proposes a discrimination against large numbers of intelligent, worthy and patriotic foreigners and in favor of the negro." Similarly, Johnson denounced the "discriminating protection" afforded to blacks by requiring that they be clothed with the same rights as whites to contract, own property, sue, and testify in court. These and kindred provisions, Johnson warned, "operate in favor of

invalidated the public-accommodations provision of the final civil-rights law of the Reconstruction era. In 1883, the Court chastised blacks and their allies for seeking what the justices perceived as illicit immunity from the regular workings of the legal system. "When a man has emerged from slavery . . ." the Court declared, "there must be some stage in the progress of his elevation when he takes the rank of a mere citizen, and ceases to be the special favorite of the laws"—this when blacks were being subjected to ruthless efforts to reduce them to serfdom. "Reverse discrimination," "special privileges," and "preferential treatment" are thus traditional expressions of hostility or contempt and time-tested rhetorical tools useful for inciting and directing resentment against reforms aimed at advancing the fortunes of colored people. For Buchanan, Limbaugh, and others of like mind, affirmative action is not only a target of complaint; it is also a convenient cudgel with which to go about their business of beating back challenges to the racial status quo.

Third, while many enemies of affirmative action insist upon putting a deflating asterisk on the résumés of racial-minority beneficiaries, they avoid putting a deflating asterisk on the résumés of whites whose accomplishments were achieved against a backdrop of antiblack exclusions.* No racial issue regarding merit or fairness intruded upon public discourse for most of the period when

---

the colored against the white race." See Andrew Johnson, "Veto of the Civil Rights Bill," March 26, 1867, available at TeachingAmericanHistory.org.

Johnson's veto was overridden by Congress.

* Note the comments of Patrick Buchanan for a vivid illustration of the mind-set that sees just deserts in the domination of white men and illicit favoritism or some other baleful influence in the promotion of those who are not white men. Asked about the long-lasting monopolization of the Supreme Court by white men, Buchanan refused to concede one iota of disquiet, declaring that, after all, "white men were 100 percent of the people who signed the Declaration of Independence" and "100 percent of the people who died at Gettysburg." See Noel Shepperd, "Pat Buchanan and Rachel Maddow Debate Sonia Sotomayor," NewsBusters.org, July 17, 2009.

whites monopolized the ranks of Supreme Court justices. *That* appalling outcome seems to have been acceptable, or at least tolerable, to many of the most vociferous opponents of affirmative action. Their racial sensibilities are only affronted when the white monopoly is challenged.

Hostility to the advancement of people of color is by no means the full story of opposition to affirmative action. Among the ranks of opponents are also people who vocally resisted Jim Crow segregation and other forms of open, formal racial hierarchy. That does not change the fact, however, that prominent among affirmative action's detractors are those who are opposed to virtually *any* policy that undermines white racial privilege. For them, the mantra of color blindness is merely an expedient tool for continuing the long struggle to keep whites on top and "others" below.

Fourth, supporters of affirmative action should acknowledge that it (like any social policy) does exact costs. Stigmatization of affirmative action's beneficiaries is one such expense. When onlookers suspect that a person has been helped by affirmative action, they do often discount that person's credentials to some extent. A poignant reflection of this devaluation is the indignation that many beneficiaries of affirmative action display when asked whether they are beneficiaries. A reason many resent being seen as such is that they know association with that status will devalue their hard-earned credentials.*

Often contributing to the indignation is a belief that the discounting is racist or otherwise illicit. Is this belief valid? It all depends on the circumstances. Imagine a scenario in which an airline announced that, because of the historical absence of

---

* For a particularly insightful description and analysis of this feeling, see Stephen L. Carter, *Reflections of an Affirmative Action Baby* (1991).

blacks from piloting, it had decided to install fifty blacks as pilots *immediately*, notwithstanding the fact that while a traditional requirement for that post entailed acquiring a thousand hours of flight training, the average amount of flight training acquired by the fifty beneficiaries of the new program was only five hundred hours. Let's also suppose that there existed no clear, easy way to differentiate between affirmative-action beneficiaries and black pilots certified before the new policy. Under this scenario, in the absence of specific knowledge about the career of any individual pilot, it would make perfect sense to be uneasy about any black person piloting that airline's aircraft. This hypothetical raises the specter of relatively undertrained people being promoted to a sensitive position that acutely affects the public welfare.* It underscores real dangers that accentuate why it is important to design affirmative action smartly, making sure to minimize the drawbacks that attend such programs.

In the case of Sotomayor, however, there was no good reason to suspect her intellectual and professional bona fides. By the time of her nomination she had been tested repeatedly in tough, exacting roles. With respect to college admission, her record may well have been less strong in certain dimensions than the records of some who unsuccessfully vied for a coveted seat in Princeton's freshman class in 1970. But the applicant from the Bronx was demonstrably highly motivated and clearly capable of performing satisfactorily the tasks that Princeton demanded. More important, after having shone spectacularly at Princeton, and performed ably in law school, she created an estimable record for herself as an attorney and a judge. All of that should have stilled the anxious talk about her status as an affirmative-action baby.

---

* Cf. *Spurlock v. United Airlines* 475 F.2d 216 (CA 10 1973) (affirming dismissal of lawsuit challenging college degree and flight hours requirements that had a disproportionate adverse effect on blacks seeking to become airline pilots).

Sotomayor was also attacked for her racial politics. The case principally cited to exemplify her bias was *Ricci v. DeStefano*. That case featured a white working-class plaintiff who claimed that he was victimized by a New Haven, Connecticut, bureaucracy that thwarted his promotion as a firefighter in order to give black candidates a better chance of getting ahead. When Ricci and a class of other white or Latino candidates outperformed black test-takers, city officials disregarded the scores, scrapped that test, and searched for another that might generate a more "racially diverse" outcome. Alleging "reverse discrimination," Ricci sued. A federal trial court ruled against him. That ruling was upheld summarily by a three-judge panel of the Second Circuit Court of Appeals, a panel on which Sotomayor sat. Although several judges sought to have the case reconsidered by the entire circuit, their efforts fell short—but not without attracting the attention of the United States Supreme Court. In a ruling handed down soon before Sotomayor's confirmation hearing, the Supreme Court reversed the lower court decision. Detractors, of course, seized upon the high court's ruling as evidence that Sotomayor was unfit to join it as an associate justice. They argued that she had gotten the case wrong, that she had therefore facilitated reverse racial discrimination against a hardworking white man, and that she had done all of this sneakily in a way designed to avoid review by the Supreme Court.

Sotomayor responded that she was merely following precedent in voting as she did. She did not argue with the validity of the Court's conclusion. She and her White House handlers probably believed that doing so would be impolitic since her opponents would likely portray a substantive defense as only further evidence of her headstrong disregard for the law. She could rightly have noted, however, that the Court was deeply divided over the matter; it ruled for Ricci only by the slimmest of margins, five to four. If Sotomayor was wrong and lawless, she had plenty of judicial company. Furthermore, of course, the Court is not always "correct." The same people who derided Sotomayor for taking a position subsequently rejected by the Supreme Court are only too happy to denounce the Court's conclusions on other issues, such as abortion or flag burning.

Another complaint arose from claims Sotomayor made in speeches about the relationship of her racial and gender identity to her judicial performance. On a number of occasions she asserted that her race and gender had inevitably influenced her judging. "I accept," she declared in a speech at a law school, "that our experiences as women and people of color affect our decisions."[24] Such statements, as mere description, caused relatively little controversy, as most observers conceded that one's background will inevitably condition one's performance as a judge (though the effect of given conditions on particular individuals can vary tremendously). What did generate controversy were remarks that not only acknowledged the influence of her racial and gender identity but applauded that influence, portraying her Latina identity not as a potential impediment to objectivity but as a resource for enlightened decision-making. As she put it in words repeated time and again during her confirmation grilling, "I would hope that a wise Latina woman with the richness of her experiences would more often than not reach a better conclusion than a white male who hasn't lived that life."[25]

This remark generated much criticism. Newt Gingrich invoked it as a basis for calling her a "racist"; Rush Limbaugh, as a basis for calling her a "reverse racist." Some of Sotomayor's supporters maintained gamely that she was merely stating inartfully the obvious: that one's background inevitably affects one's judgments (even though she was clearly saying more than that). Other supporters reminded the country that during his confirmation hearing Samuel Alito had claimed that he consciously thought of his

Italian immigrant forebears when considering immigration cases and maintained that doing so leavened his deliberations with an empathy that was good for rendering decisions that were both just and lawful. If what he said was permissible, they argued, why not what she said? Still others took the position that what Sotomayor stated in a speech or, indeed, a series of speeches is far less indicative of her future course as a justice than the voluminous record she had made as a judge—a record that contains little or no sign of the aggressive identity politics to which her detractors fearfully alluded.

In the end, for her own part, Sotomayor retreated from the positions for which she had come under fire. Dismissing her "wise Latina" line as "a rhetorical flourish that fell flat," Sotomayor expressly rejected the notion "that any ethnic, racial, or gender group has an advantage in sound judging," adding "that every person has an equal opportunity to be a good and wise judge regardless of their background or life experiences."[26] She even eschewed the purely descriptive claim that a judge's socialization will inevitably affect her judgments, telling the Judiciary Committee that an important goal of the justice system was "to ensure that the personal biases and prejudices of a judge [never] influence the outcome of a case."[27] Reminded of President Obama's previous emphasis on "empathy" and "heart," nominee Sotomayor countered with, "I wouldn't approach the issue of judging the way the president does. . . . Judges cannot rely on what's in their heart. . . . The job of a judge is to apply the law." "My personal and professional experiences help me to listen and understand," Sotomayor told her inquisitors. But it is "the law always commanding the result in every case."[28]

Sotomayor acted rightly in renouncing her "wise Latina" remark. It is indefensible. It was clearly aimed at conveying the idea that, as a judge, a "wise Latina" would not only perform differently but better than those of some other background, particularly white, male Anglos. This was an assertion of racial and gender superiority that should have been challenged and that should have been retracted. It was galling, to say the least, to see Sotomayor hectored on this point by politicians whose own records are notably deficient in matters of social justice. I think here in particular of Senators Mitch McConnell of Kentucky and Jeff Sessions of Alabama, both of whom are typically indifferent to struggles for racial and gender equality but both of whom adopted a hostile stance toward Sotomayor, premised largely, so they claimed, on the basis of her "wise Latina" utterances. Their hypocrisy, however, does not lessen the wrongfulness of her remark.

Should Sotomayor have been rejected on account of her "wise Latina" statement? No. I believed her when she explained that her remark had been aimed at inspiring Latino listeners who too often suffer from feelings of marginalization and inferiority on predominantly white Anglo campuses. I believed her when she confessed that her comments amounted to a type of pandering to the perceived biases of at least some of her listeners—a way to establish credibility, authenticity, and solidarity with them. I believed Sotomayor when she repudiated her offending comment and feel confident in that belief because her life seems to be bereft of other indications that she really believes that certain people are more just, insightful, talented, or worthy than others on account of race, gender, or some kindred trait.

A number of observers remarked that a white man making an analogous comment would have received a harsher response. That is probably true. An apt revulsion against white supremacist beliefs and practices has made many Americans keenly sensitive to any actions or statements that even hint of adherence to any notion of white racial superiority. Many people, like me, gave Sotomayor a break they would not have given a white man because, against the backdrop of American history, suspicion of white supremacist sentiments appropriately occasions a more intense, unforgiving fear than that generated by other race-related suspicions. People should be on guard to resist *any* obnoxious racial sentiment. Given that in the United States the most influential and hurtful of the bad racial sentiments has been and remains white racial superiority, it makes sense to be more strict in dealing with that particular social malady. When Latinas have been on top for generations it will be time to be as impatient with Latina-oriented narcissism as many are currently and rightly impatient with white male narcissism.*

In situations like these there is a tendency to interpret statements in their worst light and to play "gotcha" with remarks that are uncharacteristic of the speaker. This tendency has been on display continuously—from the tendentious interpretations of Hillary Clinton's King-Johnson remark to the numerous allegations that John McCain was playing the race card against Barack Obama to the calls to censure Harry Reid for his "Negro dialect" comment. It is a good thing that people are intolerant of racial bigotry or even racial "insensitivity." It is a bad thing that this laudable development is being manipulated opportunistically.

Having acted rightly in repudiating the "wise Latina" quip, Sotomayor acted wrongly in repudiating statements she had previously made which recognized what ought to be obvious: that judges are indeed policymakers as they fill in legislative or constitutional gaps, make inferences from complicated evidentiary records, interpret vague terms ("equal protection," "due process"), and apply legislative and constitutional directives to new contexts unfore-

* Responding to Senator Lindsey Graham's remark that his career would have been over had he said something analogous to what Sotomayor said, the columnist Eugene Robinson replied, "That's true. But if Latinas had run the world for the last millennium, Sotomayor's career would be over, too." "Whose Identity Politics?," *Washington Post*, July 14, 2009.

seen by those who drafted or ratified the provisions being applied. In regurgitating the inanities that have become the expected responses of Supreme Court nominees, however, Sotomayor was simply following precedent. For a long time justices have solemnly pledged to interpret, not make, law, earnestly vowed to recognize the supposedly clear difference between law and politics, and somberly refrained from answering all sorts of questions about their beliefs on the grounds that offering answers would somehow compromise their ability to properly adjudicate cases that might come before them in the future. In other words, Sotomayor was not the first candidate for a justiceship to debase herself in the hopes of winning confirmation. At Thurgood Marshall's hearing, James Eastland, the chair of the Senate Judiciary Committee, asked the nominee whether he was aware that in an opinion he had authored as a court of appeals judge he had cited a book written by a communist. Marshall answered that he did not know of the author's affiliation and that if he had known he would *not* have cited the book.[29] This was, of course, a pathetic gesture. There are, after all, communists who have contributed brilliantly to the illumination of all sorts of subjects. In this instance, the person in question was Herbert Aptheker, an admirable and important figure in American historiography, and the book in question was *A Documentary History of the Negro People in the United States*, an instructive compilation of materials that is rightly offered in many research libraries.

The Sotomayor confirmation hearings made appallingly clear that such proceedings, as currently structured, are a ridiculous sham. As the journalist Howard Fineman bluntly but aptly observes, the hearings "make everyone involved look bad. They are worse than a waste of time, because they confuse the public about what the Supreme Court does and undermine respect for law and judges."[30] How could the hearings not undermine respect for judges as they lie *and are expected to lie* in order to secure confirmation? Previously Sotomayor had argued (correctly) that "policy is made" by appellate courts and that there is "no escape from choice in judging." At her confirmation hearing, however, Sotomayor voiced adherence to a very different conception of judging, a mechanistic jurisprudence "with the law always commanding the result in every case."[31] A possible explanation for this turnabout is that she had simply changed her mind. The more realistic is that she was displaying "confirmation conversion," saying whatever she calculated it was expedient to say regardless of what she actually believed. That the latter explanation caused little uproar* indicates the extent to which confirmation conversion has become yet another expected part of the ritual. "Supreme Court confirmation hearings," Fineman observes, "consist primarily of people saying things they do not mean. . . . This is not good advertising for the basic honesty of judges."[32]

The deepening racial integration of the government of the United States through the presence of its first Latino justice is a development worthy of applause. It is unfortunate, though, that this advance proceeded on such unsatisfactory terms even though Obama was probably stronger at that moment than he will be for the remainder of his presidency. After all, he was making an appointment in the first year of his term with a Senate that was

---

* To be sure, there were some observers who were deeply affronted. Professor Michael Louis Seidman remarked, for instance, that he

> was completely disgusted by Judge Sotomayor's testimony. . . . If she was not perjuring herself, she is intellectually unqualified to be on the Supreme Court. If she was perjuring herself, she is morally disqualified.

Professor Seidman clearly believed that Sotomayor was prevaricating. "What does it say about our legal system," he asked, "that in order to get confirmed Judge Sotomayor must tell the lies that she told . . . ?" Relenting a bit, he concluded, however, that perhaps she should be excused "because our official ideology about judging is so degraded that she would sacrifice a position on the Supreme Court if she told the truth." See "The Federalist Society Online Debate Series: The Sotomayor Nomination, Part II," July 13, 2009, at fed-soc.org.

controlled by a supermajority of fellow Democrats. That under such favorable circumstances Obama felt the need to cloak a liberal selection with conservative rhetoric* suggests that in the future, with diminished political weaponry, he and his nominees will be even less willing or able to challenge the status quo.

---

* See Amy Goldstein and Paul Kane, "Little for Liberals in Confirmation Hearings," *Washington Post*, July 19, 2009. Goldstein and Kane quoted Professor Geoffrey R. Stone, who said that the hearings "did serious damage to the cause of progressive thought in constitutional law," and Doug Kendall of the Constitutional Accountability Center, who complained that with the Sotomayor confirmation hearings "the progressive legal project [had] hit rock bottom." See also Terry Eastland, "Sotomayor v. Obama: A Pseudo Confirmation Conversion," *Weekly Standard*, July 27, 2009 ("the Sotomayor hearings have made it politically harder for Obama to advance via his nominees a judicial philosophy that . . . embraces some new 'constitutional vision,' one that seeks to address what he described during his campaign as the country's 'empathy . . . deficit' ").

7

Addressing Race "the Obama Way"

In February 2009, in a speech marking Black History Month, Attorney General Eric Holder chastised Americans for evading candid discussion of racial issues. "In things racial," he maintained, "we have always been and continue to be . . . essentially a nation of cowards." He posited that "if we are to make progress . . . we must feel comfortable enough with one another, and tolerant enough of each other, to have frank conversations about the racial matters that continue to divide us."[1] Perhaps the attorney general was following up on candidate Barack Obama's declaration that "race is an issue . . . this nation cannot afford to ignore." If this is what Holder was doing, he should be ridiculed for naïveté: after Obama made that statement in his "A More Perfect Union" address he dodged racial issues. He continued that tack after winning the White House, expressly distancing himself from his attorney general's remarks. President Obama has consistently attempted to evade racial issues. If he cannot avoid them, he reframes them, minimizing the racial element. If forced to confront a racial issue squarely, he does so in a fashion calculated to assuage the anxieties of whites. This is the Obama way.

To take a closer look at the Obama way, its virtues, vices, and consequences, let's consider a couple of revealing episodes: the arrest of Henry Louis Gates, Jr., and the "You lie!" outburst of Representative Joe Wilson.

On July 16, 2009, Sergeant James Crowley, a Cambridge, Massachusetts police officer, arrested Harvard University professor Henry Louis Gates, Jr., for "disorderly conduct." What led to the arrest was a scenario that sounds like a hypothetical drafted by a law professor for a final examination on criminal procedure. A neighbor who saw two men fiddling with the front door to Gates's house called the police, noting that the men might be engaged in a burglary. The men in question were, in fact, Gates himself and a driver who was ferrying the professor home from the airport. They were fiddling with the door because it was jammed. A few minutes after forcing his way in, Gates found himself on the receiving end of an investigation as Crowley asked him to step outside of the house and onto the porch. According to the arrest report, Gates replied, "No, I will not," and asked the officer to identify himself. The officer did so and informed Gates that he was investigating a report of a possible burglary in progress. At that point, according to Crowley, Gates questioned why the officer was demanding identification and suggested the answer: "Because I'm a black man in America?" Eventually, after telling Crowley that he didn't know who he was "messing" with, Gates showed the officer a Harvard identification card. As the officer was leaving the house, Gates repeatedly asked him for his name and accused him of being a racist. When the officer told Gates that he would speak with him outside the house, the professor said, according to Crowley, "I'll speak with your momma outside." As Crowley was leaving, Gates followed, continuing to yell that the officer was racially biased. When, after repeated warnings, Gates refused to "calm down" and continued yelling, Crowley arrested the professor in front of "police officers and citizens who appeared surprised and alarmed by Gates's outburst."*

---

* See Cambridge Police Department Incident Report #9005127, July 16, 2009. See also Charles Ogletree, *The Presumption of Guilt: The Arrest of Henry Louis Gates Jr. and Race, Class and Crime in America* (2010).

Almost immediately the arrest emerged as a major news story. It became even more prominent when, during a news conference about health-care reform, President Obama was asked for his opinion about the dispute. By that time, charges against Gates had been dropped and local officials and the professor had issued a joint statement calling the incident "regrettable and unfortunate."[2] When asked what the episode said about race relations in America, President Obama noted that Gates was a friend and that therefore he might be biased. He then went on to say:

> Now, I don't know, not having been there and not seeing all the facts, what role race played in that, but I think it's fair to say, number one, that any of us would be pretty angry; number two, that the Cambridge police acted stupidly in arresting someone when there was already proof that they were in their own home; and, number three, what I think we know, separate and apart from this incident, is that there is a long history in this country of African-Americans and Latinos being stopped by law enforcement disproportionately. And that's just a fact.

Obama mentioned later that the character of the controversy following the incident was "a sign of how race remains a factor in this society."[3]

Obama did not charge that Gates's arrest was racially discriminatory. He did acknowledge historical tensions between law-enforcement officials and blacks and Latinos. But with respect to this particular altercation the president expressly stated that he did not know whether race had played a role in the arrest. He merely ventured the opinion that "the Cambridge police acted stupidly in arresting someone when there was already proof that they were in their own home."

Even that relatively mild rebuke, however, was sufficient to ignite a powerful backlash that was laced with racial overtones. Within forty-eight hours, President Obama was backtracking. He announced that he had personally called and spoken with Crowley, who impressed him as an "outstanding police officer and a good man"—a far cry from the characterization that he "acted stupidly." The president also told reporters that he wished he had calibrated his words differently because the language he had used had ratcheted up the controversy and suggested, inaccurately, that he meant to malign the Cambridge Police Department or Sergeant Crowley. "To the extent that my choice of words didn't illuminate, but rather contributed to more media frenzy, I think that was unfortunate."[4]

Obama tried to make it seem that he was *not* backing down. "I continue to believe," Obama declared, "that there was an overreaction in pulling Professor Gates out of his home to the station." But—and here Obama voiced a countervailing criticism of Gates for the first time—"I also continue to believe . . . that Professor Gates probably overreacted as well. My sense is you've got two good people in a circumstance in which neither of them were able to resolve the incident in the way it should have been resolved and the way they would have liked it to be resolved." That the incident garnered so much attention, Obama remarked, is "testimony to the fact that those are issues that are still very sensitive. . . . Even when you've got a police officer who has a fine track record on racial sensitivity, interactions between police officers and the African-American community can sometimes be fraught with misunderstanding." Allowing that he hoped that the controversy would end up becoming "a teachable moment," Obama urged everyone "to focus on how we can generally improve relations between police officers and minority communities" and to "be a little more reflective in terms of what we can do to contribute to more unity." Rejecting the argument that he ought not to have become involved in what some saw as a purely local issue, Obama maintained that "contributing to constructive . . . understandings about [the race issue] is part of my portfolio." Several days later, following up on a suggestion initiated by Sergeant Crowley, the president hosted Gates and the officer at the White House for a chat over beer, an occasion dubbed the Beer Summit.

Whether Gates's behavior actually constituted "disorderly conduct" was never authoritatively determined. That the local prosecutor dropped the charges does not necessarily mean that the police were wrong. Deciding whether to prosecute involves somewhat different considerations than those involved in deciding whether to arrest. A prosecutor might conclude that while charges are warranted, a prosecution is unwise given competing demands for time, energy, and other resources. A decision to drop the charges, however, could also mean that the charges were judged to be ill-founded and likely to be rejected at trial.

My own impression is that the officer acted wrongly in arresting Gates. Surely "disorderly conduct" should require more than merely being rude to a police officer in public. Gates's real offense was not a statutory infraction but a breach of etiquette, what the columnist Clarence Page termed "contempt of cop."[5] The likely aim of the arrest was not to secure Gates for the purpose of determining whether he had committed an offense for which he should be punished, but to punish him by imposing upon him the indignities and inconveniences that attend arrest, including handcuffing, mug shots, negative publicity, and confinement in jail.

If my impression is correct, Sergeant Crowley acted wrongly, unlawfully, and alarmingly. Police ought not be permitted to create their own rules and then enforce them through the illicit use of their delegated power. It is noteworthy that, with some exceptions, conservatives in particular almost reflexively rally around the police in circumstances like the Crowley-Gates imbroglio despite their putative commitment to personal liberty, limited government, and attentiveness to the ever-present danger that public officials will succumb to corruption and tyranny. No government officials are more susceptible to these seductions than police officers. Yet our politicians and judges, abetted by a frightened, disorganized citizenry, routinely tolerate police misconduct.

I did not say, and cannot say, that Crowley acted in a racially discriminatory fashion. The record is too thin to make such a charge confidently. It would be foolhardy, however, to dismiss as wholly implausible the possibility that Crowley treated Gates differently than he would have treated a similarly situated white man.* Policies that posit coloredness itself as a sign of increased risk of criminality have been so pervasive, police actions meant to harass people of color have been so numerous, police deception has been so corrosive, that it should come as no surprise that many observers, including those with no penchant for injecting race into a dispute baselessly, believe that Officer Crowley's perception of Professor Gates's blackness played some hard-to-identify but appreciable role in the decision to arrest him.† Such a belief does not negate the possibility that other considerations were at work as well: Gates's own racially inflected perception of white policemen, his "You don't know who you're messing with" attitude, a recognition by both men of a large class and prestige gap between them,

---

* "I can't prove that if the Big Cheese in question had been a famous, brilliant Harvard professor who happened to be white . . . the outcome would have been different. I'd put money on it, though. Anybody wanna bet?" Eugene Robinson, "Pique and the Professor," *Washington Post*, July 25, 2009.

† After reading about Gates's arrest in a local newspaper, a police officer in Boston sent an e-mail to colleagues saying that had he been the officer on the scene he would not only have arrested Gates but would also have showered him with pepper spray. This officer referred to Professor Gates as a "banana-eating jungle monkey." The officer was immediately suspended. Maria Cramer, "Hearing Set for Officer in E-mail Case," *Boston Globe*, December 5, 2009.

the effect of onlookers whose very presence might have prompted the officer to feel still more keenly the need to display his authority. Race almost always works in conjunction with other factors; almost never nowadays does it generate a racially discriminatory decision on its own. It is important to note, though, that a decision is racially discriminatory even if race is not the only or even the dominant ingredient in the decision-making process. If a racial consideration is influential at all, the decision stemming from it can rightly be labeled as racially discriminatory.

Although Obama never claimed that the arrest was racially discriminatory—he only maintained that it was stupid—detractors nonetheless accused him of "playing the race card." And even some who absolved him of that particular sin nonetheless chastised him for getting involved in a local issue when, by his own admission, he lacked mastery over all the pertinent facts.

Was there anything wrong with what Obama said? I don't think so. He acknowledged that he was friendly with Professor Gates and that, at that point, the facts of the controversy were not altogether clear. He thereby put listeners on notice that he was partial and that any impressions he had were necessarily provisional. Some contend that he should have deferred comment since he admitted that he did not know everything relevant to the case. Seldom, however, does a person—even a president—know "all" of the facts pertinent to a given controversy. To demand full knowledge before speaking is to demand silence about most things.* Many who rallied to the side of Sergeant Crowley acted as if it was blasphemous for the president to criticize the action of a police officer. But why should that be? Why not criticize the police when they appear to have erred? Are they infallible?

---

* Most people know relatively little about Hitler, Stalin, or Pol Pot. The little they do know, however, provides a quite sufficient predicate for rightly damning these murderous tyrants.

Some supporters seem to think so. One official stated that the Cambridge Police Department would support Officer Crowley whatever was unearthed by investigation. In other words, some observers took the position that Officer Crowley was entitled to unconditional support. It is precisely that attitude that has helped create institutional arrangements and habits of mind that, to a dangerous extent, insulate police authorities from scrutiny and criticism, thereby encouraging a culture of police lawlessness.

Was there anything racial about Obama's backpedaling? Yes, there was. First, one of the ingredients fueling the fierce backlash that Obama sought to tamp down was the belief that the president had made common cause with Professor Gates in attributing a racial motive to the arrest. This belief was inaccurate; Obama, as we have seen, refrained from describing Crowley's conduct as racially discriminatory. But the misimpression was fanned by detractors who saw this episode as a wonderful opportunity to blacken Obama, to associate him with the likes of Al Sharpton and Jesse Jackson, to expose what they perceive as his carefully camouflaged prejudice. On a Fox News television panel Charles Krauthammer asserted that Obama "implied, and he does this always cleverly and without leaving a fingerprint, that [the arrest] was on account of racism."[6] Krauthammer did not point to anything the president said that attributed a racial motive to the arrest. He could not do so, for no such statement existed. Rather, he insisted that the president was making a charge of racism implicitly, deploying code to make his point. In other settings when observers complain with little or no evidence that politicians are making racial appeals in code, Krauthammer takes the complainants to task for demagoguery. Here, however, he did just the thing for which he has chastised others.

More provocative than Krauthammer's comments were remarks offered by Glenn Beck, who has become, along with Rush Limbaugh, among the most visible and vociferous of the right-wing enemies of the Obama administration. Soon after Obama made his comments, Beck remarked on a Fox Television show that the president's reaction revealed a "deep-seated hatred for white people or the white culture." When a co-participant on the program, *Fox & Friends*, noted that most of the highest-ranking people in the Obama administration are white, Beck initially retreated—"I'm not saying he doesn't like white people"—only then to restate his initial point: "This guy [Obama] is, I believe, a racist."*[7] Is there anything to that charge? No. But that doesn't matter to Beck. The charge is an excellent vehicle for grabbing attention. Moreover, for a right-wing propagandist, charging that the president is a racist has the added benefit of seizing the rhetoric of liberalism and flipping it: No, it's not conservatives who are racist but liberals!

Responding to opposition is always tricky for a president. He naturally wants to defend himself but in a fashion that is befitting of his office. For Obama the difficulty is even greater. The first black president must simultaneously address supporters who will be tempted to see racial bias in opposition—whether or not bias is actually present—and detractors who will be tempted to see opportunism in all complaints against racial prejudice—whether or not the complaints are justified. Obama seeks to appease the latter more than the former. He is deeply hesitant to claim that a criticism of him is in any way racially discriminatory. He is keenly attentive to the reality that racial discrimination is often hard to identify clearly and that the very effort to make the identification is often politically costly.

---

* Rush Limbaugh told his huge radio audience, "What we learned last night, ladies and gentlemen, is that President Obama did, after all, listen to Reverend Wright all those twenty years." Obama, Limbaugh complained, was "quick to condemn the cop, the whole police department, and white America." "Limbaugh Blasts Obama's Reaction to Gates Arrest," Newsmax.com, July 23, 2009.

Racial discrimination—disfavoring an individual or group because of perceived racial affiliation—is a stigmatized behavior: it is generally viewed as morally wrong. That was not always so. Until the 1960s, many Americans were altogether willing to say openly that they believed that whites are morally and intellectually superior to blacks and that it was perfectly appropriate to discriminate against blacks on a racial basis in competitions for employment, housing, education, and other endeavors. One of the great achievements of the Civil Rights Revolution was its delegitimization of racial prejudice. It placed a moral as well as a legal cloud over racial discrimination. It made racial bigotry not only unfashionable but contemptible. It made racism an object of scorn and a target for ostracism. A result is that the prevalence of racial discrimination has been diminished. It has by no means been eradicated. But when people consciously engage in racial discrimination now, they typically deny that they are doing so and often take care to hide their tracks. Identifying their racial misbehavior then becomes treacherous. After all, deciphering ambiguous conduct is a complex, time-consuming, uncertain business. Consider the relatively simple case of a black customer in a store. A white cashier says something nasty to the customer. Racial discrimination? Maybe. On the other hand, perhaps the cashier has just received terrible news that made him angry. Or maybe the cashier is a jackass who treats everyone rudely. The problem, though, is still more complicated. People who engage in racial discrimination not only hide their prejudice from observers; they also often hide their prejudice from themselves. Many who engage in racial discrimination believe with all sincerity that they do not.

As it becomes socially hurtful to label someone as racially prejudiced, it also becomes incumbent to make such charges carefully to avoid wrongful accusations. The stigmatizing force of the charge thus becomes an inhibition upon making it. Nowadays, to make an unsubstantiated charge of racial prejudice is nearly as discrediting as engaging in racial discrimination yourself. Nothing has more besmirched the reputations of certain black leaders—Jesse Jackson and Al Sharpton come immediately to mind—than charges that they make allegations of racial discrimination opportunistically and irresponsibly.

The difficulty of identifying racial prejudice and the cost of attempting to do so is highlighted by an episode that unfolded on television at the Capitol. From the outset of his presidency, Obama had pressed the Congress to enact health-care reforms. In September 2009 he did so again, this time in a nationally telecast speech before both houses of Congress. During the speech, Joe Wilson of South Carolina, a Republican member of the House of Representatives, interrupted, screaming, "You lie!"

This unusually brazen act of disrespect elicited widespread condemnation, including the disapproval of most prominent Republican politicians. There was, then, little controversy over whether Joe Wilson had acted badly; most politicians and commentators agreed that he had.* There was controversy, however, regarding whether Wilson's conduct was racially discriminatory. Maureen Dowd, the acerbic columnist for *The New York Times,* concluded that race did play a role in Wilson's outburst. "I've been loath to admit," she declared, "that the . . . frantic efforts to paint our first black president as the Other, a foreigner, socialist, fascist, Marxist, racist, Commie, Nazi . . . had much to do with race. . . . But Wilson's shocking disrespect for the office of the president . . . convinced me: Some people just can't believe a black man is president and will never accept it." Dowd suggested that what Wilson

---

* On the other hand, Wilson did become a folk hero in some quarters, raised large amounts of money, and won reelection. See Byron York, "In S.C., Joe Wilson Outruns His 'You Lie!' Moment," *Washington Examiner,* October 13, 2010; Roddie Burris, "Wilson Turns Back Strong Miller Bid," *State,* November 3, 2010.

meant to say but left unsaid out of deference to political sur-
vival was "You lie—boy!" According to Dowd, "Wilson clearly
did not like being lectured and even rebuked by the brainy black
president."[8]

Another observer who identified Wilson's conduct as racially
discriminatory was former president Jimmy Carter. Asked about
"You lie!" Carter remarked, "Racism . . . still exists and I think
it has bubbled up to the surface because of a belief among many
white people, not just in the south but around the country, that
African-Americans are not qualified to lead this great country. It's
an abominable circumstance and grieves me and concerns me very
deeply."[9]

On the other hand, there were those who viewed Wilson's
shout as mere rudeness, a regrettable, even egregious, lapse into
incivility but a gesture which should not have been tagged with the
stigmatizing label "racist." Decrying what she views as Americans'
"hair-trigger response to any remark or action involving an
African American," the columnist Kathleen Parker asserted that
"it is profoundly irresponsible . . . to call Wilson a racist." Pressing
her point, Parker averred that "it is the height (or depth) of racism
to suggest that any opposition to Obama's policies is race-based."[10]
Similarly, the columnist Kevin Ferris charged that those who
accused Wilson of racial discrimination were themselves making
race an issue, because the evidence in support of the allegation
against Wilson was, in Ferris's estimation, "slim to none." All that
the political-correctness police could point to, Ferris asserted, was
that Representative Wilson was Southern, white, conservative,
and Republican.[11]

Actually, those who accused Wilson of racial discrimination
did point to other considerations. They noted Wilson's membership in the Sons of Confederate Veterans and that he was a leader
of the effort to keep the Confederate flag waving atop the South

Carolina State Capitol. Many who defend flying the Confederate flag claim that it has nothing to do with a defense of slavery or white supremacy. They maintain that flying the Confederate flag is mainly an assertion of pride in Southern traditions and local heritage. It is true that flying that flag does not necessarily denote allegiance to the racial slavery that the Confederacy was formed to protect; symbols can be transformed and given any meaning.* Most of the time, however, and certainly in the case of the South Carolina State House, flying the Confederate flag is an appreciative nod to the Lost Cause and a sign of defiant opposition to both the First and Second Reconstructions.† For some onlookers, however, these considerations add little or nothing to the case against Wilson for racial discrimination. It may be that, for them, the absence of any express reference to race on Wilson's part absolves him of racial misconduct.

President Obama distanced himself from the Dowd-Carter indictment. Responding to questions about the shout, Obama said that he appreciated that Wilson had "apologized quickly and without equivocation." Continuing, Obama remarked that "we have to get to the point where we can have a conversation about big, important issues that matter . . . without vitriol, without name-calling, without the assumption of the worst in other people's motives."[12]

Obama's response, eschewing any hint of racial accusation, was wholly in keeping with his image as a dignified, careful, nonangry, nonresentful statesman who happens to be black. Obama knew that he would have paid a stiff price for even mildly suggesting what is highly likely—that an affronted sense of racial privilege

* See Randall Kennedy, *Nigger: The Strange Career of a Troublesome Word* (2003).
† See Eric Foner, "Rebel Yell," *The Nation*, January 27, 2000. See also James W. Loewen and Edward H. Sebesta, eds., *The Confederate and Neo-Confederate Reader: The "Great Truth" About the "Lost Cause"* (2010).

played some part in Wilson's rudeness. During the campaign for the presidency, detractors harshly chastised Obama when he jokingly remarked that the McCain camp would try to dissuade voters from supporting him because, among other things, he did not "look like" previous presidents. Obama sought to avoid a repeat of that experience.

Glenn Beck's accusation that Obama "hates" whites has no plausible foundation. But it generated publicity that fueled nervousness and facilitated overreactions. This is the back story to one of the Obama administration's most embarrassing gaffes. In July 2010, a right-wing blogger, Andrew Breitbart, accused Shirley Sherrod, a black employee in the United States Department of Agriculture, of having withheld assistance from white farmers because of racial bias. Administration officials were so keen to deprive Glenn Beck, Bill O'Reilly, and the rest of the Fox News apparatus of a talking point that they pressured Sherrod into resigning without hearing her account of the matter. It turned out that Breitbart's portrayal was grossly inaccurate.* He posted a truncated videotape of an address by her delivered to a local branch of the NAACP. The snippet he offered made it seem that, for racial reasons, she withheld aid to white farmers in need of her help. The complete videotape showed, by contrast, Sherrod's determination to assist the white farmers fully and her attainment of a new level of understanding and empathy for their plight.† Almost immediately after the truncated video

---

* Ironically, Beck escaped besmirchment in the Sherrod affair. He refrained from publicizing the Breitbart videotape and called for Sherrod's reinstatement. For his part, Bill O'Reilly apologized to Mrs. Sherrod for failing to put her remarks "into the proper context." See Adam J. Rose, "Shirley Sherrod Scandal: Democrats, Republicans United to Insist She Be Rehired," HuffingtonPost.com, July 21, 2010; Danny Shea, "Bill O'Reilly Apologizes to Shirley Sherrod," HuffingtonPost.com, July 22, 2010.

† Adding poignancy to the affair were certain facts about Sherrod. Her father had been killed by a white man who was never prosecuted. She and her husband had long been involved in civil-rights activism. They had also been victimized by racial discrimination

was aired, the NAACP denounced Sherrod and officials in the Agricultural Department demanded that she resign, which she did. Soon thereafter the full video surfaced. The NAACP and the Agricultural Department both retracted their previous statements. The Secretary of the U.S. Department of Agriculture also publicly apologized and offered new employment to Sherrod. This was followed by a call to her from President Obama himself.[13]

Some observers contended, in the wake of the Sherrod debacle, that Obama should bring more race-experienced blacks into his inner circle, allow himself to address racial matters more directly, and elevate race relations to a higher plane in his administration's priorities. Maureen Dowd chided that Obama seems to feel "that he and Michelle are such a huge change for the nation to absorb that he can be overly cautious about pushing for other societal changes. . . . At some level, he acts like the election was enough; he shouldn't have to deal with race further."[14]

Dowd is correct when she maintains that, in Obama's view, his election was a "huge change" that will take time for the nation to digest fully and that therefore it would be mistaken to push *now* for advances on the racial front. More questionable is her assertion that he *should* be more ambitious in terms of pushing a racial agenda. Given the antiblack racism that is so ingrained in American culture, Obama's reticence is probably the most realistic course of action under the circumstances. Adopting a Lincolnian posture, Obama is determined to avoid venturing beyond what he perceives as the comfort zone of a majority of voters. On no topic is his caution more evident than race relations. Because

---

by the U.S. Agricultural Department, for which they were compensated in a settlement. When Mrs. Sherrod was hired in 2009 as the Georgia director of rural development, she was the first black person to occupy that post. See Krissah Thompson, "Despite Adversity, Shirley Sherrod Has History of Civil Service," *Washington Post,* July 22, 2010.

that topic remains volatile and because his blackness makes him particularly vulnerable to demagoguery, Obama avoids confronting the American race question, thus underscoring its central but repressed and paradoxical presence in the political culture of the United States.

8

Obama and the Future
of American Race Relations

Barack Obama's ascent is American history's most dramatic instance of upward mobility by a politician of color. Over the past quarter century, others, too, have starred in both elective and appointive posts—Colin Powell, the first black secretary of state; Condoleezza Rice, Powell's successor, the first black female secretary of state; Charles Rangel, the first black chair of the House Ways and Means Committee; John Conyers, the first black chair of the House Judiciary Committee; and Douglas Wilder, the first black popularly elected governor. But it is the ascendancy of Obama that has provoked talk of transformational "breakthroughs."* Is this talk of transformation on to something real and sustainable? Or is continuity the more important part of the story?

One development embodying elements of both continuity and change is the increasing presence of people of color in the higher echelons of the Republican Party. In 2009, on the heels of Obama's presidential triumph, the Republican Party chose as its new chairman Michael Steele, who was the first African American elected

---

* See, e.g., Gwen Ifill, *The Breakthrough: Politics and Race in the Age of Obama* (2009), and Matt Bai, "Is Obama the End of Black Politics?," *New York Times Magazine*, August 10, 2008.

to statewide office in Maryland, where he served as lieutenant governor.[1] The deficient performance of the Republicans' answer to Obama, however, caused initial supporters to abandon him. His casual resort to racial stereotypes, financial mismanagement, spats with important allies, and blunders regarding important issues dramatically diminished his stature, leading some observers to believe that the Republican Party's desire to avoid firing its first *black* chairman was the only explanation for his retention.[2] Eventually, in January 2011, Steele removed himself as a candidate for another term, even though he had been the Republican Party's titular head when it made historic advances in the midterm elections of 2010, narrowing the Democrats' majority in the Senate and retaking the majority in the House of Representatives.

In the landslide of 2010, a number of Republicans of color emerged as big winners.[3] Tim Scott became the first black Republican congressman from South Carolina since Reconstruction. His victory was particularly resonant in that an overwhelmingly white Republican electorate chose him to be their standard-bearer in the general election over Paul Thurmond, the son of the Dixiecrat legend who, as a governor and a senator, was the state's dominant political personality for half a century. Strom Thurmond anticipated the exodus of white Southerners from the Democratic Party when he abandoned it in 1948 to protest Harry Truman's support for blacks' civil rights. On the floor of the Senate he filibustered against the Civil Rights Act of 1957 for over twenty-four hours, sought to stymie the Civil Rights Act of 1964, and assailed Thurgood Marshall's nomination to the Supreme Court. He was a stubborn, canny, and effective champion of black disenfranchisement and white supremacy and was a revered figure among many white South Carolinians until his death in office, in 2003, at the age of 100. Yet, in 2010, in the very area in which Confederates fired on Union forces, igniting the Civil War, conservative white

Republicans preferred dark-skinned Scott to Thurmond's white son.* Then, in the general election, in a jurisdiction in which only about 20 percent of the residents are black, the voters of the state's First Congressional District selected Scott over his white Democratic rival. This was a district in which McCain beat Obama by fourteen percentage points.[4]

The other black Republican elected to the House of Representatives in 2010 is Allen West, who represents a district in Florida. A decorated, retired military officer who served in Iraq and Afghanistan, West became a favorite of Tea Party activists, distinguishing himself with clear, unequivocal rhetoric that situates him on the right edge of conservative Republicanism. Describing himself as a "right-wing extremist," he sweepingly denounces the Obama administration: "If we don't pay attention to what's going on right now, we will find ourselves once again becoming slaves to a tyrannical government."[5]

November 2010 also witnessed the triumph of several Republican candidates who are widely perceived as nonwhite but also nonblack—many observers place them in an "other" category of shifting boundaries. Nikki Haley became South Carolina's first female governor and the country's second Indian-American governor, following Louisiana's Bobby Jindal (who was elected in 2007).† Susana Martinez won the gubernatorial race in New Mexico, thus becoming the nation's first Latina governor. Marco Rubio of Florida won election to the Senate. The son of Cuban

---

* It is not stating the obvious to say that Thurmond's son is white. After all, as is now conceded after decades of denial, the elder Thurmond fathered a child by his family's teenaged black maid. See Jack Bass and Marilyn Thompson, *Strom: The Complicated Personal and Political Life of Strom Thurmond* (2005).
† During her gubernatorial campaign, Haley repeatedly told of how she was disqualified from a children's beauty contest because she could be neither the white queen nor the black queen. See Sarah Jaffe, "Nikki Haley: A New Face for Old Politics in South Carolina," *The Nation*, November 1, 2010.

immigrants, Rubio became the Senate's only Latino Republican (a place that had been occupied by Florida's Mel Martinez, who retired in 2009).

What does this outburst of Republican "diversification" signify? It shows that under certain circumstances among Republicans ideology does trump race. Republican voters in the First District of South Carolina preferred the black Tea Party right-winger to the staid conservative even if the latter was white and named Thurmond. Does that preference mean that the predominantly white electorate was indifferent to the race of the contestants? Indisputable evidence is hard to come by. My impression, though, is that race did—and does—matter. Race matters, for instance, if an African-American candidate obtains votes but only after having overcome his blackness in the eyes of supporters. I suspect that this was what happened, in part, to Scott and West. Voters were not indifferent to the race of the candidates; it's just that the weight of race was overmatched by other considerations. That represents an advance over the thinking that, not so long ago, categorically rejected blacks for significant positions of authority regardless of anything else. Voting for a black candidate, however, does not necessarily mean that the voter harbors no prejudice against blacks in general or black candidates in particular.

It is also probably the case that some of the whites who support African-American Republicans like Tim Scott do so in part not despite but because of their blackness. Although many Republicans say that they eschew the racial selectivity of "affirmative action" and "diversity," in practice they, too, are especially solicitous of blacks who wish to join their ranks. A reason—*not* the entire reason, but an important reason—that Scott and West are stars in the eyes of many Tea Partiers is that they are black. Their race serves as a balm to soothe the consciences of those Tea Partiers and Republicans who, at some level, feel guilty about the long-standing mistreatment of African Americans. Their race also serves as evidence that can be used to rebut charges of Tea Party or Republican racism.

In order to be eligible for racial affirmative action conservative style, the African American in question must be a black of the right sort. Typically, he or she must, like Scott and West, minimize historical and current racism, decry affirmative action, embrace antigay bias, and insist upon "small" government (except when it comes to the regulation of sex, reproduction, policing, and national security). So long as a black candidate fulfills these requirements, he is especially welcome in the Republican Party.

Do Steele, Scott, and West presage a significant partisan shift among black voters? No. Blacks in appreciable numbers are unlikely to follow the new black conservative "stars" for a variety of reasons. One is that on key matters the positions taken by black conservatives are (correctly) seen by most African Americans as contrary to their interests. Black conservatives, like their white peers, inveigh against federal governmental intrusion upon "states' rights." In black America, however, it is widely understood that federal authority has often been the only effective counterweight to private bigotry or local racialized tyranny. An example is the Civil Rights Act of 1964, which some conservatives have long decried as an illicit intrusion on the prerogatives of ownership. Another example is the Voting Rights Act of 1965, which numbers of conservatives have denounced as an unwarranted usurpation of the states' rightful authority. By contrast, most black Americans perceive that "states' rights" is often a code meaning "leave 'our' minorities to us to treat as we deem proper even if our treatment is beneath federal standards." Most African Americans also understand that the small-government ambitions of conservatives directly threaten black America since, proportionately, blacks are much more dependent than whites on governmental services and employment.

It is true that there are increasing numbers of relatively affluent blacks who might directly benefit from the fiscal policies of conservatives (for instance, the Bush tax cuts) and that some blacks of all socioeconomic categories harbor certain social attitudes that might, under different circumstances, render them susceptible to conservative capture. Republicans, however, have been unable (or perhaps unwilling) to capitalize on these potential openings. That record is unlikely to be changed by the new black conservative politicos. For one thing, some of them may well eschew engaging in racial outreach for fear of labeling themselves as mere "black" politicians, for fear of offending the putatively color-blind sensibilities of their white supporters, and, frankly, for fear of diluting their own rarity. Prized for their scarcity, black conservatives might cease to be so celebrated in a more racially integrated Republican Party. Some of the black conservative politicos perceive, moreover, that even a modest increase in the number of active African-American Republicans might quickly hit the racial tipping point, making their white peers uncomfortable. A small number of blacks is one thing, even if one or more of them are leading figures. Altogether different is a situation in which conservative whites would have to accommodate a substantial influx of blacks. Black conservatives intuit this problem. They know that their value to the Republican Party resides more in what they signify to whites—that the Party is not racist—than in what they signify to blacks.

The unlikeliness of substantial numbers of blacks migrating to the Republican Party anytime soon is rooted in more, however, than matters of class interest, cultural views, or the calculations of black conservative politicos. Many African-American voters have a deeply ingrained and understandable belief that, to paraphrase the rapper Kanye West, the Republican Party simply does not care about them. They perceive the Republican Party to be, implicitly, a white man's party that is welcoming, to be sure, of a few (but, please, not too many) blacks, so long as they harbor right-wing views and accept the notion that blacks have no good reason to complain about the country's racial situation. Most African Americans will continue to reject this mythology and leave the Tim Scotts and Allen Wests in splendid isolation as black right-wing curiosities.

Obama has been joined in the winners' circle of Democratic Party electoral politics by a cadre of other African Americans who came of age after the Civil Rights Revolution. Dubbed the "Joshua generation," these politicians are pursuing ambitions that were out of bounds for their elders, "the Moses generation," who faced and demolished de jure segregation. Among the significant figures in the Joshua generation are Massachusetts governor Deval Patrick, California attorney general Kamala Harris, Representatives Terri Swell and Jesse Jackson, Jr., and former representative Artur Davis.

Their record thus far is mixed. On the up side, Patrick decisively won reelection in 2010 as governor (a black first) in a contest in which the race question was probably as insignificant a factor as it can be in modern America. In 2010 Harris won a cliff-hanger in which her opponent prematurely announced that he had won. In prevailing, she became the first woman and the first person of color to ascend to the office of attorney general in the nation's most populous state. Seen by some as a "female Obama" (for one thing, she is the daughter of an Indian immigrant mother and a black American father), Harris is nicely positioned to run for the governorship of California in a few years. Sewell, hailing from Selma, the spiritual home of the Voting Rights Act, won election in 2010 as the first black woman to represent Alabama in Congress.

On the down side are stalled careers or precipitous failures. Jesse Jackson, Jr., appeared to have an inside lane to political advancement. He owned a legendary name. He was an early and much-publicized Obama supporter. He demonstrated admirable independence by publicly reprimanding his father. The younger Jackson was tainted, however, by the ugly shenanigans that surrounded the appointment of a senator to replace Obama once he assumed the presidency. Perhaps Jackson was wrongly tarnished and maybe he will regain his former promise. That he has been diminished, however, is evident.

Artur Davis seemed poised to traverse new terrain for a black politician when he sought the governorship of Alabama. Winning statewide office has proven difficult for black politicians. To reiterate a stark and sobering fact: in all of American history, blacks have won gubernatorial elections on only three occasions. Davis compounded the degree of difficulty by seeking to become the first popularly elected black chief executive of a Deep South state.

Davis failed, losing to a white rival in the Democratic Party primary. He lost in a revealing fashion. He eschewed the old black establishment. He declined to support key liberal initiatives, including health-care reform. He distanced himself from Obama (though he had previously been an avid supporter). He tried ostentatiously to make himself palatable to white moderates or even conservatives while taking for granted completely the black electorate. In the end he found himself abandoned by black voters who displayed their own independence, preferring the white nominee by a large margin. Davis lost, David Wilkins aptly observes, "because he attempted to take a page out of the President's playbook without fully understanding the play."[6] Obama is always careful to offer his black constituents signals that he identifies with them and seeks to advance their interests even if he cannot deliver benefits immediately or in a race-specific fashion. In other words, if nothing else, Obama always offers fellow blacks psychic satisfaction. Davis rather defiantly stopped doing that and paid the price at the polls.[7]

One cannot confidently make large inferences based on the

outcome of a few contests in disparate contexts. Two predictions, however, can be realistically ventured. One is that black and other politicians of color are likely to remain a presence at all levels of electoral competition in the coming years. They have become an entrenched part of the Democratic Party as voters, delegates, and nominees. They are not nearly as influential or welcomed on the Republican side. But even Republicans who sneer at diversity in theory seek it in practice as they celebrate their rare Tim Scotts, Nikki Haleys, and Susana Martinezes. The second prediction is that racial sentiments will continue to affect politicians of all sorts far into the future. Race matters. The color line persists.

Americans are divided over the racial regime they want to create. They paper over conflicts with banalities—"We all want racial justice" or "We all want racial equality." These anodyne generalities lull Americans into thinking that they share the same ends and differ only over means. Actually, though, Americans differ markedly over ends as well as means. Many say that they envision a society in which racial differences have withered away or in which the differences that exist are unrecognized. In this scenario race is no longer a uniform that triggers socially significant responses but becomes no more important than, say, eye color. This idea seems to have animated the (mainly white) supporters of Barack Obama who chanted excitedly at his campaign rallies, "Race doesn't matter! Race doesn't matter! Race doesn't matter!" Individuals who embrace this perspective often champion "color blindness" as an aspiration and welcome the prospect of a "postracial America," although they differ over strategy. Some contend that the best way to attain the color-blindness ideal is to reject virtually *all* racial selectivity immediately, even when the purpose of the selectivity is to maintain racial integration or to ensure the presence of racial minorities in influential forums from which they might otherwise be excluded.[8] Others embrace color blindness as an ultimate goal but contend that that aim can best, or maybe only, be attained by policies that are temporarily race conscious.[9] Others see nothing wrong with people expressing pride in and support for their racial "own."[10]

Racial pluralists of a certain sort see the disciplined cultivation of racial affinities as good foundations upon which to build respect for multicultural differences. They reject the thinking associated with "color blindness" and dismiss as ill-conceived the aspiration for a "postracial" America. Not only do they associate these slogans with ignorance about the continuation of racial mistreatment and indifference to the present harms caused by past injustices,[11] but, more fundamentally, they perceive the proponents of color blindness and postracialism as positing the erasure of nonwhite difference as a condition for "progress." They want organizations such as the Black Law Students Association or the Latino Law Students Association to exist in perpetuity, not temporarily as mere transient stopgaps disposable after acceptance has been achieved. They see the color-blindness and postracialism tropes as the latest in a long line of initiatives—"the melting pot," "Americanization," "assimilation," "acculturalization," "integration"—aimed at coercing conformity to a white, Anglo, Christian, heterosexual normalcy.

Examples abound that reveal the latent conflicts dividing Americans over the sort of racial regime to which they aspire. Consider the following question: When, if ever, and for what reason, if any, is it appropriate to take race into account in deciding for whom to vote? Answering this question is difficult and provokes a wide range of responses.

There is no law limiting the criteria by which one may decide to vote for candidate X as opposed to candidate Y. Without fear of legal repercussions one can openly confess to preferring or opposing candidate X or Y for any reason whatsoever, including whim ("eenie, meenie, miny, moe"), ideology, physical attractiveness, religion, party affiliation, or race. Many laws prohibit racial selectivity in the selling of food, automobiles, houses, insurance, and other goods and services. Without exception, however, one may legally vote for or against someone wholly or partially on a racial basis. Furthermore, a voter is not only free of legal regulation; a voter is also free of the regulatory force of public opinion because of the anonymity that enshrouds the casting of secret ballots. In the sanctuary of the voting booth, the voter is free of public scrutiny; she can vote as she pleases without fear of any external gaze.*

A key question—perhaps *the* key question—posed by the presidential election of 2008 was whether a sufficient number of voters would be willing to support a black candidate to enable Barack Obama to capture the White House.[12] That question was answered in the affirmative. Obama did not win a majority of the white electorate. He did, however, win a sufficient number of white voters to prevail. That he did so was largely what made the election of November 4, 2008, so momentous. It evidenced a remarkable diminution in the Negrophobia and white racial narcissism that had long made the prospect of a black president incredible. Obama's success stemmed in part from a broadening consensus that ethical voting requires electors to refrain from categorically dismissing a candidate *solely* on the basis of his or her race. In 1958,

---

* How people vote collectively, however, may have legal repercussions. The presence of racially polarized voting, for instance, is an important factor in determining whether legislative districting violates the Voting Rights Act. See, for example, *Thornburg v. Gingles*, 478 U.S. 30 (1986). The law does not penalize any individual voter, no matter the basis of her vote. The law does require the redrawing of district boundaries, however, if it is determined that bloc voting by a racial majority, in conjunction with other circumstances, deprives a racial minority of a fair opportunity to participate meaningfully in the electoral process. Under certain conditions, in other words, the Voting Rights Act counters racially polarized voting.

the Gallup Organization first asked whether Americans would be willing to vote for a qualified black presidential candidate nominated by their own party. Three in five white Americans answered that, even under those circumstances, they would *not* be willing to vote for a black candidate—any black candidate. The proportion fell to below one in five by 1980 and to below one in ten by 1990. "At least in principle," observe the distinguished political scientists Lawrence D. Bobo and Michael Dawson, "the overwhelming majority of White voters consistently express a willingness to consider voting for a Black presidential candidate and have said so for at least a decade."[13]

Of course, in the election of 2008, there were more than racial dynamics at play. Voters were influenced by party affiliation, religious beliefs, symbolic cues, stances toward salient issues, perceptions of individual character, and all manner of other considerations. Amid the many mysteries that continue to fascinate students of electoral behavior, however, one thing is clear: at least 43 percent of white voters were willing to vote for a black candidate under certain conditions. Some of these voters supported Obama despite racial affinities that would ordinarily prompt them to side with the white candidate. Even with a preference for "one of their own," some white voters embraced Obama-Biden over McCain-Palin. Some of these voters concluded that Obama successfully rebutted their presumption against black candidates. Some of them voted for "the black guy" only out of a sense of desperation, given the economic downturn and the utter unacceptability of the McCain-Palin alternative. The election of Obama, in short, did not usher forth a new day in which black politicians are free of the burden of race. It only documented that racial selectivity no longer absolutely precludes the possibility of a black presidential candidate prevailing.

Race still matters!

But blackness matters now in ways that are not always detrimental. Identifying as black can also *assist* a candidate. Consider that Obama received about 95 percent of the black vote. Had John Kerry been able to do that he would have become president of the United States.

That a much larger percentage of blacks preferred Obama to McCain is unremarkable. Michael Dukakis (1988) received 90 percent of the black vote, Bill Clinton (1992 and 1996) 83 percent and 84 percent, Al Gore (2000) 90 percent, and John Kerry (2004) 89 percent. But Obama topped all preceding Democratic candidates by a substantial margin. Explaining their votes, many black supporters cited Obama's programmatic commitments (ending the war in Iraq and promoting social equity), his record (an excellent education and demonstrated devotion to public service), and his personal qualities (eloquence, dignity, poise). People disagree over the accuracy of these assessments. But there is relatively little controversy over the underlying legitimacy of taking such considerations into account.

But what about other considerations? More specifically, what about blacks who voted for Obama, at least in part, because of sentiments such as the following:

> There is a piece of me that thrills to the Obamas because of a red-blooded racial loyalty. . . . The messy tribal feelings have not been my main reason for supporting Obama. But it's been roiling underneath. . . . There's going to be a brother in the White House! Yeah—I feel it, too![14]

This person said that he did not vote for Obama *solely* on the basis of "racial loyalty." But he did expressly cite feelings of kinship and solidarity as an ingredient of his support.

The racial loyalist in question is John McWhorter, a generally conservative commentator best known for his acerbic critiques of affirmative action, protest politics, and black cultural tendencies he views as self-defeating.* McWhorter was not alone among conservative-minded blacks who, pulled by sentiments of racial affinity, felt drawn to Obama. Their ideological differences with him clarify the presence and dilemma of racial loyalty. Liberal Democratic black voters encountered no dissonance in voting for Obama; their partisan and ideological tendencies were aligned with any sentiments of racial loyalty that they felt. By contrast, black conservative Republicans did encounter dissonance. But like McWhorter, despite strong ideological disagreement they nonetheless voted for Obama in part on the basis of racial kinship and solidarity—"he looks like me." [15]

What do people say in response to black voters' assertions of racial loyalism? Some repudiate it. Barack Obama did when he said that he sought no votes on grounds of racial affinity but only on the basis of his superior ability to provide the leadership the country needed. Oprah Winfrey implicitly repudiated it, too, when, in endorsing Obama, she said that she supported him *not* because he was black but because he was brilliant and committed to policies and priorities that would benefit the country as a whole. [16] She disclaimed any sort of racial tribalism as a basis of her support and instead invoked a meritocratic criterion.

Additional examples of repudiation surfaced in the aftermath of the controversy that ensued when Colin Powell endorsed Obama. Several conservatives, most notably Patrick Buchanan and Rush Limbaugh, alleged that racial affinity played a role in prompting Powell to make the endorsement. [17] They charged that Powell supported Obama because the general, out of loyalty, wanted to assist

* See John McWhorter, *Losing the Race: Self-Sabotage in Black America* (2000); *Authentically Black: Essays for the Black Silent Majority* (2003); *Winning the Race: Beyond the Crisis in Black America* (2005).

his racial "brother." The reason this charge was deemed news-worthy is that electoral favoritism stemming from racial-group loyalty is seen by many as wrong. Some observers agreed with Buchanan and Limbaugh and condemned Powell, while others defended Powell from what they saw as a baseless calumny. Common to both sets of observers was a conviction that the racial favoritism alleged to have transpired is bad.

A substantial number of African Americans say openly and without apology, however, that they do take racial affiliation into account in deciding for whom to vote—that, yes, one of the things that prompted them to support Obama is that he is black like them, that he is their racial kinsman, that he is a "brotha." They concede that it would be unwise to view race as the *only* criterion. But they insist that giving some deference to racial commonality is defensible or maybe even obligatory. In their view, to forgo the thought, practice, and emotions of black solidarity would be shamefully self-destructive. Such a course, they contend, would amount to unilateral disarmament in an environment in which black collective defense and uplift remains imperative. Proponents of this view insist upon distinguishing white racial loyalism from black racial loyalism, maintaining that they are different historically, sociologically, and normatively. Black racial loyalism, they contend, was called into being by white racial oppression. It is the defensive adaptation of a besieged racial minority. To them, therefore, black racial loyalism is morally good while white racial loyalism is morally bad.*[18]

There are, however, grounds other than racial loyalty on which people take race into account in deciding for whom to vote. Some

---

* "It is OK to vote your race when doing so is a historic milestone for a race that has been systematically disenfranchised and marginalized in this country for nearly 500 years. . . . I think it's just fine for black people to be a little bit racist towards white people until true equality has been achieved, until a black candidate for President is just another candidate and not a historical novelty." Anonymous respondent to Stephen J. Dubner in "When Is It OK to Vote Your Race?," NewYorkTimes.com, October 17, 2008.

see blackness as a proxy that signals the likely presence of certain valued experiences, sensibilities, and sympathies.* Voters put race to work in other ways as well. For example, some counted Obama's blackness as a plus, anticipating that partly because of his race his election would inspire marginalized minority youth, display undeniably a repudiation of white supremacist traditions,† generate new respect for the United States abroad, and elevate the status of blacks who have as a group been cruelly stigmatized for so long.

The controversies that surround all of these rationales are indicative of our society's ambivalence and confusion regarding ultimate racial aims. It is commonplace to hear exhortations urging Americans forward toward the grand destination of "racial equality." [19] Less common, but badly needed, is acknowledgment that Americans share little consensus regarding what "racial equality" entails or what landmarks or boundaries constitute that destination. Leaders speak of the racial "promised land" but offer little toward identifying its spiritual or political or socioeconomic whereabouts.

Assessments of the Obama administration generate numerous examples of conflicting racial aspirations. Consider the rancorous discussion that attended remarks made by the television commentator Chris Matthews after Barack Obama's first State of the Union address.

Matthews declared:

He [Obama] is post-racial. . . . I forgot he was black tonight for an hour. He's gone a long way to become a leader of this country and past so much history in just a year or two. I mean

---

* See Jane Mansbridge, "Should Blacks Represent Blacks and Women Represent Women? A Contingent 'Yes,'" *Journal of Politics* 61 (1999): 627.

† Responding to the question "When is it OK to vote your race?" one person remarked, "I believe that there is extra utility in proving that a non-(completely) white person can be president—for all of us. It demonstrates something very hopeful about American democracy and the maturity of American voters of all races." NewYorkTimes.com, October 17, 2008.

it's something we don't even think about. I was watching and I said, wait a minute, he's an African-American guy in front of a bunch of other white people and there he is, president of the United States, and we've completely forgotten that tonight— completely forgotten it. I think it was in the scope of the discussion, it was so broad ranging, so in tune with so many problems and aspects of American life. That you don't think in terms of the old tribalism and the old ethnicity. It was astounding in that regard, a very subtle fact. It's so hard to even talk about it. Maybe I shouldn't talk about it, but I am.[20]

Later, elaborating on his comment, Matthews said that the main point he had been attempting to make was that Obama had "taken us beyond black and white in our politics, wonderfully so, in just a year."[21]

Matthews's statement became the most widely noted of all the commentary on Obama's speech. Some observers found nothing wrong with it. They heard Matthews as saying, essentially, that it was a positive and noteworthy thing for *this* president to be able and willing to deliver a State of the Union speech that reached way beyond any parochial obsession with racial issues. Defenders also maintained that Matthews was right to note approvingly that this State of the Union occasion was essentially similar to those that had come before notwithstanding the unprecedented nature of the president's race.

Matthews, however, was also widely criticized. Some observers chastised him for insufficient color blindness. Why, they asked, make mention of Obama's race at all? Why, moreover, should Matthews forget about Obama's race for only an hour as opposed to forever?

An opposing critique took Matthews to task for supposing it a good thing that he had forgotten (albeit only temporarily) that

Obama is black. These critics heard Matthews's statement as a confession that he is only able to see an African American as presidential when he is blind to that person's blackness.[22]

Some detractors also heard Matthews as saying that assertions of blackness constitute an impediment to the realization of a postracial America and that it is the absence of such assertions that enables Obama to be a transcendent figure. They find this message to be insulting since it depicts blackness as a problem warranting minimization or elimination.* These critics discern in Matthews's comment a reprise of Joe Biden's musings about Obama being "clean" and "articulate"—applause for a black man seen as atypical. As one observer put it, Matthews's commentary "exposed the subconscious lowered expectations that many white men harbor about people of color."[23] Matthews fulsomely praised Obama's speech for being "so broad ranging, so in tune with so many problems and aspects of American life." But, of course, the speech in question was the State of the Union address. What did Matthews expect—a speech limited to the state of Harlem, Compton, and the Ninth Ward?

What are President Obama's racial politics? That there is a need to pose this question might seem odd given that Obama has written a much-praised memoir and delivered a speech that some observers put alongside the most illuminating explorations of race relations in American history. Obama's statements on race, however, are strikingly *un*instructive.

Early on in his presidency, Obama was pressed by some activists and politicians to offer race-specific policies to address the dispro-

---

* Cf. W. E. B. Du Bois, *The Souls of Black Folk* (1903). ("How does it feel to be a problem?")

THE PERSISTENCE OF THE COLOR LINE

portionately high rates of unemployment that have long plagued black and other racial-minority communities. He steadfastly refused to do so, declaring on one occasion, "I think it is a mistake to start thinking in terms of particular ethnic segments of the United States rather than to think that we are all in this together and we are all going to get out of this together."*[24] Obama, however, has been allowed to leave obscure the basis for his refusal. Was it a matter of electoral prudence—a perception that he would pay an unacceptably high price at the ballot box if he were to do anything suggestive of racial favoritism? Was it a matter of programmatic pragmatism—a perception that any race-specific policy he could conceivably implement would be inadequate to bring substantial relief to the black unemployed (regardless of the political cost exacted)? Was it a matter of political principle—the belief that it would be wrong for the president of the United States to distinguish among the ranks of the unemployed on racial grounds?

My impression is that all three of these considerations play a role in Obama's aversion to race-targeted programs. "I can't pass laws that say I'm just helping black folks," he responded when asked about Congressional Black Congress (CBC) criticism of his employment policy. "I'm the President of the United States. What I can do is make sure that I am passing laws that help all people, particularly those that are most vulnerable and most in need. That in turn is going to help lift up the African American community."[25] Here Obama was engaging in the old trick of creating a straw man to knock down. The CBC was not requesting policy aimed at "just helping black folks." It was requesting policy that would be

* Obama has expressed the same idea in a variety of ways: "The most important thing I can do for the African American community is the same thing I can do for the American community, period, and that is get the economy going again and get people hiring again." Quoted in David Jackson, "Obama Rejects Congressional Black Caucus Criticism," *USA Today*, December 3, 2009.

intended to assist America as a whole but "particularly those who are most vulnerable" in economic downturns—the last-hired and first-fired racial minorities. The CBC was not disputing that the president should seek to "help all people." It was questioning, and rightly so, whether the president's unemployment policy could be shaped in such a way as to provide quicker relief to those sectors of the workforce that are most in jeopardy—sectors in which racial minorities show up in disproportionate numbers.*

Although some members of the CBC threatened to cause trouble for Obama if he failed to address their concerns, their grumbling soon subsided. Obama did not further respond substantively. He did respond symbolically, however, by inviting several prominent African-American "leaders" (Al Sharpton, Ben Jealous, Marc Morial) to the White House to discuss unemployment. This meeting, of course, produced no new knowledge or initiatives. But that was never its actual purpose. Its aim was public relations: to signal that the White House cared about the grumbling (and to bestow upon the invitees the favor of presidential attention—a favor reciprocated by the invitees' subsequent expressions of gratitude and support).

The black-left critique of President Obama reiterates preelection complaints that he wrongly avoids confronting racial issues, marginalizes the poor, relies too much on white male elite power brokers such as Lawrence Summers and Timothy Geithner, and pursues a foreign policy that, in its essentials, conforms to the militaristic, Eurocentric, pro-Israel framework that he inherited.

---

* It is worth recalling that when Richard Nixon was elected president in 1968, his secretary of labor–designate, George P. Schultz, announced that the country's most pressing labor problem was black unemployment—most important, the "appalling unemployment experience of black teen-agers." This problem, Schultz declared, called for "special measures," because employers could simply not be allowed to conduct business as usual. See Hugh Davis Graham, *The Civil Rights Era: Origins and Development of National Policy, 1960–1972* (1990), 322–323.

These critics are aggrieved, for instance, by the Obama administration's decision in April 2009 to boycott the United Nations' World Conference Against Racism. The administration claimed that the conference was clearly going to be openly and wrongly hostile to Israel. Critics contend that the administration's stance displayed a continued thralldom to the Israel lobby that was accentuated by Obama's knowledge that certain sectors of Israeli and Jewish-American public opinion view him with an apprehension colored by long-standing black-Jewish tensions.

Most of Obama's critics on the black left are radicals who have little traction outside of small constituencies that read Black AgendaReport.com, the BlackCommentator.com, *NewPolitics*, *The Progressive*, and similar magazines or Web sites. A bit more influential are intellectuals who have been able to gain popularity not only in left-wing venues, academia, and politically active churches but also in the black glossies (*Ebony* and *Essence*, for example), black radio, commercial book publishing, and cable television. Two such figures have been heard from previously in these pages: Cornel West and Michael Eric Dyson.

Dyson vocally supported Obama's presidential campaign, often warding off criticism from detractors on the left. After Obama moved into the White House, however, Dyson's attitude changed. He began to voice the very criticisms he had previously rebutted. Irked by what he viewed as Obama's failure to pay sufficient homage to heroes of the black liberation movement, especially Martin Luther King, Jr., Dyson complained that the new president seemed to suffer from "an incapacity . . . to explicitly embrace blackness."[26] Later, after the dustup over Harry Reid's portrayal of Obama as a light-skinned black free of a Negro dialect, Dyson expressed disappointment with the president's disinclination to offer racial instruction to the country. "This president," Dyson remarked, "runs from race like a black man runs from a cop."[27]

The odd thing about Dyson's sharp turnabout is that it seems not to have been triggered by any substantial change in Obama's mode of operation; he was as diffident regarding race prior to his election as after it. Rather, it seems that an important, perhaps key, factor in Dyson's about-face was the long delay of an invitation to the White House.*

West, as noted previously, was quite critical of Obama during much of the election campaign, though he always said that he would vastly prefer Obama to McCain. After Obama assumed power, West continued to criticize him. He assailed, for instance, Obama's selection of certain people for pivotal positions in his administration. Especially galling for West was Obama's choice of Lawrence Summers to be his chief adviser on economic matters. When Summers was the president of Harvard University he and West had a highly publicized dispute, which led to West leaving Harvard (for Princeton) and to Summers being widely disparaged in black intellectual and activist circles. Despite his bad reputation within the black intelligentsia, however, Summers was chosen by Obama to be director of the National Economic Council. By contrast, neither West nor anyone in his circle received any comparable presidential appointment.†

---

* "I ain't been to the White House . . . I ain't been invited . . . I endorsed him in New Orleans at the Essence Festival, 60,000 people. [*Ebony* magazine said] that that was the first major endorsement by a major black figure . . . I ain't been nowhere." "Michael Eric Dyson vs President Obama," YouTube, posted on May 29, 2009, by mrdaveyd.

† The most prominent leftish black appointee in the Obama administration was Anthony K. "Van" Jones, who served as the special adviser for green jobs, enterprise, and innovation at the White House Council on Environmental Quality. A founder of ColorOfChange, a black political organization, in 2005, Jones became a leading voice in the environmental-justice movement. His tenure at the White House, however, was brief. After only five months on the job, he resigned under fire from conservatives because of statements disparaging Republicans; expressions of support for Mumia Abu-Jamal, a death-row prisoner convicted of having killed a police officer; and allegations that he had signed a petition charging that President Bush had allowed the 9/11 attacks to occur to provide a basis for U.S. military interventions abroad. See John M. Broder,

During Obama's campaign for the presidency, he repeatedly alluded to the far-flung and diverse character of his extended family as a source of knowledge and inspiration that would assist him in serving as a conciliator of America's racial tensions. Given his background, and given the obsessions that have surrounded interracial sex and marriage, it would be revealing to know more precisely Obama's views regarding intimate transracial relationships. A reporter once asked him what he thought about the propriety of his daughters receiving a racial affirmative-action edge when they apply to college. I'd like to know what he thinks about the prospect of his daughters perhaps dating (or marrying) white boys (or girls). Will he be indifferent to the race of their romantic companions? If so, why so? Would he prefer them dating blacks? If not, why not?

Even a formulaic response would be instructive, as it would indicate what the president considers to be a politic answer. That he would publicly object to his daughters crossing the race line for romance is inconceivable, for such an attitude is widely perceived as backward, if not bigoted. More imaginable, but still highly unlikely, is that he would publicly express a preference for his daughters to marry other blacks, perhaps on the grounds that group solidarity is an accepted, indeed respected, tradition of American pluralism and that black communities are in special need of black married couples.* If the president offered any response to this question, the most likely would be that he is agnostic regarding the race of

---

"White House Official Resigns After G.O.P. Criticism," *New York Times*, September 7, 2009, and Van Jones, "Shirley Sherrod and Me," *New York Times*, July 24, 2010.
* See Charles W. Mills, "Do Black Men Have a Moral Duty to Marry Black Women?," *Journal of Social Philosophy* 25 (1994): 131. See also Karyn Langhorne Folan, *Don't Bring Home a White Boy and Other Notions That Keep Black Women From Dating Out* (2010).

his children's boyfriends or girlfriends, that he is concerned only about the content of their character, not the color of their skin. This position is, at least in theory, probably the most popular in America—the position which holds that there is no black America or white America or Latino America or Asian America, but only the United States of America, the position which holds that race should no longer serve the function of a uniform, the position which holds that regardless of race, Americans should perceive one another just as Americans. Of course, in practice Americans act far differently, and interracial marriages between whites and blacks (especially white men and black women) remain quite rare.*

Obama said as a candidate that, if elected, his administration would fight invidious racial discrimination. As president, his Justice Department is doing so with considerably more vigor than was the case under his predecessor. The Obama Justice Department increased funding to its Civil Rights Division and took steps to arrest that division's plummeting morale and standing. That is all to the good and warrants praise. It would be naïve to conclude, however, that enhanced antidiscrimination efforts will substantially alter the racial demographics of privilege and deprivation. Stark racial gaps would continue to exist even if, miraculously, *all* illegal racial discrimination ceased immediately. That is because current unlawful racial discrimination, while bad,[28] is not the biggest source of the widely divergent outcomes in wealth, income, education, health, and mortality that differentiate racially the conditions of life in the United States.† The deprivation imposed by new, "fresh," unlawful racial discrimination pales in comparison

---

* See R. Richard Banks, "The Aftermath of *Loving v. Virginia*: Sex Asymmetry in African American Intermarriage," *University of Wisconsin Law Review* 2007: 533; Ralph Richard Banks, *Is Marriage for White People?: How the African American Marriage Decline Affects Everyone* (2011).

† As of 2003, white women could expect to live 4.54 years longer than black women, while white men could expect to live 6.33 years longer than black men.

with the suffering imposed by the vestigial consequences of racial oppression in the past, including lost opportunities stemming from the exclusion of racial minorities from social networks—friendships, dating, marriages, private clubs—that are largely outside the jurisdiction of governmental regulation.

Obama is aware of all of these sources of racial inequality and seeks to address them, albeit cautiously, within the boundaries of what he perceives to be conducive to his political well-being.

Let's consider certain key issues. Obama is undoubtedly aware that, even without racial animus, social inertia tradition will often exclude racial outsiders from coveted, influential decision-making positions. With that in mind, Obama has made sure that, with respect to anything he has a hand in shaping, racial minorities receive careful attention as candidates. He hasn't dramatized or publicized this aspect of his process. Doing so would be counterproductive. Recall the controversy that engulfed Bill Clinton when he openly declared that he sought to construct a Cabinet that "looked like America."[29] He was harassed on one front by those who sneered that he was engaging in quota hiring and on another by those who charged that his move toward diversification did not

---

There are 13.5 infant deaths for every 1,000 births by black women, compared to 5.7 for white women and 6.8 for a national average.

In 2004, 24.7 percent of black households were below the poverty level, while the comparable figures for other races were 10.8 percent (white), 9.8 percent (Asian), and 21.9 percent (Hispanic or Latino). The national average was 12.7 percent.

For every dollar of wealth held by a typical white family, the African-American family has only one dime.

See Sam Harper, John Lynch, Scott Burris, and George Davey Smith, "Trends in Black-White Life Expectancy Gap in the United States, 1983–2003," *Journal of the American Medical Association* 297 (2007): 1224–1232; "Health, United States, 2006," U.S. Department of Health and Human Services Centers for Disease Control and Prevention, November 2006, available at http://www.cdc.gov/nchs/data/hus/hus07.pdf#027; Brian K. Bucks, Arthur B. Kennickell, Traci L. Mach, and Kevin B. Moore, "Changes in U.S. Family Finances from 2004 to 2007: Evidence from the Survey of Consumer Finances," *Federal Health Bulletin* 95 (February 2009): A1–A55. See, generally, Ray L. Brooks, *Racial Justice in the Age of Obama* (2009).

go far enough. Obama makes no dramatic statements about race and recruitment in his administration. But his actions show that he is attentive to the social demography—the "diversity"—of his appointments. It is not accidental that in addition to nominating the first Latina Supreme Court justice and selecting the first black attorney general, he also appointed the first black administrator of the Environmental Protection Agency (Lisa Jackson) and the first black administrator of NASA (Charles Bolden). All of these individuals are capable. But in each instance, there were also lots of capable whites who could easily have been chosen instead—and, in previous times, would have been chosen instead.

Of course, Obama was not entering uncharted territory in hiring people of color to high positions. Every president since Lyndon Johnson has had at least one African American in his Cabinet, even presidents who condemned "quota hiring." And, of course, in the administrations of George W. Bush, two of the most important members of the Cabinet were black—Colin Powell and Condoleezza Rice. Still, in no previous administration have the most desirable positions in the federal government been more accessible to people of color than in the Obama administration. Obama has not only elevated himself to the highest office in America. He has also elevated a whole cadre of people of color who, strengthened by the certification and experience they receive from stints in his administration, will undoubtedly emerge as key actors in local and national politics for decades to come.

As I noted earlier, affirmative action is not a good issue for Obama.[30] It is in tension with the transracial "universalism" that he prefers to voice and that many of his followers prefer to hear. In debate over employment policy, Obama has repeatedly rejected what amounted to pleas for affirmative action in employment relief. If racial selectivity was inappropriate in that context, however, why is it not inappropriate in others, maybe all? Obama doesn't say.

What Obama does say is notably laconic and noncommittal. In the chapter called "Race" in his precampaign manifesto *The Audacity of Hope*, Obama does not so much embrace affirmative action as indicate a grudging toleration of it. He describes it as "a useful, if limited, tool to expand opportunity to under-represented minorities,"[31] but refrains from offering it any more praise than that. Moreover, the sort of affirmative action that he defends is so narrowly defined that one can fairly doubt whether, in that form, it can be said to exist at all. "Affirmative action programs," he writes, "when properly structured, can open up opportunities otherwise closed to qualified minorities without diminishing opportunities for white students."[32] How can that be? If a program is at all constrained by scarcity, special efforts made on behalf of racial minorities will necessarily diminish opportunities for whites, even if only minimally. Obama, here, is simply obscuring the dilemmas that affirmative action inescapably poses. Racial affirmative action *does* distinguish between people on a racial basis. It *does* redistribute resources. It *does* subject preferred candidates to lower standards than those who are unpreferred. It *does* generate stigma and resentment.

Affirmative action, like any social program, has costs. The issue is whether those costs are justified by countervailing gains. In *The Audacity of Hope* and on subsequent occasions, Obama has suggested, without elaborating, that he has his doubts. He repeatedly contends that progressives ought to allocate their investments elsewhere. Ensuring that all children perform at grade level and graduate from high school, he has declared, "would do more than affirmative action to help those black and Latino children who need it the most."[33] Likewise, he has averred that the most effective ways to close the gap between minority and white workers may have "little to do with race," that the things that would most help minority workers are the same things that would most help white workers: education and training, good jobs, and government policies "that restore some balance to the distribution of the nation's wealth. . . . This pattern—of a rising tide lifting minority boats—has certainly held true in the past. . . . The same formula holds true today."[34]

Is Obama correct? Yes and no. There are nonracial redistributivist measures imaginable that would, if fully implemented, help racial-minority communities as a whole more than existing affirmative-action programs. Such measures would include excellent and accessible public schooling and a full employment policy providing an entitlement to work paying decent wages. If a quid pro quo was on offer, blacks and other racial minorities would be well advised to trade affirmative action for such reforms. Obama, however, is in no position to ensure the deliverability of such initiatives. In today's environment, with severe fiscal constraints and the continued ascendancy of a conservative ideology of political economy and governance, it would be foolhardy for progressive-minded folk to relinquish productive affirmative-action programs, despite all their liabilities, in exchange for "universal" programs that, if implemented at all, would likely be underfunded. This is one of the reasons Obama will leave affirmative action alone. He won't champion it conspicuously, but he will maintain the affirmative-action status quo.

While affirmative action requires grappling with the legitimacy and wisdom of using racial distinctions expressly in allocating *benefits*, another big issue on the racial front involves the legitimacy and wisdom of allocating *burdens* by following rules that in form are nonracial but impose adverse effects disproportionately upon racial minorities.* This issue is pervasive. Formally nonracial crite-

---

* An interesting twist on this theme features those who charge that an Obama-supported tax on tanning salons is "racist" because the clientele of such salons is made up disproportionately of whites. This complaint is fatuous. The government wanted to raise revenues and discourage excessive tanning because of attendant health hazards. There has been no evidence uncovered which suggests that the real reason for the tax is to disad-

ria have the effect of disproportionately excluding minority candidates from education and employment opportunities.[35] They also expose racial minorities disproportionately to toxic dumps and other disagreeable or dangerous social excrescences.[36]

The most striking and consequential example of formally nonracial regulations that generate racially disproportionate adverse consequences is criminal sentencing. "Crime and punishment in America have a color," Professor Glenn Loury declares. "The extent of racial disparity in imprisonment rates is greater than in any other major area of American social life: at eight to one the black-white ratio of incarceration rates dwarfs the two-to-one ratio of non-marital childbearing, the two-to-one ratio of infant mortality rates and one-to-five ratio of net worth. While three out of two hundred young whites were incarcerated in 2000, the rate for young blacks was one in nine. A black male resident of the state of California is more likely to go to a state prison than a state college."[37]

Mass incarceration represents a singularly destructive governmental intervention that disproportionately burdens poor, inner-city, minority communities. To an excessive degree it has exiled young men and women from their neighborhoods; removed them from relatives, friends, lovers, and spouses; subjected them to inhumane prison conditions; neutered them as participants in politics (since in many states ex-convicts are not allowed to vote); and stigmatized them ruinously, preventing them from gaining economic security and thereby making them more vulnerable to recidivism.* Communities should be protected from dangerous

---

vantage white people. See N. C. Aizenman, " 'Tan Tax' Discussions Include Allegations of Reverse Racism," *Washington Post*, July 8, 2010.

* In previous work—see especially *Race, Crime, and the Law* (1997)—I erred in minimizing the communal injury inflicted by the hyper-punitiveness that is, unfortunately, an all-too-familiar feature of criminal-justice systems in America. I regret that oversight.

criminals—murderers, rapists, robbers—through deterrence and incapacitation; some people, alas, *must* be imprisoned. But there is good reason to doubt the morality as well as the efficacy of the war on drugs—a misguided campaign that has played a large role in blackening prison populations over the past several decades.

The aspect of the war on drugs that has most engaged proponents of a racial critique of mass incarceration is the singling out of crack-cocaine offenses as the infractions most warranting harsh punishments. Until recently, when the Supreme Court freed judges to depart somewhat from congressional directives in sentencing, federal law had decreed that a person convicted of possession with intent to distribute fifty grams or more of crack cocaine must be imprisoned for no less than ten years. By contrast, only if a person was convicted of possession with intent to distribute at least five thousand grams of powder cocaine was he subject to a mandatory minimum sentence of ten years—a hundred-to-one ratio in terms of the intensity of punishment. Moreover, a person caught merely possessing one to five grams of crack cocaine was subject to a mandatory minimum sentence of five years in prison. Crack cocaine was the only drug for which there existed a federal mandatory minimum penalty for a first offense of simple possession. This striking difference in punishment is joined by an arresting disparity in the racial demographics of those subjected to the harsh crack laws. In 1992, 92.6 percent of the defendants convicted for crack-cocaine offenses nationally were black, and only 4.7 percent were white. By contrast, 45.2 percent of defendants sentenced for powder-cocaine offenses were white, and only 20.7 percent were black.[38] More than a decade later the racial disparity held firm. In 2006, 82 percent of those sentenced under federal anticrack laws were black while only 8.8 percent were white—even though according to the United States Sentencing Commission, whites constitute more than two-thirds of those who use crack.[39]

Many have argued that, especially against the backdrop of these racial demographics, the federal government's peculiarly harsh punishment of crack-cocaine offenses is unwise and unfair, and violates the equal-protection clause of the Constitution.* President Obama is aware of mass incarceration, the war on drugs, and their racial consequences. In *The Audacity of Hope* he rejects the claim that those caught up in the drug hustle typically *prefer* drug-dealing to the discipline of earning a wage. Along with expressing a recognition of the essential humanity of people caught up in street life—an understanding that what makes them tick is essentially the same as what makes "regular" Americans tick—Obama hinted that he favored investing more resources in steering the most vulnerable away from criminality and reclaiming the fallen. Moreover, he gave reason to believe that, because of his own personal circumstances, he might bring to bear upon policy-making an active empathy for the multitudes whose lives have been blighted by the war on drugs. After all, he admitted to dabbling in marijuana and cocaine as a youth. "It seems reasonable to assume," Professor Michelle Alexander observes, "that Obama . . . would have a 'there but for the grace of God go I' attitude about millions of [men of color] imprisoned for drug offenses comparable to his own."[40]

I doubt, though, that Obama will expend much political capital addressing America's shameful penal policies and conditions. There is good reason to reform comprehensively the administration of criminal justice, particularly the war on drugs. The prosecution of that war is a classic instance of a "cure" being worse than the

---

* See, e.g., David A. Sklansky, "Cocaine, Race, and Equal Protection," *Stanford Law Review* 47 (1995): 1283, and David Cole, "The Paradox of Race and Crime: A Comment on Randall Kennedy's 'Politics of Distinction,' " *Georgetown Law Journal* 73 (1995): 2547. For an account that questions aspects of the racial critique of punishment for crack-cocaine infractions see Randall Kennedy, *Race, Crime, and the Law* (1997), 364–386.

disease. Obama, however, is highly unlikely to invest the resources that would be necessary to push crime control and punishment policy in a substantially more just and humane direction. He will be unwilling to risk being charged with racial partiality and being "soft" on crime.

My doubt that Obama will act decisively regarding this issue is nourished by what he has done and refrained from doing as a candidate and (thus far) as president. During the campaign, Obama kept his distance from racially inflected controversies involving civilians and law-enforcement officials. One of these controversies involved black teenagers in Jena, Louisiana—the Jena Six—who were charged with attempted murder for beating a white youngster. Though the black kids were by no means blameless*—indeed, their conduct was thuggish—it is clear that local authorities punished them excessively and subjected them to far harsher treatment than misbehaving white youth would have been subjected to. Prominent black activists, most notably Jesse Jackson, Sr., sought to enlist Obama in a campaign to mobilize public opinion in support of the Jena Six and in opposition to what they saw as old-fashioned law-and-order racism. They failed. Obama kept his distance. He mentioned the Jena Six when asked about their plight, commented on the case via press releases, and alluded to the issue briefly at appearances before black audiences. But Obama clearly resisted associating himself closely with the Jena Six protest. Jackson complained disapprovingly that Obama's standoffishness was tantamount to "acting like he's white."[41] Jackson likened the Jena Six protest to the protest in Selma, Alabama, in the 1960s and maintained

---

* See Richard Thompson Ford, "The Wrong Poster Children: Why the Jena 6 Protests Have Gone Awry," *Slate*, September 24, 2007. ("The 21st century civil rights movement will need more sympathetic poster children than the Jena 6. These young men weren't exactly engaged in peaceful civil disobedience when they ran afoul of the law.")

that if he had been running for president, he would have been "all over" the teenagers' case. Obama's white Democratic rivals for the nomination, especially Hillary Clinton, were also more aggressive and racially focused than he was willing to be. Clinton told attendees at an NAACP dinner in South Carolina that the Jena Six case "reminds us that the scales of justice are seriously out of balance when it comes to charging, sentencing, and punishing African Americans."[42] Obama was decidedly more understated. Reacting to Jackson's taunt, Obama averred that outrage at an injustice such as the one transpiring in Jena "isn't a matter of black and white. It's a matter of right and wrong."[43] Sticking to his strategy of deracialization, Obama sought as much as he could to avoid dirtying himself with the racial messiness of the dispute without alienating his African-American base. He saw deep engagement in the controversy as a losing proposition, a racial quagmire that, for many white voters, would only blacken him.

As president, Obama's first highly publicized encounter with racial conflict in the administration of criminal justice involved the Gates-Crowley fracas that led to the lamentable Beer Summit. This episode vividly underscores the power of certain continuities despite the Obama ascendancy. As one observer sardonically put it, a white police officer "made a bogus arrest and received an apology from the President of the United States and an invitation to the White House."[44] Obama's retreat from his correct chastisement of the officer involved in that episode of misused police power suggests that he is unlikely to do anything far-reaching about the problems of police misconduct and mass incarceration.

This is not to say that Obama will do nothing. He will generally refrain from taking steps that worsen the situation.* He will typi-

---

* It is important to recall, however, that during his first presidential campaign, Obama did criticize the Supreme Court when, in *Kennedy v. Louisiana*, 554 U.S. 407 (2008), it invalidated a state law that authorized capital punishment for the rape of minors.

cally appoint judges and other officials who will be more attuned to issues implicating racial justice than others who would be selected by a different president. Obama's Department of Justice, for instance, has urged an end to the singling out of crack-cocaine offenses.[45] It has recommended that crack cocaine be treated the same as powder cocaine, a reform which, if adopted, would save thousands from the especially severe punishments inflicted upon those caught up in possessing or dealing crack. The Obama administration did prompt Congress to lessen the crack-powder sentencing differential from 100 to 1 to 18 to 1. The president, however, made no statement personally when he signed the Fair Sentencing Act. Clearly he sought to avoid being closely associated with it and the issues from which it grew.

Despite the huge importance of the mass-incarceration disaster, Obama will decline to address it directly and comprehensively. That is because Obama is a professional politician first and last. For the sake of attaining and retaining power, he is willing to adopt, jettison, or manipulate positions as evolving circumstances require. Supporters call it adaptability, detractors opportunism.

Reminiscent of Bill Clinton's superintendence of an execution in Arkansas during the presidential campaign of 1992, Obama's critique of the Court's ruling in *Kennedy* was obviously intended to immunize him further against any charge that he is soft on crime. See Liliana Segura, "Obama's Draconian New Death Penalty Stance," *AlterNet*, June 27, 2008; and Michelle Alexander, *The New Jim Crow: Mass Incarceration in the Age of Colorblindness* (2010), 239–240.

The most dramatic example of tolerated racial discrimination in the administration of punishment occurs in the infliction of the death penalty. Capital punishment for rape has been an area in which racial discrimination has been repeatedly revealed but judicially denied. See Randall Kennedy, *Race, Crime, and the Law* (1997), 311–350.

Challenging the law authorizing the death penalty for the rape of a minor, the black defendant's attorneys in *Kennedy* adverted to the long-standing pattern whereby black men are virtually the only rapists sentenced to death. In an amicus curiae brief, the NAACP Legal Defense Fund and the American Civil Liberties Union noted that "Louisiana has executed only fourteen defendants for rape since 1941, and all fourteen were black." See Brief Amicus Curiae of the American Civil Liberties Union, the ACLU of Louisiana, and the NAACP Legal Defense and Educational Fund in Support of Petitioner, *Kennedy v. Louisiana*, 07–343, at 11.

He has liberal instincts and will effectuate progressive reforms—but only if he can do so without getting uncomfortably close to what he perceives to be too high a political price. That is why progressives need to put grassroots movements on the ground to serve as blockers. If they clear space for Obama on the left he will follow. But he will not himself lead the way.

Obama's cautiousness has prompted him on occasion to cede excessive ground to the right. In the course of nominating Sonia Sotomayor he carelessly reinforced conservative dogma about apolitical judging. To cite another example: Obama erred in backing away from his initial criticism of Officer Crowley. The facts were on Obama's side; the officer had behaved in a deeply objectionable fashion. The political price for sticking by his criticism, moreover, did not appear to be prohibitive. I hasten to reiterate what I have said before: any assessment of Obama must be made in acknowledgment of uncertainty. I do not know for sure what the balance of forces looked like from the perspective of the White House at that time. I would not want Obama to stick by his criticism of Officer Crowley under any circumstances—for example, if doing so would do him substantial long-term damage. In criticizing Obama I am simply expressing the view that he seems to have retreated in an unseemly way unnecessarily. At the same time, I hope that Obama will continue to be carefully attuned to public opinion. He must if he is to survive and flourish politically. I don't want him to be overly concerned with displaying "courage" or ideological purity—indicia of virtue that some of his detractors on the left admire and require. My requirements are different. I demand that he be a president who governs as progressively as circumstances will allow. Where that line rests at any particular point is difficult to assess, which is yet another reason for judging Obama's decisions deferentially.

Excessive deference, however, can also breed problems. It can breed complacency. If Obama is given a free pass by progressives, it is almost inevitable that he will fail to be as progressive as might otherwise be possible. The problem of excessive deference is all too evident. Consider commentary by the distinguished social scientist Lawrence Bobo. Alarmed by what he sees as misguided discontent, Professor Bobo states that he is "not just surprised by all the carping on the left, but bewildered and disappointed by it."[46] "The critique from the left," Bobo writes, "is as misplaced, self-indulgent, and politically naïve as the critique . . . from the right has been intransigent, irrational, and corrosive of the democratic process." Obama's leftist opponents, Bobo complains, appreciate all too little that he is "the best hope for a progressive agenda in these times, particularly on these issues likely to be of greatest concern for African American and Latino/a voters and communities." I partly agree with Bobo. I, too, fault some on the left who, in criticizing Obama, have allowed idealism to become an enemy of beneficent reform. Bobo, however, praises Obama too much. If Cornel West is too stingy in assessing Obama, Bobo is too generous. Relieved by the defeat of the Republicans in 2008, Bobo applies to Obama a standard of assessment that is too low. "What the left fails to acknowledge," Bobo declares, "are the enormous progressive accomplishments that Obama and his Administration are already achieving."

"Enormous" accomplishments?

The progressive reforms attributable to Obama are surely praiseworthy. But to laud them as "enormous" is to indulge in grade inflation. It is only because conservatism has driven left-liberal aspirations down so steeply that Obama's deeply compromised initiatives can possibly be perceived as remarkable. "Especially in areas affecting . . . racial and ethnic minorities," Bobo maintains, "there is unambiguous evidence [that the Obama administration] has charted a profoundly different course from that of its predecessor." That is true. But focusing the comparison on Bush sets up a woefully diminished baseline and is bound to make Obama look good.

How does Obama compare to his Democratic presidential predecessor Bill Clinton? Their racial politics are similar. Like Clinton, Obama abjures any policy smacking of invidious racial discrimination (in contrast to the indifference displayed by Republican presidents). Like Clinton, Obama takes pains to appoint people of color to high offices. Like Clinton, Obama is willing to do more than Republican politicians to ameliorate the plight of the truly disadvantaged. Like Clinton, Obama is comfortable around black folk, has close black friends, and knows intimately the gestures and inflections, jokes and allusions that will elicit the attention, respect, and support of blacks, especially the churchgoing sort. Like Clinton, Obama is adept at ceremonies at which he can pay homage to African-American icons or remedy oversights in public memory.

Obama is also like Clinton in that he makes sure to inoculate himself periodically against charges of Negrophilia by castigating blacks for illegitimacy, criminality, and other moral failings—sermons that would be easy to overlook were it not for their consequence of legitimating the notion that the predicament of the colored poor results primarily from their own conduct and not from the deformative deprivations imposed on them by a grievously unfair social order. Also like Clinton, Obama is unwilling to press hard and take risks to do what is necessary to create a true possibility for full employment and a real end to poverty, which is especially pronounced among people of color.

Clinton enjoys the reputation of having been a progressive president with special solicitude for blacks.* Yet he wrongly signed a deeply flawed welfare bill that hurt colored communities disproportionately. Moreover, in keeping with his sponsorship of

* See Randall Kennedy, "The Triumph of Robust Tokenism," *The Atlantic*, February 2001.

hyper-punitiveness, Clinton supported capital punishment despite the obvious fact that racial selectivity plays a major, though subtle, role in determining the unlucky few the State deems fit for killing. With respect to these and other similarly race-inflected issues, the differences between Presidents Clinton and Obama are minimal. Clinton initiated a national "Conversation on Race." It was a dud. But Clinton's Conversation did show a president who was at least willing to make some investment in educating the public about the American race question. Burdened by his blackness and inhibited by his caution, Obama is unlikely to make a comparable investment.

Obama's principal contribution to American race relations will derive not from any policies he initiates or decisions he makes but from the symbolic power of his example as a black man who became president. That he climbed to the apex of political power has irrevocably changed the imagination of America and, indeed, the world. Among colored folk, his ascendancy has raised expectations of what is possible for them to achieve in a "white" Western modern democracy. It has also affected the expectations of white folk, habituating them, like nothing before, to the prospect of people of color exercising power at the highest levels. There are many who still chafe at this turnabout—witness the racial component of the denial, resentment, and anger that has fueled reaction against the Obama administration.

The racial backlash, however, is eclipsed by the lesson being daily and pervasively absorbed—the message that a person of color can responsibly govern. Americans should not be boastful about learning that lesson at this late date; it should have been taken for granted long ago. But given the tragic cast of American race relations, a popular recognition of African-American inclusion, legitimacy, and competence in the White House is a substantial step forward. It is an advance that will forever be associated with Barack Obama, earning him a well-deserved place in American, indeed global, history.

Acknowledgments

I have received help with this book from many quarters. My colleagues at Harvard Law School, led by our wonderful dean, Martha Minow, create an excellent environment for all manner of intellectual endeavor. I learned much from the students who made so memorable the course I taught on the presidential election in 2008 as it unfolded before our eyes day by day. I shall always remember the class we had on November 6, 2008, as participants, often overcome by tears, voiced their feelings within hours of witnessing Barack Obama's victory.

The staff of the Langdell Library has been unfailingly useful. I am especially grateful for the assistance provided by Janet Katz, Michelle Pearse, Terri Gallego O'Rourke, Lisa Junghahn, Meg Kribble, George Taoultsides, and Melinda Kent.

Morgan Rucker Kennedy, Marianna Jackson, Tarun Chhabra, and Pamela Usukumah provided rewarding editorial and research assistance.

I benefited tremendously from responses I received to the lectures I delivered in Lyon, France, at forums organized by the Villa Gillet. I am deeply grateful for the warm hospitality offered to me on those occasions by Guy Walter and Cedric Duroux.

Four people, now deceased, provided me with buoyant memories and a legacy of generous lives well-lived: my father, Henry

Harold Kennedy, Sr.; my father-in-law, William E. Matory, Sr.; my wife, Yvedt Love Matory; and my splendid teacher John F. McCune.

Over the course of this project I have been able to count on the counsel of numerous friends and relatives who have been willing to read and reread my work. I am deeply grateful to Angela Acree, Richard Banks, David Barron, Gary Bell, Thaddeus Bell, Danielle Conway, Gary Chafetz, Justin Driver, Roger Fairfax, Richard Fallon, Eric Foner, Richard Ford, Lani Guinier, Jennifer Hochschild, Samuel Isaacharoff, Altomease Kennedy, Henry Kennedy, Jr., Sanford Levinson, Glenn Loury, Pope McCorkle, Darrell Miller, Eric Miller, Courtland Milloy, David Prather, Benjamin Sears, Michael Louis Seidman, Tommie Shelby, and David B. Wilkins.

Erroll McDonald, Altie Karper, Michiko Clark, and Andrew Wylie have enabled me to overcome procrastination. Henry William Kennedy, Rachel Kennedy, and Thaddeus Kennedy have helped me to escape despair. Alondra Nelson has been a tremendous source of encouragement and insight, love and happiness.

Notes

Introduction

1. See Henry Louis Gates, Jr., "In Our Lifetime," TheRoot.com, November 4, 2008.
2. Professor Angela Davis, AALSMinorityListServ, November 5, 2008.
3. Betsy Karasik, "Letter to a New Neighbor," *Washington Post*, November 23, 2008.
4. Posting of Bernie P. to http://comments.realclearpolitics.com/read.php?1,2588 61,259089,quote=1 (posted on November 5, 2008).
5. James Adler, Letter to the Editor, "Obama, History, and the Task Ahead," *New York Times*, November 5, 2008, http://www.nytimes.com/2008/11/06 /opinion/lo6elect.html.
6. Posting of deebee to http://jackandjillpolitics.disqus.com/wednesday _evening_open_thread/ (posted on November 5, 2008).
7. "Trouble with the Humans. Working-Class Whites Are Angry with the Democrats for Lots of Reasons. Race Is Not One Of Them." *The Economist*, Lexington column, October 21, 2010.
8. See, e.g., Lawrence Bobo, "It's Time for President Obama to Become a Leader," TheRoot.com, December 7, 2010 ("We still don't know who Obama is, what he is committed to and what he truly stands for"). Katrina vanden Heuvel, "Obama: On the Way to a Failed Presidency?," *Washington Post*, December 7, 2010.
9. Michael Tesler and David O. Sears, *Obama's Race: The 2008 Election and the Dream of a Post-Racial America* (2010), 5.
10. Ibid., at 159.
11. Dan Balz, "Biden Stumbles at the Starting Gate," *Washington Post*, February 1, 2007.
12. Ben T. Sweet, "Race Relations and the Presidential Election of 2008" (final paper, Harvard Law School, December 18, 2008). See also Andrew Gelman

and John Sides, "Stories and Stats: The Truth About Obama's Victory Wasn't in the Papers," *Boston Review*, September/October 2009.

13. CNN national exit polls. See results at http://www.cnn.com/ELECTION /2008/results/polls/#USP00p1 (retrieved on February 20, 2010).

14. John Heilemann, "The Glow of Obama's Mandate Is Good Enough for Now," *New York*, November 6, 2008. See also David Paul Kuhn, "Exit Polls: How Obama Won," *Politico*, November 5, 2008; Chris Kromm, "Election 2008: The Generation Gap: Young White Voters in the South," *Facing South*, November 12, 2008.

15. Barack Obama, "A More Perfect Union," speech given on March 18, 2008.

16. News conference by the president given on July 22, 2009.

17. See Michael D. Shear and Perry Bacon, Jr., "Black Lawmakers Call on Obama to Do More on Behalf of Blacks," *Washington Post*, December 9, 2009; Sheryl Gay Stolberg, "For Obama, Nuance on Race Invites Questions," *New York Times*, February 9, 2010.

18. Robert Kuttner, "Saving Progressivism from Obama," HuffingtonPost.com, November 21, 2010.

19. Remarks by the president and vice president at signing of the Don't Ask, Don't Tell Repeal Act of 2010, December 22, 2010.

20. Quoted in Geoffrey R. Stone, "Same-Sex Marriage and Interracial Marriage: What Do Barack Obama and Abraham Lincoln Have in Common?," HuffingtonPost.com, August 12, 2010. See also James Downie, "What Does Obama Really Think About Gay Marriage? A Telling Timeline," *The New Republic*, August 19, 2010.

21. See, e.g., William N. Eskridge, Jr., *The Case for Same-Sex Marriage: From Sexual Liberty to Civilized Commitment* (1996); Michael Mello and David L. Chambers, *Legalizing Gay Marriage* (2004); George Chauncey, *Why Marriage?: The History Shaping Today's Debate Over Gay Equality* (2004).

22. See, e.g., Stephen R. Haynes, *Noah's Curse: The Biblical Justification of American Slavery* (2002).

23. Quoted in *Loving v. Virginia*, 388 U.S. 1, 3 (1967). See also Fay Botham, *Almighty God Created the Races: Christianity, Interracial Marriage, and American Law* (2009).

24. Geoffrey R. Stone, "Same-Sex Marriage and Interracial Marriage: What Do Barack Obama and Abraham Lincoln Have in Common?," HuffingtonPost .com, August 12, 2010.

25. Downie, "What Does Obama Really Think About Gay Marriage?"

26. See Perry Bacon, Jr., "Obama Says His Views on Same-Sex Marriage Are 'Evolving,'" *Washington Post*, December 23, 2010.

27. See "Read/React: Michael Eric Dyson on Obama," TheRoot.com, January 11, 2010.

1. The Obama Inaugural

1. David Nakamura and Debbi Wilgoren, "A Massive Crowd Embraces the Moment," *Washington Post*, January 20, 2009.
2. Constance M. Green, *The Secret City: A History of Race Relations in the Nation's Capital* (1967).
3. See Steven F. Lawson, ed., "To Secure These Rights: The Report of Harry S. Truman's Committee on Civil Rights" (1947, 2004), at 118.
4. Harry S. Jaffe and Tom Sherwood, *Dream City: Race, Power, and the Decline of Washington, D.C.* (1994).
5. See Chuck Todd and Sheldon Geiser, *How Barack Obama Won: A State-by-State Guide to the Historic 2008 Presidential Election* (2009).
6. See Kenneth O'Reilly, *Nixon's Piano: Presidents and Racial Politics from Washington to Clinton* (1995), and Clarence Lusane, *The Black History of the White House* (2011).
7. See Henry Wienacek, *An Imperfect God: George Washington, His Slaves, and the Creation of America* (2003).
8. Lusane, *The Black History of the White House*, 35–47.
9. Ibid., 80–81.
10. Thomas Jefferson, *Notes on the State of Virginia* (1782); Thomas Jefferson to Thomas Cooper, September 1814.
11. See Winthrop D. Jordan, *White Over Black: American Attitudes Towards the Negro, 1550–1812* (1968), and John Chester Miller, *The Wolf by the Ears: Thomas Jefferson and Slavery* (1991).
12. See Robert V. Remini, *The Life of Andrew Jackson* (1988), and Robert V. Remini, *The Legacy of Andrew Jackson: Essays on Democracy, Indian Removal and Slavery* (1988).
13. O'Reilly, *Nixon's Piano*, at 36–37. See also William Dusinberre, *Slavemaster President: The Double Career of James Polk* (2003).
14. Quoted in James McPherson, "What Did He Really Think About Race?," *New York Review of Books*, March 27, 2007.
15. Quoted in O'Reilly, *Nixon's Piano*, at 50. See also David Warren Bowen, *Andrew Johnson and the Negro* (1989).
16. See "John McCain's Speech to the NAACP," *New York Times*, July 16, 2008; "McCain's Concession Speech," *New York Times*, November 5, 2008.
17. Quoted in Edmund Morris, *Theodore Rex* (2001), 54.
18. Ibid., 55.
19. Quoted in O'Reilly, *Nixon's Piano*, at 96.
20. See Dewayne Wickham, *Bill Clinton and Black America* (2002).
21. See Eric Foner, *Freedom's Lawmakers: A Directory of Black Officeholders During Reconstruction* (1996), at xvii.

22. Ibid., at xv.
23. See Richard A. Primus, "The Riddle of Hiram Revels," *Harvard Law Review* 119 (2005): 1681, 1682.
24. Quoted in ibid., at 1694.
25. See Edmund L. Drago, *Black Politicians and Reconstruction in Georgia: A Splendid Failure* (1992, 1982).
26. See William Gilette, *The Right to Vote: Politics and the Passage of the Fifteenth Amendment* (1965).
27. Foner, *Freedom's Lawmakers*, at xxvii.
28. Ibid., at xxviii.
29. Ibid.
30. James S. Pike, *The Prostrate South: South Carolina Under Negro Government* (1874), at 11–12.
31. E. Merton Coulter, *The South During Reconstruction, 1865–1866* (1947), at 141–144.
32. See Morton Stavis, "A Century of Struggle for Black Enfranchisement in Mississippi: From the Civil War to the Congressional Challenge of 1965— and Beyond," *Mississippi Law Journal* 57 (1987): 591.
33. Rep. George Henry White, "Address to Congress," January 29, 1901.
34. See Nancy Weiss, *Farewell to the Party of Lincoln: Black Politics in the Age of F.D.R.* (1983).
35. See Raymond H. Geselbrecht, ed., *The Civil Rights Legacy of Harry S. Truman* (2007).
36. See Nick Kotz, *Judgment Days: Lyndon Baines Johnson, Martin Luther King, Jr., and the Laws That Changed America* (2005), and Robert Mann, *The Walls of Jericho: Lyndon Johnson, Hubert Humphrey, Richard Russell, and the Struggle for Civil Rights* (1996).
37. See Dan T. Carter, *The Politics of Rage: George Wallace, the Origins of the New Conservatism, and the Transformation of American Politics* (2000), and Dean J. Kotlowski, *Nixon's Racial Rights: Politics, Principle, and Policy* (2001).
38. Quoted in David R. Colburn, "Running for Office: African-American Mayors from 1967 to 1996," in David R. Colburn and Jeffrey S. Adler, eds., *African American Mayors: Race, Politics, and the American City* (2001), 47.
39. See Colburn and Adler, *African American Mayors*.
40. "Douglas Wilder and the Continuing Significance of Race: An Analysis of the 1989 Gubernatorial Election," *Journal of Political Science* 23 (1995): 87; J. L. Jeffries, *Virginia's Native Son: The Election and Administration of Governor L. Douglas Wilder* (2000); and R. A. Strickland and M. L. Whicker, "Comparing the Wilder and Gantt Campaigns," *Political Science & Politics* 25 (1992): 204.
41. See, e.g., Jason Carroll, "Will Obama Suffer from the 'Bradley Effect?'" CNN.com, October 13, 2008, available at http://articles.cnn.com/2008

-10-13/politics/obama.bradley.effect_1_bradley-effect-bradley-campaign
-exit-polls?_s=PM:POLITICS.

42. Quoted in Henry Louis Gates, Jr., *Thirteen Ways of Looking at a Black Man* (1997), at 99.

43. See Shirley Chisholm, *Unbought and Unbossed* (1970), and the film documentary *Chisholm '72: Unbought and Unbossed*, Shola Lynch, director (2005).

44. Shirley Chisholm, speech given on June 4, 1972, quoted in Gloria Steinem, "The Ticket That Might Have Been," *Ms.* (January 1973).

45. See Marshall Frady, *The Life and Pilgrimage of Jesse Jackson* (1996); Lucius J. Barker and Ronald W. Walters, eds., *Jesse Jackson's 1984 Presidential Campaign: Challenge and Change in American Politics* (1989); Frank Clemente with Frank Watkins, eds., *Keep Hope Alive: Jesse Jackson's 1988 Presidential Campaign; A Collection of Major Speeches, Issue Papers, Photographs and Campaign Analysis* (1989); and Adolph L. Reed, Jr., *The Jesse Jackson Phenomenon* (1986).

46. See "Behind the Hero: Black History," *New York Times*, July 22, 1988. See also Michael Oreskes, "Voters and Jackson: Confronting Racial Limitations and Lifting Them, a Bit," *New York Times*, August 13, 1988.

47. See William Jelani Cobb, *The Substance of Hope: Barack Obama and the Paradox of Progress* (2010), at 49.

48. See, e.g., Larry J. Sabato, "Jesse Jackson's 'Hymietown' Remark—1984," WashingtonPost.com (1998), available at http://www.washingtonpost.com/wp-srv/politics/special/clinton/frenzy/jackson.htm.

49. On Louis Farrakhan see Arthur J. Magida, *Prophet of Rage: A Life of Louis Farrakhan and His Nation* (1996); Amy Alexander, ed., *The Farrakhan Factor: African American Writers on Leadership, Nationhood and Minister Louis Farrakhan* (1998); and Mattias Gardell, *In the Name of Elijah Muhammad: Louis Farrakhan and the Nation of Islam* (1996).

50. See Mattias Gardell, *In the Name of Elijah Muhammad: Louis Farrakhan and the Nation of Islam* (1996), 245–271.

51. On Colin Powell see Karen DeYoung, *Soldier: The Life of Colin Powell* (2006), and Colin Powell with Joseph E. Persico, *My American Journey* (2003).

52. See Martin Plissner, "Ready for Obama Already," *New York Times*, February 7, 2007.

53. See Jacob Javits, "Integration from the Top Down," Esquire.com (originally published in the December 1958 issue of *Esquire*).

54. Quoted in "Obama Proved Them Wrong: Historical Speculation on the Prospects of a Black President," *Journal of Blacks in Higher Education*, Winter 2009/2010.

55. Ibid.

56. Ibid.

57. Ibid.

58. William Jelani Cobb, *The Substance of Hope: Barack Obama and the Paradox of Progress* (2010), 10. Similarly, Cobb maintains that "Obama knew something about race that [few] knew in 2007: that the country was prepared to elect an African American to the highest office in the land." Ibid., at 32.

59. Quoted in Greg Mitchell, "Racial Incidents and Threats Against Obama Soar: Here Is a Chronicle," HuffingtonPost.com, November 15, 2008.

60. See Milton J. Valencia, "Post-election Fire at Springfield Church Raises Questions," *Boston Globe*, November 5, 2008.

61. See Alex Koppelman, "Nader Refers to Obama as 'Uncle Tom,'" Salon.com, November 5, 2008, http://www.salon.com/news/politics/war_room/2008/11/05/nader.

62. Quoted in Breyten Breytenbach, "Obamadela," *Harper's Magazine*, March 2009.

2. Obama Courts Black America

1. See Dawn Turner Trice, "Obama Unfazed by Foes' Doubts on Race Question," *Chicago Tribune*, March 15, 2004 (quoting Barack Obama as saying, "My view has always been that I'm African-American"), and see "Remarks of Senator Barack Obama," Howard University, September 28, 2007 (Obama refers to himself as "a black man named Barack Obama").

2. See Adam Serwer, "He's Black, Get Over It," *American Prospect*, December 5, 2008.

3. See Kathy Russell, Midge Wilson, and Ronald Hall, *The Color Complex: The Politics of Skin Color Among African Americans* (1992), and Trina Jones, "Shades of Brown: The Law of Skin Color," *Drake Law Journal* 49 (2000): 1487; Darrick Hamilton, Arthur H. Goldsmith, William Darity, Jr., "Shedding 'Light' on Marriage: The Influence of Skin Shade on Marriage for Black Females," *Journal of Economic Behavior and Organization* 72 (2009).

4. Quoted in Robert Brent Toplin, "Between Black and White: Attitudes Towards Southern Mulattoes, 1830–1861," *Journal of Southern History* 45 (1979): 185, 197–198.

5. Ibid.

6. See *Perez v. Sharp*, 198 P.2d 17 (1948).

7. Quoted in Toplin, "Between Black and White," at 192.

8. See, e.g., E. B. Reuter, "The Superiority of the Mulatto," *American Journal of Sociology* 23 (1917): 83.

9. See Jeff Zeleny and Joseph Berger, "GOP Chairman Urges Reid to Step Down Over Remarks," *New York Times*, January 10, 2010.

10. Jennifer L. Hochschild and Vesla Weaver, "The Skin Color Paradox and the American Racial Order," *Social Forces* 86 (2007).

11. See *Plessy v. Ferguson*, 163 U.S. 537 (1896).
12. See Thomas Dixon, *The Leopard's Spots: A Romance of the White Man's Burden, 1865–1900* (1902).
13. Christine B. Hickman, "The Devil and the One Drop Rule: Racial Categories, African Americans and the U.S. Census," *Michigan Law Review* 95 (1997): 1161, 1166.
14. See cbsnews.com/stories/2007/02/09/60minutes.
15. W. E. B. Du Bois, *Dusk of Dawn: An Essay Toward an Autobiography of a Race Concept* (1940, 1992), 153.
16. See Marie Arana, "He's Not Black," *Washington Post*, November 30, 2008.
17. See "Many Insisting That Obama Is Not Black," HuffingtonPost.com, December 14, 2008.
18. See James Hannaham, "Multiracial Man," Salon.com, February 2, 2008 (quoting Joy Zaremba: Obama ought to "come out and be a proud biracial American").
19. Trice, "Obama Unfazed."
20. See Hannaham, "Multiracial Man."
21. Barack Obama, *The Audacity of Hope: Thoughts on Reclaiming the American Dream* (2006), 231.
22. Barack Obama, "The America We Love," June 30, 2008.
23. See Gary Younge, "Is Obama Black Enough?," *Guardian*, March 1, 2007.
24. See Dan Terry, "The Skin Game: Do White Voters Like Barack Obama Because He's Not Really Black?," *Chicago Tribune*, October 24, 2004.
25. Stanley Crouch, "What Obama Isn't: Black Like Me," New York *Daily News*, November 2, 2006.
26. See Debra J. Dickerson, "Colorblind," Salon.com, January 22, 2007.
27. See "Historians' First Draft on Obama," MSNBC.com, November 5, 2008.
28. See Younge, "Is Obama Black Enough?" See also Leonard Pitts, "'Black Enough' and Liberal Too," *Sacramento Bee*, August 16, 2007 ("Obama is upwardly mobile, Harvard educated and beloved by many white liberals. So he is regarded by some [blacks] with suspicion"). Salim Muwakkil, "Barack Obama Made Smashing National Debut," *Progressive*, July 28. 2004; Ted Kleine, "Is Bobby Rush in Trouble?," *Chicago Reader*, March 17, 2000; Ben Smith, "Obama's Introduction: Black Enough," *Politico*, June 17, 2007.
29. Quoted in David Mandell, *Obama: From Promise to Power* (2007), 131. See also Salim Muwakkil, "Ironies Abound in 1st District," *Chicago Tribune*, March 20, 2000. See also Timothy Stewart-Winter, "Before Obama Was a Favorite Son," RealClearPolitics.com, April 7, 2008.
30. Quoted in Mandell, *Obama*, at 131.
31. See Rachel L. Swarns, "So Far, Obama Can't Take Black Vote for Granted," *New York Times*, February 2, 2007. See also Jonathan Tilove, "Obama and Race," *Post-Standard* (Syracuse, N.Y.), and Michael Paul Williams, "Is

Barack Obama Black Enough?," *Richmond Times-Dispatch*, February 16, 2007.

32. See David Mendell, *Obama: From Promise to Power* (2007), 189–190.

33. Lawrence Otis Graham, *Member of the Club: Reflections on Life in a Racially Polarized World* (1995), 41.

34. See Ryan Lizza, "Making It," *The New Yorker*, July 21, 2008.

35. Ta-Nehisi Coates, "A Deeper Black," *The Nation*, May 1, 2008.

36. See Dahlia Lithwack, "A Complicated Record on Race," *Newsweek*, April 7, 2008.

37. Obama, *Audacity of Hope*, at 244.

38. Quoted in Richard Kahlenberg, "Obama's RFK Moment," Slate.com, February 4, 2008.

39. Ibid.

40. See, e.g., Richard Kahlenberg, "Barack Obama and Affirmative Action," InsideHigherEd.com, May 12, 2008 ("Obama's suggestion that he may be ready to change the focus of affirmative action policies in higher education— away from race to economic class—could prove pivotal in his efforts to reach working-class whites").

41. Stephen Carter, *Reflections of an Affirmative Action Baby* (1991), 101; Orlando Patterson, "Affirmative Action: The Sequel," *New York Times*, June 22, 2003.

42. See Kelefa Sanneh, "What He Knows for Sure," *The New Yorker*, August 4, 2008.

43. Denise Watson Batts, "Tavis Smiley to Hold Annual 'State of the Black Union 2007' This Weekend," *Virginian-Pilot*, February 6, 2007.

44. Quoted in Sanneh, "What He Knows."

45. See Melissa Harris-Lacewell, "Who Died and Made Tavis King?," TheRoot.com, February 15, 2008.

46. Ibid.

47. Earl Ofari Hutchinson, "Hang in There Tavis Smiley, Don't Let the Black Thought Police Run You Out," HuffingtonPost.com, April 11, 2008.

48. Gloria Steinem, "Women Are Never Front-Runners," *New York Times*, January 8, 2008.

49. Ibid.

50. Ibid.

51. Ibid.

52. See "Race and Gender in Presidential Politics: A Debate Between Gloria Steinem and Melissa Harris-Lacewell," *Democracy Now*, January 14, 2008. See also Betsy Reed, "Race to the Bottom," *The Nation*, May 1, 2008, and Kimberlé Crenshaw and Eve Ensler, "Feminist Ultimatum: Not in Our Name," HuffingtonPost.com, February 5, 2008; Allison Samuels, "The Legacy of My Grandmother," *Newsweek*, March 17, 2008.

53. See Robert L. Allen with the collaboration of Pamela P. Allen, *Reluctant*

Reformers: Racism and Social Reform Movements in the United States (1983), and Winifred Breines, *The Trouble Between Us: An Uneasy History of White and Black Women in the Feminist Movement* (2006).

54. See, e.g., Reed, "Race to the Bottom."

55. See Randall Kennedy, "Marriage and the Struggle for Gay, Lesbian, and Black Liberation," *Utah Law Review* 3 (2005): 781.

56. See Reed, "Race to the Bottom."

57. Alice Walker, "Lest We Forget: An Open Letter to My Sisters Who Are Brave," *The Black Scholar* 38 (Spring 2008): 44.

58. Thomas Sowell, "The Audacity of Rhetoric," RealClearPolitics.com, March 25, 2008.

59. Thomas Sowell, "A Living Lie," RealClearPolitics.com, April 15, 2008.

60. Shelby Steele, "Why Jesse Jackson Hates Obama . . ." *Wall Street Journal,* July 22, 2008.

61. Shelby Steele, "The Obama Bargain," *Wall Street Journal,* March 18, 2008.

62. For descriptions and analysis of black conservatism see Michael Dawson, *Black Visions: The Roots of Contemporary African-American Political Ideologies* (2003), and Christopher Bracey, *Savior of Sellouts: The Promise and Peril of Black Conservatism, from Booker T. Washington to Condoleezza Rice* (2008).

63. Juan Williams, "Obama's Color Line," *New York Times,* November 30, 2007.

64. Ibid.

65. Ibid.

66. Juan Williams, "Obama and King," *Wall Street Journal,* April 4, 2008.

67. Ibid.

68. Juan Williams, "Face It, Democrats: Barack Obama's Got a Growing Problem with Whites," New York *Daily News,* May 11, 2008.

69. Juan Williams, "It's Time for Another Obama Race Speech," *Wall Street Journal,* June 6, 2008.

70. Ibid.

71. Kathleen Wells, "A Conversation with Dr. Cornel West," *Race-Talk,* February 23, 2010.

72. *Drs. Julianne Malveaux and Cornel West* (PBS television broadcast August 28, 2008), http://www.pbs.org/kcet/tavissmiley/archive/200808/20080828_drs juliannemalvea.html.

73. Ibid.

74. Adolph Reed, Jr., "Obama No," *Progressive,* May 2008.

75. Bruce Dixon, "Obama's Multiracial Coalition and the Politics of 'Racial Reconciliation,'" BlackAgendaReport.com, March 19, 2008.

76. Glen Ford, "Obama Won't Address Specific Black Concerns," BlackAgenda Report.com, August 6, 2008.

77. Glen Ford, "Why Barack Obama Needs a Whuppin': Honest Abe, He Ain't," BlackAgendaReport.com, June 13, 2007.

78. For an illuminating version of this perspective see Paul Street, *Barack Obama and the Future of American Politics* (2009).
79. See Randall Kennedy, "The Triumph of Robust Tokenism," *The Atlantic*, February 2001.

3. Obama and White America: "Why Can't They All Be Like Him?"

1. See James Hannaham, "Obama and the Rules for Angry Black Men," Salon .com, September 18, 2008.
2. Barack Obama, "A More Perfect Union," speech on March 18, 2008 (transcript available at http://www.nytimes.com/2008/03/18/us/politics/18text -obama.html).
3. Obama, "A More Perfect Union."
4. Barack Obama, *The Audacity of Hope: Thoughts on Reclaiming the American Dream* (2006), 247.
5. See, e.g., Jeremy I. Levitt and Matthew Whitaker, eds., *Hurricane Katrina: America's Unnatural Disaster* (2009).
6. Obama, *Audacity of Hope*, 229.
7. See, e.g., Maria Gavrilovic, "Obama Talks of Family's Military Service," CBS News, May 26, 2008.
8. Richard Cohen, "Obama's Farrakhan Test," *Washington Post*, January 15, 2008.
9. Quoted in Jason Linkins, "Richard Cohen Suggests Obama Has a 'Farrakhan Test,' Obama Responds," HuffingtonPost.com, January 15, 2008.
10. Quoted in "Russert Plays the Farrakhan Card," YouTube.com, February 26, 2008. See also the interesting commentary by Ann Althouse, "Obama, Farrakhan, and How Hillary Clinton Took the Opening and Then Squandered It," Althouse.com, February 27, 2008.
11. Althouse, "Obama, Farrakhan, and Clinton."
12. Quoted in Mary Mitchell, "Why Obama 'Denounced' Farrakhan," *Chicago Sun-Times*, March 2, 2008.
13. Ibid.
14. See Kelefa Sanneh, "Project Trinity," *The New Yorker*, April 7, 2008.
15. See Brian Knowlton and Jodi Kantor, "Obama Camp Caught up in Minister's Controversial Remarks," *New York Times*, March 17, 2008.
16. See "The Reverend Jeremiah Wright Was an Early Concern, Obama Aide Admits," LATimesBlog.LATimes.com, March 16, 2008.
17. Brian Ross and Rehab El-Bari, "Obama's Pastor: God Damn America, U.S. to Blame for 9/11," ABC News, March 13, 2008.
18. Quoted in Nedra Pickler and Matt Appuzzo, "Obama Confronts Racial Division," Associated Press, March 18, 2008.

19. John McCain, interview with Chris Matthews, *Hardball* College Tour at Villanova University, April 15, 2008.
20. Newt Gingrich, "The Obama Challenge: What Is the Right Change to Help All Americans Pursue Happiness and Create Prosperity?," Newt.org, March 26, 2008.
21. Quoted in Jake Tapper, "Huckabee Defends Obama . . . and the Rev. Wright," ABCNews.com, March 19, 2008.
22. Peggy Noonan, "A Thinking Man's Speech," *Wall Street Journal*, March 21, 2008.
23. Charles Murray, "Have I Missed the Competition?," *National Review Online*, March 18, 2008.
24. "Moment of Truth," *Washington Post*, March 19, 2008.
25. George Packer, "Native Son," *The New Yorker*, March 31, 2008.
26. Frank Rich, "The Republican Resurrection," *New York Times*, March 23, 2008.
27. Nicholas Kristof, "Obama and Race," *New York Times*, March 20, 2008.
28. See "Progressives for Obama," *The Nation*, March 2, 2008.
29. See Howard Kurtz, "A Complex Speech, Boiled Down to Simple Politics," *Washington Post*, March 20, 2008.
30. Charles Krauthammer, "Justifying a Scandalous Dereliction," *National Review Online*, March 21, 2008.
31. Ibid.
32. Victor Davis Hanson, "The Obama Crash and Burn," *National Review*, March 24, 2008.
33. Ibid.
34. See "Obama Weathers the Wright Storm, Clinton Faces Credibility Problem," survey report, PEW Research Center for the People and the Press, March 27, 2008.
35. Joan Morgan, "Black Like Barack," in T. Denean Sharpley-Whiting, ed., *The Speech: Race and Barack Obama's "A More Perfect Union"* (2009), 55–56.
36. Andrew Sullivan, "The Speech," TheAtlantic.com, March 18, 2008, andrewsullivan.atlantic.com/the_daily_dish/2008/03/the-speech.html.
37. Richard Thompson Ford, *The Race Card* (2009), 365.
38. See "Obama's Father's Day Speech Urges Black Fathers to Be More Engaged in Raising Their Children," HuffingtonPost.com, June 15, 2008.
39. See Jeff Zeleny, "Jesse Jackson Apologizes for Remarks on Obama," *New York Times*, July 10, 2008.
40. Kevin Alexander Gray, "Why Does Barack Obama Hate My Family?," *Counterpunch*, July 11, 2008.
41. Gary Younge, "Internet Conversations," *The Nation*, August 4/11, 2008.
42. See John Judis, "Is Obama Al Smith or John F. Kennedy?," *The New Republic*, June 4, 2008.
43. See Christopher M. Finan, *Alfred E. Smith: The Happy Warrior* (2002).

44. Ibid., at 213.
45. Quoted in Thomas J. Carty, *A Catholic in the White House? Religion, Politics, and John F. Kennedy's Presidential Campaign* (2004), 55.
46. Quoted in Shaun A. Casey, *The Making of a Catholic President: Kennedy vs. Nixon 1960* (2009), 191.
47. Ibid.
48. Ibid., at 151.
49. Ibid., at 168.
50. Quoted in George J. Marlin, "JFK's Houston Speech at 50: Three Views," TheCatholicThing.org, September 9, 2010.
51. Quoted in Casey, *Making of a Catholic President*, at 169.
52. Quoted in Carty, *Catholic in the White House?*, at 94.
53. Ibid., at 1.
54. Ibid., at 1–2.

4. The Race Card in the Campaign of 2008

1. Quoted in Kate Phillips, "Bill Clinton: 'I Am Not a Racist,'" *New York Times*, August 4, 2008.
2. "Running While Black," *New York Times*, August 2, 2008.
3. Tali Mendelberg, *The Race Card: Campaign Strategy, Implicit Messages, and the Norm of Equality* (2001), 39.
4. Quoted in Forrest G. Wood, *Black Scare: The Racist Response to Emancipation and Reconstruction* (1968), 71.
5. Quoted in Dan T. Carter, *The Politics of Rage: George Wallace, the Origins of the New Conservatism and the Transformation of American Politics* (1995), 96.
6. See Donald R. Kinder and Lynn M. Sanders, *Divided by Color: Racial Politics and Democratic Ideals* (1996), 223. See also Carter, *Politics of Rage*.
7. Quoted in Kinder and Sanders, *Divided by Color*, at 227.
8. Bob Herbert, "Righting Reagan's Wrongs?," *New York Times*, November 13, 2007. See also David Greenberg, "Dog Whistling Dixie," Slate.com, November 20, 2007, and Kinder and Sanders, *Divided by Color*.
9. See Mendelberg, *Race Card*.
10. See Richard Thompson Ford, *The Race Card: How Bluffing About Bias Makes Race Relations Worse* (2008).
11. See Robert D. McFadden et al., *Outrage: The Story Behind the Tawana Brawley Hoax* (1990).
12. See Jeffrey Toobin, *The Run of His Life: The People v. O. J. Simpson* (1996).
13. Quoted in Sarah Wheaton, "Clinton's Civil Rights Lesson," *New York Times*, January 7, 2008.
14. "Unite, Not Divide, Really This Time," editorial, *New York Times*, January 9, 2008.

15. See "Bill Moyers on Clinton, Obama, King, and Johnson: A Bill Moyers Essay," January 18, 2008, PBS.org.

16. See "Bill Clinton on Barack Obama," YouTube.com, January 26, 2008.

17. See, e.g., Jake Tapper, "Bubba: Obama Is Just Like Jesse Jackson," ABC News: Political Punch blog, http://blogs.abcnews.com/politicalpunch/2008/01/bubba-obama-is.html (January 26, 2008).

18. Kathy Kiely and Jill Lawrence, "Clinton Makes Case for Wide Appeal," *USA Today*, May 7, 2008.

19. See Joe Conason, "Was Hillary Channeling George Wallace?," Salon.com, May 9, 2008.

20. Bob Herbert, "Seeds of Destruction," *New York Times*, May 10, 2008.

21. Orlando Patterson, "The Red Phone in Black and White," *New York Times*, March 11, 2008.

22. Response 34 of 737 readers' comments to Patterson, "The Red Phone in Black and White," posted March 11, 2008.

23. See DailyHowler.com, March 11, 2008.

24. Quoted in Jayson K. Jones and Ana C. Rosado, "Obama Campaign Criticizes Ferraro Comments," *New York Times*, March 11, 2008.

25. See Ta-Nehisi Coates, "Playing the Race Card," Slate.com, March 14, 2008.

26. Quoted in Jones and Rosado, "Obama Campaign Criticizes Ferraro."

27. Ibid.

28. See Calvin Trillin, "The Essence of Geraldine Ferraro's Explanation of Why Barack Obama Is in the Lead for the Democratic Nomination," *The Nation*, April 7, 2008.

29. See Andrew Sullivan, "Goodbye to All That: Why Obama Matters," *The Atlantic*, December 2007.

30. See, e.g., Christopher Hitchens, "Fool Me Thrice," Slate.com, January 28, 2008 ("How can one equal Bill Clinton for thuggery and opportunism when it comes to the so-called 'race card'?"); Eugene Robinson, "The Card Clinton Is Playing," *Washington Post*, May 9, 2008; Bob Herbert, "Seeds of Destruction," *New York Times*, May 10, 2008. See also Chris Cillizza and Shailegh Murray, "Racial Undercurrent Is Seen in Clinton Campaign," WashingtonPost.com, December 23, 2007.

31. See Herbert, "Seeds of Destruction."

32. See Sean Wilentz, "Race Man: How Barack Obama Played the Race Card and Blamed Hillary Clinton," *The New Republic*, February 27, 2008.

33. Quoted in Alex Koppelman, "Obama Co-chairman: Clinton Didn't Cry for Katrina," Salon.com, January 9, 2008.

34. "Politics of Attack," *New York Times*, October 8, 2008.

35. Derrick Z. Jackson, "McCain Plays the Race Card," *Boston Globe*, October 14, 2008.

36. Quoted in Elisabeth Bumiller, "Congressman Rebukes McCain for Recent Rallies," *New York Times*, October 11, 2008.

37. Quoted in Kate Phillips, "Palin: Obama Is 'Palling Around with Terrorists,'" *New York Times*, October 4, 2008.

38. See, e.g., Rachel Weiner, "Obama Hatred at McCain-Palin Rallies: 'Terrorists!' 'Kill Him!,'" HuffingtonPost.com, October 6, 2008; El Zicho, "McCain Rally Racism: 'I'd Never Vote for a Black Man.' Complete with Veiled Assassination Threats," DailyKos.com, October 29, 2008; Frank Rich, "The Terrorist Barack Hussein Obama," *New York Times*, October 11, 2008.

39. See Drew Westen, *The Political Brain: The Role of Emotion in Deciding the Fate of the Nation* (2007), 243–245.

40. See Bill Press, "John McCain Plays the Race Card," HuffingtonPost.com, July 31, 2008.

41. Bob Herbert, "Running While Black," *New York Times*, August 2, 2008.

42. Hendrik Hertzberg, "Race, Lies, and Videotape," *The New Yorker*, August 6, 2008.

43. See "Dukakis: McCain Using Same Race Tactics as 'Willie Horton' Ad," HuffingtonPost.com, September 22, 2008.

44. Karen Tumulty, "McCain Plays the Race Card," Time.com, September 18, 2008.

45. Ford, *The Race Card*, at 339.

46. See Holly Bailey, "Do the Wright Thing," *Newsweek*, October 27, 2008, and William Kristol, "The Wright Stuff," *New York Times*, October 6, 2008.

47. See Michael Cooper, "McCain Criticizes Remarks by Obama's Former Pastor," *New York Times*, April 28, 2008, and Sam Stein, "Rick Davis: Campaign Rethinking Playing the Rev. Wright Card," HuffingtonPost.com, October 20, 2008.

48. See Michael Scherer, "The Anti-Obama Campaign That Didn't Happen," Time.com, November 24, 2008 ("Davis says that concern about race played a major role in the entire aesthetic of McCain's ads").

49. Quoted in Jayson K. Jones and Ana C. Rosado, "McCain Campaign Says Obama Is Playing the 'Race Card,'" *New York Times*, July 31, 2008.

50. Ibid.

51. Ibid.

52. Quoted in Michael Cooper and Michael Powell, "McCain Camp Says Obama Is Playing 'Race Card,'" *New York Times*, August 1, 2008.

53. "Who's Playing the Race Card?," *Washington Post*, October 17, 2008.

54. Quoted in Cooper and Powell, "McCain Campaign Says Obama Playing 'Race Card.'"

55. Michael Powell, "With Genie out of Bottle, Obama Is Careful on Race," *New York Times*, August 2, 2008.

5. Reverend Wright and My Father:
Reflections on Blacks and Patriotism

1. Quoted in Jake Tapper, "Michelle Obama: 'For the First Time in My Adult Lifetime, I'm Really Proud of My Country,'" ABCNews.com, February 18, 2008.

2. Quoted in Michael Cooper, "Cindy McCain's Pride," *New York Times*, February 19, 2008.

3. See David Greenberg, "Waving the Flag," Slate.com, July 2–3, 2008.

4. See Evan Thomas, "Alienated in the USA," *Newsweek*, March 13, 2008.

5. Andrew C. McCarthy, "The Company He Keeps," *National Review*, April 11, 2008.

6. See Merle Curti, *The Roots of American Loyalty* (1946, 1968).

7. See Julianne Malveaux and Reginna A. Green, eds., *The Paradox of Loyalty: An African American Response to the War on Terrorism* (2002), 47.

8. Alasdair MacIntyre, "Is Patriotism a Virtue?" in Igor Primoratz, ed., *Patriotism* (2002), 210–211.

9. John F. Kennedy, Inaugural Address, January 20, 1961.

10. See, e.g., Igor Primoratz, ed., *Patriotism* (2002); Joshua Cohen and Martha Nussbaum, *For Love of Country: Debating the Limits of Patriotism* (1996).

11. George Santayana, *The Life of Reason* (1905).

12. Leo Tolstoy, *On Patriotism* (1894).

13. George Bernard Shaw, *World*, November 15, 1893.

14. Michael Eric Dyson, "Understanding Black Patriotism," *Time*, April 24, 2008.

15. Quoted in Ray Raphael, *Founding Myths: Stories That Hide Our Patriot Past* (2004), 180.

16. See Gary Nash, Introduction to Benjamin Quarles, *The Negro in the American Revolution* (1991), xv.

17. Quarles, *Negro in the American Revolution*, xxvii.

18. Frederick Douglass, "Why Should a Colored Man Enlist?," *Douglass' Monthly*, April 1863.

19. See Sterling Brown, "Count Us In," in Rayford Logan, *What the Negro Wants* (1944, 2001), 331.

20. Quoted in "Documents: James Madison's Attitude Toward the Negro" and "Advice Given Negroes a Century Ago," *Journal of Negro History* 6 (1921): 74, 79, 103. See also Drew McCoy, *The Last of the Fathers: James Madison and the Republican Legacy* (1989), 253–322.

21. David Walker, *Appeal to the Coloured Citizens of the World* (1829), available at http://www.pbs.org/wgbh/aia/part4/4h2931t.html.

22. Quoted in Theodore Draper, *The Rediscovery of Black Nationalism* (1980), 15.

23. Ibid., at 10.

24. Ibid., at 42.

25. Catherine Ellis and Stephen Drury Smith, eds., *Say It Plain: A Century of Great African American Speeches* (2005), 13–14.

26. Quoted in James M. McPherson, "The Negro's Civil War: How American Blacks Felt and Acted During the War for the Union" (1967), 20.

27. Ibid., at 21.

28. "Close Ranks," in David Levering Lewis, ed., *W.E.B. DuBois: A Reader* (1995), 697.

29. Quoted in Gail Lumet Buckley, *American Patriots: The Story of Blacks in the Military from the Revolution to Desert Storm* (2001), 211.

30. See, e.g., Richard M. Dalfiume, "The 'Forgotten Years' of the Negro Revolution," *Journal of American History*, June 1968: 90, and Peter Kellogg, "Civil Rights Consciousness in the 1940's," *The Historian*, November 1979: 42.

31. See Harvard Sitkoff, "African American Militancy in the World War II South: Another Perspective," in Neil R. McMillen, ed., *Remaking Dixie: The Impact of World War II on the American South* (1997).

32. Quoted in ibid.

33. See Martha Biondi, *To Stand and Fight: The Struggle for Civil Rights in Postwar New York City* (2003).

34. See Sherie Mershon and Steven Schlossman, *Foxholes & Color Lines: Desegregating the U.S. Armed Forces* (1998), 124–127.

35. Frederick Douglass, "The Meaning of July Fourth for the Negro," July 4, 1852, speech given on July 5, 1852, available at http://www.pbs.org/wgbh/aia/part4/4h2927t.html.

36. See Leonard I. Sweet, "The Fourth of July and Black Americans in the Nineteenth Century: Northern Leadership Opinion Within the Context of the Black Experience," *Journal of Negro History* 61 (1976): 256.

37. Quoted in Buckley, *American Patriots*, at 163.

38. Quoted in ibid., at 317.

39. Quoted in ibid., at 323.

40. See Douglas R. Egerton, *Death or Liberty: African Americans and Revolutionary America* (2009), 72; Henry Wieneck, *An Imperfect God: George Washington, His Slaves, and the Creation of America* (2003), 113; Graham Russell Hodges, ed., *The Black Loyalist Directory: African Americans in Exile After the American Revolution* (1996), 112, 196; Gary B. Nash, *The Forgotten Fifth: African Americans in the Age of Revolution* (2006); and Sylvia R. Frey, *Water from the Rock: Black Resistance in a Revolutionary Age* (1991).

41. Graham Russell Hodges, *Slavery and Freedom in the Rural North: African Americans in Monmouth County, New Jersey, 1665–1865* (1997), 97.

42. See L. Scott Philyaw, "A Slave for Every Soldier: The Strange History of

Virginia's Recruitment Act," *Virginia Magazine of History and Biography* 109 (2001): 376; Miller, *Wolf by the Ears,* at 24–25.

43. See Egerton, *Death or Liberty,* at 13 ("a majority of African Americans ultimately cast their lot with the British").

44. See William H. Becker, "In God and Country Do We Trust?," in Otto Reimherr, ed., *Quest for Faith, Quest for Freedom* (1987), 142.

45. Frederick Douglass, "Country, Conscience, and the Anti-Slavery Cause," speech given on May 11, 1847, available at http://www.yale.edu/glc/archive/1088.htm.

46. Malcolm X, "The Ballot or the Bullet," speech given on April 3, 1964.

47. Randall Robinson, *Quitting America: The Departure of a Black Man from his Native Land* (2004).

48. See An Observer, "The Gulf War and the Wounds of Race," *Reconstruction* 3 (1991).

49. See Gary Kamiya, "Rev. Wright Isn't the Problem," March 25, 2008, Salon .com.

50. www.guardian.co.UK/commentisfree/2008/mar/27/thedayofjerusalemsfall

51. See Philip Nobile, ed., *Judgment at the Smithsonian* (1995).

52. See Michael Scherer, "Swampland," *Time,* April 4, 2009.

53. "Text: Obama's Remarks on His Choice of Sotomayor," *New York Times,* May 26, 2009, www.nytimes.com/2009/05/26/us/politics/26obama.sotomayor .text.html.

6. The Racial Politics of the Sotomayor Confirmation

1. Quoted in Robert Dallek, *Flawed Giant: Lyndon Johnson and His Times, 1961–1973* (1998), 44.

2. The literature on the battle over Thomas's confirmation is large. See, e.g., Kevin Merida and Michael A. Fletcher, *Supreme Discomfort: The Divided Soul of Clarence Thomas* (2007); Randall Kennedy, *Sellout: The Politics of Racial Betrayal* (2008); Jane Meyer and Jill Abramson, *The Selling of Clarence Thomas* (1994); and Toni Morrison, ed., *Race-ing Justice, Engendering Power: Essays on Anita Hill, Clarence Thomas, and the Construction of Social Reality* (1992).

3. See Kevin R. Johnson, "On the Appointment of a Latina/o to the Supreme Court," *Harvard Latino Law Review* 5 (2002): 1 (serious discussion of the elevation of a Latino to the Supreme Court "represents an acknowledgment of the growing Latina/o presence, and a movement away from Latina/o invisibility").

4. Barack Obama, announcement of Sonia Sotomayor for associate Supreme Court justice, May 26, 2009 (transcript available at http://articles.cnn.com

/2009-05-26/politics/obama.sotomayor.transcript_1.justice-souter-supreme
-court-highest-court?_s=PM:POLITICS).

5. Senate Committee on the Judiciary, *Hearing on the Nomination of Sonia Sotomayor as Associate Justice to the United States Supreme Court,* 111th Congress,
2009 (statement of Senator Jeff Sessions), available at http://www.washington
post.com/wp-srv/politics/documents/sessions_openingstatement_soto
mayor.html.

6. Senate Committee on the Judiciary, *Hearing on the Nomination of John G.
Roberts as Chief Justice to the United States Supreme Court,* 107th Congress
2005 (statement of the Honorable John G. Roberts), available at http://www
.nytimes.com/2005/09/13/politics/politicsspecial1/13ctext.html.

7. Christopher L. Eisgruber, *The Next Justice: Repairing the Supreme Court
Appointments Process* (2007), 17.

8. "Remarks by the President in Nominating Judge Sonia Sotomayor to the
United States Supreme Court," The White House, May 26, 2009.

9. Ibid.

10. Jeffrey Toobin, "Diverse Opinions," *The New Yorker,* June 8, 2009.

11. "Remarks by the President in Nominating Judge Sonia Sotomayor."

12. Jeffrey Rosen, "The Case Against Sotomayor," *The New Republic,* May 4,
2009.

13. Ibid.

14. Mark Hemingway, "So What Does Rosen Really Think?," *National Review
Online*: The Corner blog, May 4, 2009.

15. John Derbyshire, *National Review Online,* "Essential Jurisprudence," May 4,
2009.

16. See Joan Biskupic and Sandra Day O'Connor, *Sandra Day O'Connor*
(2005), 71.

17. Ibid.

18. Ibid.

19. Ibid., 83.

20. Rush Limbaugh, "GOP Must Go to Mat on Sotomayor or Tell Real Story
of Barack Obama" radio broadcast, May 26, 2009 (transcript available at
http://www.rushlimbaugh.com/home/daily/site_052609/content/01125106
.guest.html).

21. See Patrick J. Buchanan, "A Quota Queen for the Court," Buchanan.org,
June 2, 2009; Patrick J. Buchanan, "Sonia Sotomayor: Miss Affirmative
Action, 2009," Buchanan.org, June 12, 2009. See also Joan Walsh, "Buchanan
on Sotomayor: 'Not that Intelligent,'" Salon.com, May 27, 2009, http://www
.salon.com/news/opinion/joan_walsh/politics/2009/05/27/supreme_court.

22. See Matt Corley, "Barnes: Sotomayor 'Benefited' from Affirmative Action
'Tremendously,'" *Think Progress,* May 28, 2009, http://thinkprogress.org
/2009/05/28/barnes-sotomayor-affirmative-action/.

23. Stuart Taylor, Jr., "The View from 1987," *Newsweek*, June 29, 2009.
24. Sonia Sotomayor, "A Latina Judge's Voice," speech given in 2001 (transcript available at http://www.nytimes.com/2009/05/15/us/politics/15judge.text .html?_r=2&pagewanted=all).
25. Ibid.
26. DeNeen L. Brown and Richard Leiby, "Valerie Jarrett Cites 'Double Standard' Between Sotomayor, Alito," WashingtonPost.com, June 15, 2009, http:// voices.washingtonpost.com/44/2009/06/15/valerie_jarrett_cites_double _s.html.
27. Senate Committee on the Judiciary, *Hearing on the Nomination of Sonia Sotomayor* (statement of Sonia Sotomayor).
28. Ibid.
29. Senate Committee on the Judiciary, *The Supreme Court of the United States: Hearings and Reports on Successful and Unsuccessful Nominations of Supreme Court Justices by the Senate Judiciary Committee, 1916–1975*, Volume 7, compiled by Roy M. Mersky and J. Myron Jacobstein (1977).
30. Howard Fineman, "Advise and Shut Up Already: Let's End Confirmation Hearings," *Newsweek*, July 27, 2009.
31. See Peter Baker and Neil A. Lewis, "Sotomayor Vows 'Fidelity to the Law' as Hearings Start," *New York Times*, July 13, 2009.
32. Ibid.

7. Addressing Race "the Obama Way"

1. Attorney General Eric Holder, Remarks at the Department of Justice African American History Month Program, February 18, 2009 (transcript available at http://www.justice.gov/ag/speeches/2009/ag-speech-090218.html).
2. See Tracy Jan, "Gates Chastises Officer After Authorities Agree to Drop Criminal Charge," *Boston Globe*, July 21, 2009.
3. See Katharine Q. Seelye, "Obama Wades into Volatile Racial Issue," *New York Times*, July 23, 2009.
4. Barack Obama, Remarks Regarding the Arrest of Henry Louis Gates, Jr., July 24, 2009 (transcript available at http://www.nytimes.com/2009/07/24 /us/politics/24obama.text.html).
5. Clarence Page, "Obama's Henry Gates-gate," RealClearPolitics.com, July 26, 2009.
6. *Special Report with Bret Baier*, "'Special Report' Panel on Whether Racism Played into Arrest of Harvard Professor," July 24, 2009.
7. See "Fox Host Glenn Beck: Obama Is a 'Racist,'" HuffingtonPost.com, July 28, 2009, http://www.huffingtonpost.com/2009/07/28/fox-host-glenn -beck-obama_n_246310.html.

8. Maureen Dowd, "Boy, Oh, Boy," *New York Times*, Sept. 12, 2009, at WK17.
9. *Newshour*, broadcast September 16, 2009 (transcript available at http://www.pbs.org/newshour/bb/politics/july-dec09/rage_09-16.html).
10. Kathleen Parker, "Playing the Racial Deck," *Washington Post*, September 20, 2009.
11. Kevin Ferris, "Race Card Is a Diversion Tactic," *Philadelphia Inquirer*, October 8, 2009.
12. See Holly Bailey, "Joe Wilson Apologizes, Again, and Obama Accepts," *Newsweek,* September 10, 2009.
13. See Clarence Lusane, *The Black History of the White House* (2011), 465–475. See also Sheryl Gay Stolberg, Shaila Dewan, and Brian Stelter, "With Apology, Fired Official Is Offered a New Job," *New York Times*, July 22, 2010.
14. See Maureen Dowd, "You'll Never Believe What This White House Is Missing," *New York Times*, July 24, 2010. See also Matt Bai, "Race: Still Too Hot to Touch," *New York Times*, July 25, 2010, and Holly Epstein Ojalvo, "Why Is Race Hard to Talk About?," *New York Times*, July 27, 2010.

8. Obama and the Future of American Race Relations

1. See Adam Nagourney, "Republicans Choose First Black Party Chairman," *New York Times*, January 13, 2009.
2. See, e.g., Bradford Plumer, "RNC Debate: Michael Steele Just Won't Quit," *The New Republic*, January 3, 2011; Bradford Plumer, "One-Armed Midgets, Rejoice!," *The New Republic*, October 6, 2010; Ralph Z. Hallow, "RNC fails to report $7M in debt to FEC," *Washington Times*, July 20, 2010; Michael Memoli, "Michael Steele Under Fire over Afghanistan Remarks," *Los Angeles Times*, July 2, 2010.
3. See Clarence Page, "A Republican Party That's Not for Whites Only," JournalNews.com, November 8, 2010.
4. See Dana Milbank, "With GOP Primary, South Carolina Finally Buries Strom Thurmond," *Washington Post*, June 27, 2010; John Ryan, "Tim Scott," *National Journal*, November 8, 2010.
5. Profile of Allen West, on WhoRunsGov.com/WashingtonPost.
6. David B. Wilkins, "The New Social Engineers in the Age of Obama: Black Corporate Lawyers and the Making of the First Black President," *Howard Law Journal* 53 (2010): 557, 643.
7. See Jeff Zeleny, "Alabama Candidate Tries Obama Style Coalition," *New York Times*, May 31, 2010, and Thomas Spencer, "Davis Won't Run for Office Again," *Birmingham News*, June 3, 2010.
8. See, e.g., William Van Alstyne, "Rites of Passage: Race, the Supreme Court, and the Constitution," *University of Chicago Law Review* 46 (1979): 775 ("One

gets beyond racism by getting beyond it now: by a complete, resolute, and credible commitment *never* to tolerate in one's own life—or in the life of one's government—the differential treatment of other human beings by race"), and Alexander Bickel, *The Morality of Consent* (1975) ("Discrimination on the basis of race is illegal, immoral, unconstitutional, inherently wrong, and destructive of democratic society").

9. See, e.g., *Regents of the University of California v. Bakke*, 438 U.S. 265 (1978) (Justice Harry Blackmun concurring in part and dissenting in part: "In order to get beyond racism, we must first take account of race"), and *Grutter v. Bollinger*, 539 U.S. 306 (2003) (Justice Sandra Day O'Connor for the Court: "We expect that 25 years from now, the use of racial preferences will no longer be necessary").

10. See, e.g., Molfi Kete Asinte, *Afrocentricity* (1988), and Maulena Karenga, *Introduction to Black Studies* (1993). See generally Tommie Shelby, *We Who Are Dark: The Philosophical Foundations of Black Solidarity* (2005).

11. Eduardo Bonilla-Silva, *Racism Without Racists: Color-Blind Racism and the Persistence of Racial Inequality in the United States* (2006); Michael K. Brown, et al., *Whitewashing Race: The Myth of a Color-Blind Society* (2005).

12. See, e.g., Alex Koppelman, "Will Whites Vote for Barack Obama?," Salon .com, January 24, 2008; John Judis, "The Big Race: Obama and the Psychology of the Color Barrier," *The New Republic*, May 28, 2008; Stephen J. Dubner, "When Is It OK to Vote Your Race," NewYorkTimes.com, October 17, 2008.

13. See Lawrence Bobo and Michael Dawson, "A Change Has Come: Race, Politics, and the Path to the Obama Presidency," *DuBois Review* 6 (2009): 1, 5.

14. John McWhorter, "Of Course Race Mattered," *New York Post*, November 9, 2008.

15. See Frederic J. Frommer, "Black Conservatives Conflicted on Obama," Associated Press, June 14, 2008.

16. See Jeff Zeleny, "Oprah Endorses Obama," *New York Times*: The Caucus, May 3, 2007, http://thecaucus.blogs.nytimes.com/2007/05/03/oprah -endorses-obama-2/.

17. See Sam Stein, "Some Conservatives See Race in Powell's Obama Endorsement," HuffingtonPost.com, October 19, 2008.

18. See Tommie Shelby, *We Who Are Dark: The Philosophical Foundations of Black Solidarity* (2005).

19. Philip A. Klinkner with Rogers M. Smith, *The Unsteady March: The Rise and Decline of Racial Equality in America* (1999), 317.

20. See Ta-Nehisi Coates, "I Just Remembered Chris Matthews Was White," *The Atlantic*, January 28, 2010.

21. See Michael Calderone, "Matthews Clarifies: Obama's 'Taken Us Beyond Black and White,'" Politico.com, January 28, 2010, http://www.politico.com

/blogs/michaelcalderone/0110/Matthews_clarifies_Obamas_taken_us_beyond_black_and_white.html.

22. Quoted in Jesse Washington, "Matthews Remark Exposes Complexity of Transcending Race," News.Yahoo.com, January 28, 2010.

23. Natalie Holder-Winfield, "That Was Mighty White of You Chris Matthews," HuffingtonPost.com, February 1, 2010.

24. "Obama Rejects Congressional Black Caucus Criticism," USAToday.com, December 3, 2009.

25. Quoted in Sheryl Gay Stolberg, "For Obama, Nuance on Race Invites Questions," *New York Times*, February 9, 2010.

26. Quoted in Gwen Ifill, *The Breakthrough: Politics and Race in the Age of Obama* (2009), 261.

27. The Buzz, "Michael Eric Dyson Says President Obama Is Afraid to Address Race," TheRoot.com, January 11, 2010.

28. See, e.g., Ian Ayers, *Pervasive Prejudice? Non-Traditional Evidence of Race and Gender Discrimination* (2001); Michael Fix and Margery Austin Turner, eds., *A National Report Card on Discrimination in America: The Role of Testing* (1999); and Joleen Kirschenman and Kathryn M. Nickerman, "We'd Love to Hire Them, but . . . : The Meaning of Race for Employers," in Christopher Jencks and Paul E. Peterson, eds., *The Urban Underclass* (1991).

29. See George Stephanopoulos, *All Too Human* (1999), 118, 122.

30. See, e.g., David Paul Kuhn, "Obama Shifts Affirmative Action Rhetoric," Politico.com, August 10, 2008 (quoting Professor Kenneth Bickers of the University of Colorado, who noted that affirmative action "racializes the campaign in a sense that Obama has been trying to avoid").

31. Barack Obama, *The Audacity of Hope: Thoughts on Reclaiming the American Dream* (2006), 246.

32. Ibid., 244.

33. Ibid., 246.

34. Ibid., 245–246.

35. This is the issue that lends such importance to the landmark Supreme Court case *Griggs v. Duke Power Company*, 401 U.S. 424 (1971), and the struggle that led to the codification of *Griggs* in the Civil Rights Act of 1991. See generally Robert Belton, "Title VII at Forty: A Brief Look at the Birth, Death and Resurrection of the Disparate Impact Theory of Discrimination," *Hofstra Labor and Employment Law Journal* 22 (2005): 431.

36. See, e.g., Robert D. Bullard, ed., *Unequal Protection: Environmental Justice and Communities of Color* (1994), and Vicki Been, "Locally Undesirable Land Uses in Minority Neighborhoods: Disproportionate Siting or Market Dynamics?," *Yale Law Journal* 103 (1994): 1383.

37. Glenn Loury, *Race, Incarceration, and American Values* (2008), 22–23.

38. Randall Kennedy, *Race, Crime, and the Law* (1997), 364–365.

39. United States Sentencing Commission, *Special Report to Congress: Cocaine and Federal Sentencing Policy* (May 2007).

40. Michelle Alexander, *The New Jim Crow: Mass Incarceration in the Age of Colorblindness* (2010), 239.

41. See "Barack Obama Defends Response to 'Jena Six' Arrests After Reverend Jackson Criticism," Fox News, September 20, 2007.

42. See Nicholas Wapshott, "Obama Hopes Could Rest on Jena Case," *New York Sun*, September 20, 2007.

43. See Tobin Harshaw, "Obama, Jackson, and Jena," *New York Times*, September 20, 2007.

44. William Jelani Cobb, *The Substance of Hope: Barack Obama and the Paradox of Progress* (2010), 160.

45. See Statement of Lanny A. Breuer, Assistant Attorney General, Criminal Division, United States Department of Justice Before the United States Senate Committee on the Judiciary, Subcommittee on Crime and Drugs, April 25, 2009.

46. See Lawrence D. Bobo, "Obama and the Great Progressive Disconnect," *Pathways*, Spring 2010.

Index

black activists, 13, 28, 87–90, 92, 112
  alternative traditions to patriotism
    voiced by, 180–2
  Obama's response to, 87–8, 110–12,
    122–3
Black Agenda Report (Web site), 102
black conservatives, 95–101
Black Enterprise, 56
Black Entertainment Television
  (BET), 149
Black Law Students Association, 249
Black Panther Party, 78
black patriotism, 165, 168–85, 194
  alternative traditions to, 16, 113,
    176, 180–2, 183–9
  military service and, 168–9, 174–6,
    181*n*
  and resistance to proposed
    repatriation of free blacks, 170–2
  white America's views on, 164, 173
  white hostility to, 177–80
black politicians, 18, 40, 43, 45–64, 99,
  108, 152–3, 154, 240
  Bradley effect and, 55–7
  Democratic Party's presence of, 51,
    52, 246–8
  derogatory myths and stereotypical
    depictions of, 49, 152, 159
  in gubernatorial and mayoral
    elections, 12, 52–6, 240, 246,
    247
  mixed races of, 69
  in modern Republican Party, 51*n*,
    240–2, 243–6, 248
  racially polarized voting and, 8,
    53, 55
  racial obstacles and backlash to,
    7*n*, 9, 12, 15, 47–9, 53, 131, 159
  in Reconstruction era, 46–51, 52*n*
  and role of race in influencing
    voters, 7–9, 11, 55–7, 243–4,
    248, 250–5

in seeking U.S. presidency, 12,
  56–64, 89, 97
  see also Obama, Barack
Black Power Movement, 71, 176
*Blueprint for Change, The: Obama
  and Biden's Plan for America,*
  85–6
Bobo, Lawrence D., 142*n*, 143*n*, 251,
  275
Bok, Derek, 168*n*
Bolden, Charles, 265
Booth, John Wilkes, 42*n*
Bork, Robert, 22, 197–8, 205, 211
Boston Globe, 151, 229*n*
Bowen, William G., 168*n*
Bradley, Tom, 52, 53, 55
Bradley effect, 55–7
Brandeis, Louis D., 196*n*, 200, 209
Braun, Carol Moseley, 12, 52
Brawley, Tawana, 137
*Breakthrough, The: Politics and Race
  in the Age of Obama* (Ifill),
  36*n*
Breitbart, Andrew, 237
Brooke, Edward, 12, 51*n*, 52
Brown, James, 71
Brown, Sterling, 169–70
Brown v. Board of Education, 120–1,
  197, 198*n*
Brown-Williams, Irma, 36
Bruce, Blanche Kelso, 47*n*
Buchanan, Patrick J., 211, 212, 213*n*,
  253–4
Bulge, Battle of the, 176, 179
Burris, Roland, 52*n*
Bush, George H. W., 52, 58–9, 62, 135,
  184, 185, 199, 205, 209
Bush, George W., 10, 11*n*, 84, 87, 142,
  153, 157, 192, 201–2, 205, 245,
  261*n*, 265, 275
Butts, Calvin, III, 13
Byrd, Robert, 179–80

A NOTE ABOUT THE AUTHOR

Randall Kennedy received his undergraduate degree from Princeton and his law degree from Yale. A Rhodes Scholar, he served as a law clerk to Supreme Court Justice Thurgood Marshall. Kennedy is the holder of the Michael R. Klein Professorship at Harvard Law School, a fellow of the American Academy of Arts and Sciences, and a member of the American Philosophical Association.

A NOTE ON THE TYPE

This book was set in Adobe Garamond. Designed for the Adobe Corporation by Robert Slimbach, the fonts are based on types first cut by Claude Garamond (ca. 1480–1561). Garamond was a pupil of Geoffroy Tory and is believed to have followed the Venetian models, although he introduced a number of important differences, and it is to him that we owe the letter we now know as "old style."

Typeset by Scribe,
Philadelphia, Pennsylvania

Printed and bound by RR Donnelley,
Harrisonburg, Virginia

Designed by M. Kristen Bearse